THE PHILOSOPHER KING

MUSIC OF THE AMERICAN SOUTH

THE PHILOSOPHER KING

T Bone Burnett
and the Ethic of a Southern
Cultural Renaissance

Heath Carpenter

The University of Georgia Press
ATHENS

© 2019 by the University of Georgia Press
Athens, Georgia 30602
www.ugapress.org
All rights reserved
Designed by Rebecca A. Norton
Set in 10.5/14 Minion Pro

Most University of Georgia Press titles are
available from popular e-book vendors.

Printed digitally

Library of Congress Cataloging-in-Publication Data
Names: Carpenter, Heath, 1979– author.
Title: The philosopher king : T Bone Burnett and the
ethic of a southern cultural renaissance / Heath Carpenter.
Description: Athens, Georgia : University of Georgia Press, [2019] |
Series: Music of the American South ; 5 |
Includes bibliographical references and index.
Identifiers: LCCN 2018053139 | ISBN 9780820355597 (pbk. : alk. paper)
| ISBN 9780820355603 (ebook)
Subjects: LCSH: Burnett, T-Bone—Criticism and interpretation. |
Popular music—Southern States—History and criticism.
Classification: LCC ML429.B927 C37 2019 | DDC 780.92—dc23
LC record available at https://lccn.loc.gov/2018053139

To Hannah

Until philosophers rule as kings
or those who are now called kings and leading men
genuinely and adequately philosophize . . .

—PLATO, *REPUBLIC*, BOOK V

CONTENTS

ACKNOWLEDGMENTS

I could not have completed this project without the support of many people. I want to thank the administration and my colleagues at Harding University, particularly the English Department for their consistent encouragement. Similarly, I greatly appreciate the Heritage Studies faculty at Arkansas State University for their guidance throughout my time in the program. I would like to further thank Dr. Michael Bowman and Dr. Marcus Tribbett, and particularly Dr. Deborah Chappel Traylor, who I cannot adequately praise. Our lunch meetings are some of my most fond memories during this long process. Dr. Traylor's consistency, sage advice, and calm yet forthright demeanor were a constant source of comfort and inspiration. I would also like to acknowledge Melissa Hall, Joe Henry, Tyler Jones, Lance Ledbetter, Bonnie Montgomery, Laura Rogers, Lydia Rogers Slagle, and Jason Weinheimer for graciously agreeing to be interviewed for this project. A further special thanks to the University of Georgia Press, particularly Pat Allen, Walter Biggins, Katherine La Mantia, Lea Johnson, Rebecca Norton, Jordan Stepp, and the rest of the team for all their help in seeing this to fruition. I owe a big thanks to Ed Vesneske Jr. for his thorough editing eye and generosity and to Justin Duyao for his research assistance. Lastly, I am blessed to have a supportive family. My mom and dad, Doug and Pam Carpenter, my in-laws, Tom and Phyllis Alexander, my brother Harrison and sister-in-law Megan, and my extended family and friends have been a consistent source of encouragement. Lastly, I could not have accomplished this without the support of my wife Hannah and our four children (Tristin, Silas, Enid, and Thomas), who endured what must have seemed like endless talk of Southern culture and who dealt with me spending significant amounts of time away from them with understanding and grace. I love you.

THE PHILOSOPHER KING

THE TASTEMAKER

T Bone Burnett and Southern Cultures

Standing on a stage in downtown Little Rock, Arkansas, in a recently opened bar that purposefully fetishizes rural Southern culture and which stands as a contradiction to her purist roots ethic, country singer Bonnie Montgomery— a classically trained pianist and opera singer, producer, and author—and her three-piece outlaw country band play an inspired set for dozens of half-interested listeners. In New York City, two Florence, Alabama–raised sisters who grew up singing a cappella music from church pews listen, awestruck and silent, in a room alongside Elton John, Jeff Bridges, and the Brooklyn-based bluegrass band the Punch Brothers as bluegrass legend Ralph Stanley, who the girls liken to a prophet in the Bible, sings the old gospel tune "Lift Him Up That's All." Inspired, the duo return to their hotel room and write "River Jordan," a song for their soon-to-be released second album. In Atlanta, the husband-and-wife duo who comprise Dust-to-Digital work meticulously to digitally restore traditional American roots music. In Little Rock, a record producer arranges his studio to best create a live performance sound, recording songs to an analog machine before transferring them to digital. In Los Angeles, the singer-songwriter and producer T Bone Burnett takes a call from the Coen Brothers regarding a film starring George Clooney about, as they see it, the history of American music.

What do these snapshots have in common? As cultural tastemaker, what role does T Bone Burnett play? What does this have to do with the American

South? What does this say about consumer culture in America and the ever-enigmatic generational issues of identity, authenticity, and heritage? What about the twenty-first-century context provides cultural space for such a community to exist? What are the characteristics of and the spark igniting the preservationist heritage movement in contemporary roots music, and how can this music community contribute to ongoing conversations regarding contemporary Southern identity? This book's purpose is to explore these connections, the culture in which they reside, and most specifically the role T Bone Burnett plays in a contemporary cultural movement which seeks to re-present a traditional American music ethos in distinctly Southern terms.

Though Burnett is somewhat of a cult philosopher-king of roots music, garnering ample praise from rock critics and popular sources, little to no critical attention has been paid to him by the scholarly community. Save some critical attention regarding the *O Brother, Where Art Thou?* soundtrack in particular, Burnett seems to have only been studied anecdotally by traditional scholarship. Regarding popular sources, he has been given ample attention for individual projects, yet there is seemingly little done on his cumulative effect on culture. I aim to position Burnett as a cultural catalyst in the twenty-first-century popular music community, particularly the aspects of this movement with direct ties to the American South. Such investigation allows for the dissection of a community by those who help shape its parts. Studying Burnett allows for the close examination of a cultural architect while following his influence out into the broader musical and cultural landscape in which he participates. Particularly, I would like to consider Burnett's ethic by closely analyzing his soundtracks, select musical artists, producers' recording philosophies, and branding strategies, each of which could be seen as both "performing" the lo-fi ethos and purposefully participating in a community or "scene." I will set the movement within the contemporary context in which such sounds, symbols, and narratives reside. In the process, I plan to investigate how relevant cultural issues are being negotiated, how complicated discussions of history, tradition, and heritage feed the ethic, and how the American South as a perceived distinct region factors in to the equation.

There is a philosophical connection between this movement and the Southern Renascence of the early to mid-twentieth century. Led by authors like William Faulkner and the Twelve Agrarians at Vanderbilt, the Renascence, according to Richard H. King, was "engaged in an attempt to come to terms not only with the inherited values of the Southern tradition but also with a certain way of perceiving and dealing with the past." Put more simply, they had to "decide whether the past was of any use at all in the present; and if so, in what ways?"[1] Like the early Renascence, which addressed the guilt of slavery, the myths of the Lost Cause, and the consequences of technological advancement on a once-agrarian people, among other themes, this contemporary movement seeks to address the complexities of Southern identity through cultural history, with particular focus on race, class, and gender.[2] Its contributors explore that identity by creating art that best uncovers the Southern cultures standing resistant to the oversimplified, often stereotypical, and superficially homogeneous contemporary Southern identity often portrayed. This contemporary cultural renaissance reads as a complication of false dichotomies of Southern identity, where women are either "the redneck woman" or the "lily-white Southern belle," for instance.

As I analyze Burnett's community, it is not either-or; it's both-and. The case studies here argue for a complication of overgeneralized and trite assertions of Southern identity. The artists here carry conservative and liberal impulses simultaneously; some are religious *while also* politically and socially liberal. They are interested in tradition but think the Confederate flag is a scourge; they are interested in community but not in being either defined by uniformity or limited to unthinking conformity. Southern identity is rooted in the past, but these artists are resistant to moonlight-and-magnolia apologia generalizations and are eager to address the complexities of race, class, gender, religion, and politics. For them, the idea of the South or Southerners as any one thing, or as something that fits neatly with boxes to be checked for certain characteristics, loaded symbols, or tropes, is problematic.

This book does not presume, however, that such negotiations have not been ongoing since the original Renascence. On the contrary, the study of the Southern condition and Southern identity has been ongoing, involving great minds like C. Vann Woodward, Charles Reagan Wilson, Eudora Welty, William Ferris, Maya Angelou, and John Shelton Reed; respected programs of study on campuses like the University of Mississippi and the University of North Carolina at Chapel Hill; a host of specialized journals such as *Southern Cultures* and *Southern Studies* and a number of university presses; and innumerable books and reference materials, most notably *The New Encyclopedia of Southern Culture*, which currently extends to nineteen volumes. Furthermore, negotiations over what the South is or isn't and what her people and ways entail have never ended, with continuing debate via cultural forms from music, literature, and photography to television, film, and comedy. This examination argues that T Bone Burnett influenced a specific strain of this renaissance in the twenty-first century, shining a light on part of an ongoing conversation. As such, I will use his particular footprint as a key to navigation.

By doing so, I hope to show the complex inner workings of a contemporary cultural movement while also arguing that Burnett and like-minded participants are inspired by more than just nostalgia, or what Houston Baker calls a "purposive construction of a past filled with golden virtues, golden men, and sterling events." Baker contrasts nostalgia's substitution of "allegory for history" with critical memory: "the cumulative, collective maintenance of a record that draws into relationship significant instants of time past and the always uprooted homelessness of now."[3] The ability of critical memory to scrutinize and judge in order to create is at the root of Burnett's philosophy. Undoubtedly inspired by traditional American music and the cultures in which such art was born, participants in this renaissance appeal to a regenerative process to make explicit and implicit cultural declarations regarding group and self-identity, memory, preservation, regeneration, and heritage.

In the process, this book aims at utilizing several discourses and themes. Within these pages, I hope to bring together so-called popular-culture and high-culture mediums to help debate the ongoing and problematic territory between the commodified and the ever-enigmatic "authentic." Furthermore, conversations over the contested terrain of tradition will mix with the progressive impulses in the evolution of the South's people, places, and art to form a more complicated picture of how historical contexts, symbols, and themes interact within this contemporary Southern movement. Through these pages, I will rely on a hybrid mixture of literary analysis and ethnography. In some cases, I will read soundtracks, songs, cultural moments, places, and people, and in others I will let the artists speak for themselves. Since my study is driven by popular-culture analysis and ethnographic case studies, it is not meant to be a cross section or scientific sampling. Yet, such an interdisciplinary study will undoubtedly afford a depth of perspective on, context for, and perception of those artists within this particular Southern circle.

Though this study does not speak in depth for every Southern demographic, as a culture study by nature, the methods employed could be used in any other cultural environment—such as in regard to the popularity of the New Orleans hip-hop artist Lil Wayne among Southern middle-class white teenagers—and employed as a means of discovery. With the incorporation of historical scholarship, critical theory, popular-culture examples, ethnography, and contemporary and historic contexts, my aim is to serve as conduit between the producers, consumers, and those interested in studying the motivations and actions of artists and community members within this cultural setting, exploring the essential who, what, when, where, how, and why questions informing patterns of thinking and behaving.

Furthermore, Burnett is an interesting case study to pursue in regards to the success of contemporary roots music. In addition to being a backup guitarist in Bob Dylan's band in the sixties and a musician in his own right, he has most influenced the roots revival as a producer, particularly in helping produce and arrange movie soundtracks. His work on *Walk the Line* and *Crazy Heart* highlights the gritty, raw sound and ethos of "outlaw" country music. The *Cold Mountain* soundtrack does the same for traditional Appalachian roots music, and *Inside Llewyn Davis* focuses on the 1960s New York City folk scene. Furthermore, *O Brother, Where Art Thou?* arguably serves as an overview of American roots music. That soundtrack features revered folk songs reinterpreted by modern musicians, while also presenting genres such as blues, prison chants, gospel hymns, and an actual 1959 Alan Lomax prison field recording of "Po' Lazarus." Citing the millions of albums sold and the Grammy wins, historian Ronald Cohen argues that *O Brother* "demonstrated that roots music had a definite mass appeal."[4]

Burnett seems to be playing the role of Ralph Peer, Harry Smith, and Alan Lomax in equal parts. As Peer and other record executives paired existing folk songs with new artists, Burnett uses staple folk performers like Emmylou Harris and Alison Krauss alongside rockers like Jack White to reinterpret older songs for a current generation. Yet, there are differences as well. Peer was a businessman first. Barry Mazor notes that Peer was "never . . . driven by any particular desire to contribute something to traditional music, by any musical theory or ideology . . . [but by] finding an untapped opportunity that worked—an audience unaddressed, a style of music underexplored, a new way to freshen what was already available."[5] Peer recognized that "people buying records were *not* especially interested in hearing standard or folkloric music.

What they wanted was something new—built along the same lines."[6] Burnett seems to follow Peer's pattern, helping to discover and produce musicians that tap into an older past and reinvent a particular ethos. Alabama-bred duo the Secret Sisters, who Burnett produced and included on the *Hunger Games* soundtrack, sound like a modern remake of the Peer-produced Carter Family. The sisters grew up harmonizing in an a cappella church tradition, had never lived outside of the South, and had not ever been on an airplane when they were discovered, and later connected to Burnett, through a local Nashville talent competition.

Yet Burnett, using tools of popular culture like film soundtracks, seems much more interested than Peer in the philosophical and cultural implications of re-presenting and reinterpreting roots music. He seems to fall much more in line with the academic and philosophical leanings of Alan Lomax. For example, in 2016, Burnett, rocker Jack White, and Robert Redford produced a three-part documentary series for PBS titled *American Epic* exploring the early use of recording equipment in the 1920s. Following Burnett's soundtrack formula and ethos, during the film the crew "reassembles the recording machine by replicating every element of the materials—including the original microphones and amplifiers—and inviting an array of high-profile musicians [Jack White, Willie Nelson, Beck, Nas, the Avett Brothers, among others] to record in that 1920s-styled atmosphere." Regarding the documentary, Burnett says, "These musicians we profile are the real American heroes. . . . They set out from the darkness with nothing but a guitar on their backs, put out their thumbs and conquered the world."[7]

Like Harry Smith, Burnett presents songs which have since inspired others to recreate folk-based music for a contemporary audience. Like Guthrie, Dylan, and a host of musicians who studied Smith's Folkways albums for inspiration, Burnett's soundtracks have influenced bands such as Grammy winners Mumford & Sons.[8] Not surprisingly, Burnett tapped Mumford to help produce and sing on the *Inside Llewyn Davis* soundtrack, another Coen film set in the Greenwich Village 1960s folk scene. This regenerative quality connects well to the many garage bands, festivals, and folk scenes that rock journalist Richie Unterberger argues were born out of the first folk revolution.[9]

The history of roots or folk music in America tells the story of musicians, executives, and collectors amidst social movements, economic collapses, and world wars. Such historical grounding illustrates how roots music is not a static antique, relegated to dormant history. Rather, the ethos fueling such music makes it a regenerative art form in a constant state of revival and reinterpretation, promoting authenticity in an age of mass production, which partially helps to explain why it has again found widespread success with contemporary audiences. Furthermore, because many of Burnett's most noted film soundtracks and artistic productions are either set in the South or have a historic connection to the region, he becomes a unique vessel by which to study the reimagining of Southern culture in the twenty-first century.

So-called folk "purists" bristle at how some position the *O Brother, Where Art Thou?* soundtrack as the twenty-first-century spark popularizing neo-folk and Americana sounds and aesthetics. Such critics may see a George Clooney film lampooning Depression-Era Mississippians as a puddle-deep attempt to at worst stereotype and at best mass-market and commodify the august cultural heritage inspiring such sounds and musical heroes alike. Such a view is not without warrant. Scholars, critics, and consumers alike have debated the film and soundtrack to a variety of conclusions.[10] However, outside the space and time of the film, the soundtrack producer T Bone Burnett's cultural influence deserves attention. Nearly two decades removed from the soundtrack, his relationship to the bourgeoning roots, rock, and pop worlds is evident.

Yet, beyond the *O Brother* soundtrack and its awards, millions of albums sold, and a host of postmodern roots-influenced artists lies a canon of original music and select artistic productions that craft a determined philosophical treatise on the nature of music and society, grounded in the complex relationships sounds and people have to specific places, particularly those with roots in the American South. That a George Clooney film becomes the popular culture megaphone by which to speak Burnett's discourse complicates the somewhat prickly reaction to the film and its soundtrack by some, particularly in light of Burnett's artistic productions, recording philosophy, and community-building in the years to come. What was to follow were more soundtracks with the same ethic and formula. With each, something became clearer: swirling around in the soundtracks and the movement were cultural messages evoking communal and individual identity, race, class, gender, religion, politics, philosophy, ethics, and the music business, all infused with notions of the past, the present, and the future. Furthermore, the initial reaction to the *O Brother* soundtrack is not without foundation: beyond nostalgic fantasy-making, what good is such music without a sophisticated understanding of the cultural context out of which it was originally born? Additionally, is contemporary popular roots music simulated mimicry or regenerative participation in a longstanding tradition, and who has the power to decide? Cumulatively taken, these questions ask what Burnett's soundtracks and ethic offer the contemporary world. What is Burnett's cultural imprint? The key to the answer rests in the years following *O Brother*. Yet, the findings of such an examination transcend music culture alone. Burnett's soundtracks are important on their own and collectively as musical history and as instigator of popularizing roots sounds for contemporary audiences. Beyond the roots music influence, though, it is no coincidence that much of his production work has a direct connection to the American South. As such, in the decade following *O Brother*, Burnett's philosophy and ethic have become the sounds and ethos of a new Southern cultural renaissance that surpasses music, speaking directly to a reinvigorated interest in Southern culture, ethics, philosophy, and storytelling. Infused in the resurgence of roots-inspired music is renewed interest in Southern cultures. The two are inseparable, and Burnett's soundtracks, philosophy, and ethic feed and are representative of both, as the following chapters will investigate. Chapter 1 deals with both the cultural context surrounding the *O Brother* soundtrack and the work itself. Reading the soundtrack's compilation, the individual songs, and the music's placement within the film's narrative as text, while keeping in mind the music's historical context and its purposeful placement in contemporary culture, offers a perspective both on what Burnett attempts to accomplish and how the music's message is still relevant today. By looking at bands like Mumford & Sons formed in *O Brother's* wake and addressing the "folk fad" fears of scholars like Benjamin Filene, Chapter 2 opens the door on the complex negotiations between music and consumption, particularly establishing the grounds by which contemporary Southerners can use both the film's parody and the earnestness of the music's context to craft contemporary Southern identities. The first two chapters lay the groundwork for how Burnett spends his *O Brother* capital, which will be explored in Chapter 3's look at his post–*O Brother* soundtracks and Chapter 4's look at the community of artists with which Burnett has purposefully aligned himself, particularly focusing on the Secret Sisters. With this foundation established, Chapters 5 and 6 will extend Burnett's ethic to the broader community of musicians, producers, preservationists, writers, and cultural tastemakers. There I will look at the community and ethic of the outlaw country artist Bonnie Montgomery and the music producers Joe Henry and Jason Weinheimer. In the last chapter, I will extend this ethic further, looking at various cultural outlets that, abiding by and participating in Burnett's cultural milieu, make up part of the contemporary Southern cultural renaissance.

CHAPTER 1

HISTORY, IRONY, AND CULTURAL CONDUIT

The *O Brother, Where Art Thou?* Soundtrack
and Contemporary Southern Identity

> The story of the United States is this: One kid, without
> anything, walks out of his house, down the road, with
> nothing but a guitar and conquers the world.
>
> **— T BONE BURNETT**

Reading the *O Brother* soundtrack with questions of authenticity, sincerity, representation, and history in mind, particularly through the lens of contemporary Southern identity, can aid in better understanding Burnett's cultural stimulus. The Coen Brothers' 2000 Academy Award–winning film features the episodic jaunt—"fraught with peril" and "oh, so many startlements"[1]—of Delmar O'Donnell, Pete Hogwallop, and Ulysses Everett McGill as they break out of prison to seek a fictitious $1.2 million treasure. In reality, Everett needs to stop his wife Penny, played by Georgia native Holly Hunter, from marrying a suitor who is "bona fide." While pursuing the treasure and being chased by the law, the escaped convicts encounter a silver-tongued, one-eyed, crooked Bible salesman; a group of intoxicating sirens; a manic, hypersensitive bank robber; an enigmatic blind prophet; a mass baptism; a violent Klan mob; and a bluesman who sold his soul to the devil at the crossroads. There is substantial scholarship devoted to the film's historic references, Southern archetypes, Homeric allusions, and its notable hat-tip to movies like *Sullivan's Travels*, *Gone with the Wind*, and *The Wizard of Oz*, alongside how the soundtrack functions within the work. Beyond these allusions, the film and its soundtrack, written as part of the narrative structure, aim at an overarching awareness of how film and music contribute to cultural awareness, historical memory, and identity. As such, the film shines as much light on cultural consumers as it does on history. By invoking Southern myths and lore, set in the increasingly mythologized Depression Era, with satiric allusions to historical events and people, the movie—fueled by its sound—purposefully resists neatly organized categories. So, responses will remain varied. This is another great message the film delivers. Memory, historical interpretation, and identity are wrapped up in complicated personal contexts—infused with the emotion of the present. As Everett says, "It's a fool that looks for logic in the chambers of the human heart."[2] Looking at the various reactions to the film helps break down the need for precisely arranged resolution in favor of embracing the messy incongruities of history, memory, and the present. Noting the function of the music within the film and the separate success of the soundtrack sheds light on the multifaceted ways in which consumers have processed and used the sound and its cultural ethos.

The Depression Era offers modern culture consumers a space for nostalgic mythmaking in ways that other historic periods such as post–Civil War America formerly offered. *O Brother's* Depression setting is part of the film's ironic spirit: as the characters within the film often participate in the midcentury Southern mythmaking, contemporary viewers participate in an updated version of remembrance through the film itself. It's conceivable that consumers today are participating in both the myth of the South *and* the Depression at once. The Coens' formula appears to be a satiric weapon that casts light on culture's penchant for mythmaking, heroifying, stereotyping, and distorted public memory, which are fueled by a cocktail of nostalgia and "tradition" as the film recreates a parody with the same method. In this vein, the film offers several meta-narratives within a meta-mythology, with seemingly self-congratulatory irony. Burnett, too, is not above myth-provoking conflation, purposefully feeding the music's mythology into its contemporary cultural imprint: "The story of the United States is this: One kid, without anything, walks out of his house, down the road, with nothing but a guitar and conquers the world."[3]

Within the film's plot, Hugh Ruppersburg cites several "popular and deeply ingrained myths of Americana" which are "deftly interwoven": chain-gang film, Depression story, Southern tall tale, a treasure hunt, a political campaign, and the vanquished fallen South, to name a few.[4] The film simultaneously invokes a number of Southern stereotypes while playing fast and loose with historical figures and events, such as in the portrayals of Robert Johnson,

Baby Face Nelson, Governor Pappy O'Daniel, and the Great Mississippi Flood of 1927, among others. Yet, Ruppersburg notes how the Coens are purposefully not interested in historical accuracy—a decisive nudge at the ahistorical foundation of mythmaking, perhaps—as Baby Face Nelson died in 1934, three years before the film's setting, and never set foot in Mississippi. And though there was a Pappy O'Daniel, he was governor of Texas, not Mississippi. The picture features these distinctly Southern images while evoking complicated memories of poverty, racism, and classism that have always permeated the American South. As such, the movie and its soundtrack present a collage of stereotypes and lore concerning the South, implicitly channeling Faulkner's Yoknapatawpha, Twain's Huck, and Griffith's *Birth of a Nation* alongside all the countless Hollywood executives, music moguls, and cultural influencers who ever contributed to the idea of "the South," managing to celebrate and lampoon those myths simultaneously.

Tackling so much at once left film critics, viewers, and scholars with diverse responses. J. Hoberman of the *Village Voice* calls the film a "protracted Little Moron joke . . . [and] a tepid gumbo of Deep South clichés."[5] Charles Taylor argues that "if Mad [*sic*] magazine had attempted to do 'Let Us Now Praise Famous Men' the result might be 'O Brother, Where Art Thou?'"[6] Others compared it to a "Three Stooges episode featuring an even stupider version of the cast of *Hee Haw*,"[7] a "flattening pile of artifice and conceit disguised as road comedy,"[8] a "piece of pop nihilism,"[9] and "a wildly ambitious but ultimately unsatisfying goof on *The Odyssey*."[10]

In contrast, many critics loved the film, calling it a "classic myth from both literature and the movies, commingled . . . and untrammeled by any sense of predictability, urgency, realism or believability . . . hypnotic, graceful and seductive,"[11] a "cockeyed marvel of a comedy packed with amazing set pieces,"[12] and "a rambunctious and inspired ride,"[13] while marveling at how "the real siren songs of time and place turn the visual kitsch into a distilled Americana that's unexpectedly stirring."[14] Perhaps famed film critic Roger Ebert, who gave the film two-and-a-half out of four stars, provides the interlocutor between the two camps: "I left the movie uncertain and unsatisfied. I saw it a second time, admired the same parts, left with the same feeling. . . . I had the sense of invention set adrift; of a series of bright ideas wondering why they had all been invited to the same film."[15]

One thing that unites critics, scholars, and consumers alike is the essential role music plays within the film. The soundtrack, with T Bone at the helm choosing musicians, producing the sessions, and advising on the catalogue, is a roots music anthology featuring gospel, blues, bluegrass, country, chain-gang chants, and folk music—what becomes broadly noted throughout the film as "old-timey." The Coens wrote the music into the film, actually record-ing the music before filming, which left few scenes without their sounds and created a purposeful sub-narrative. In the liner notes to the soundtrack, Ethan Coen argues that the music is "compelling . . . in its own right . . . harking back to a time when music was a part of everyday life." Regarding the film's origins, Burnett recollects Ethan Coen calling and asking if he was interested in help-ing on "a film about the history of American music."[16] Coen here notes one way the music functions within the film, and implicitly another way by which the soundtrack could be judged today: as a historical treatment of the commercial interest in roots-folk sound.

Though the music existed in pockets throughout America, it was not until the recording boom of the 1920s that folk music truly got its first taste of com-mercial success. During this time, entrepreneurs like Ralph Peer created the first great popular interest in American folk music.[17] Peer scoured the South in search of folk music to be popularized for the masses on his Okeh records. He would hold tryouts where normal folks, who undoubtedly had been playing music in their homes and for community events, had the chance to record old songs for pay. Peer famously discovered the influential recording artists Jimmy Rodgers and the Carter Family in Bristol, Tennessee on the same day in 1927.[18] Burnett contends that the 1930s was one of the most amazing periods of music, from modernist classical to the blues in the South. He argues that "America began to record itself in the 1930s, and we hear the true voices of this country coming to us from those recordings."[19]

Despite the public interest in folk music, it would take the father-and-son team of John and Alan Lomax to usher in true commercial success. Using modern technology and mass communication to best "articulate a canon of American folk music," the Lomax team "enlisted the full array of mass media . . . to transform rural folk musicians into celebrities," integrating their music into popular culture.[20] With the backing of the Library of Congress, the Lomax duo lugged around a recording device in their trunk, covering thousands of miles, particularly around the South. They preferred to record black men in prisons, as they thought, often wrongly, that such men would not be tainted by the popular music outside the prison walls. In one such trip to the infamous Angola prison in Louisiana, they discovered a convicted murderer named Lead Belly who would become one of the early stars of folk blues.[21] Not surprisingly, Burnett uses a 1959 Alan Lomax recording from a prison chain gang at the Mississippi State Penitentiary in Lambert.

Furthermore, there are purposeful allusions to the imprint of the music industry and the music itself throughout the film. After the three men have escaped to the home of Pete's cousin, the stereotypically named Wash Hogwallop, they sit around at night listening to "You Are My Sunshine," Governor Pappy O'Daniel's political anthem—a reference to the song's actual political past via Louisiana governor Jimmie Davis—on the radio. In fact, both politicians depicted in the film deploy "old-timey" music in their campaigns throughout. Soon, the boys are paid by a local radio station to "sing into the can." The engineer is adamant that they sing the "old-timey songs that folks can't get enough of." After the newly named Soggy Bottom Boys lay down their hit "Man of Constant Sorrow," a record producer later hunts them up, claiming that the "record is goin' through the roof" and that the "whole damn state's goin' apey [for it]."[22] With scenes like these, the Coens show how average people, music executives, and politicians used the power of the radio to create cultural impressions.

Along with historical representation, the music also functions as a complicated conduit concerning issues of Southern identity, nostalgia, memory, and tradition, prompting questions regarding its placement within the satirical context of the film. Andrew B. Leiter focuses on how the "music functions as a multi-layered agent of nostalgia . . . moderat[ing] hard times . . . [and] softening the depictions of an otherwise miserable Southern world."[23] Leiter contends that the "'old-timey' music . . . mitigates the . . . ridicule of the South . . . [while] invit[ing] nostalgic considerations of Southern distinctiveness at a time of increasingly homogenized regional identities . . . [and] distancing that nostalgia from less savory aspects of Southern distinctiveness."[24] Christopher J. Smith calls the film a "gleefully magic-realist fable of the world of the musical South . . . a visionary rapprochement based on the *idea* of Southern music." Moving beyond nostalgia, Smith focuses on the way an imagined world exercises an influential reality. For Smith, "in the semiotic universe of southern music and in the history of American culture that imagined world . . . represents another world, one less alienated, more egalitarian, and more fully integrated (in every sense of the word)." Smith concludes that the film "intentionally abandons the historical 'reality' of southern black-white/rich-poor dichotomies in favor of a fable of social rapprochement achieved through music."[25]

Underlying ideas concerning history and nostalgia, particularly regarding the South, are complex notions of authenticity and tradition. Sean Chadwell thoroughly examines how the music serves as narrative within the film. He contends that "authenticating this music as 'old time'" and representing it as narrative raises several questions.[26] Among those are one he quotes from a scathing review of O Brother: does the film's content "support and respect the music, or does it use the music to perpetuate the negative, stereotypical hillbilly image?"[27] Furthermore, Chadwell contends that such "authentication" within the film ultimately omits or ignores connections between African American and white Southern cultures. However, while the film could be said to reinforce hillbilly stereotypes with scenes of slack-jawed yokels dancing, the music exerts enough cultural agency to complicate such a broad condemnation. Though Chadwell's concern is valid, the soundtrack's assembly of black and white musicians highlights their interrelatedness more than their separateness. This is a point Burnett is keen to make, commenting on how similar the genres of music are, and that, though the musicians "followed different muses," the sounds were "all a part of the same world."[28]

By evoking the idea of the "authentic," Chadwell raises more questions than answers, particularly when the authentication process takes place within a purposefully satirical context. Margaret Toscano recognizes the complicated relationship between history and memory, noting two camps in which such scholarship usually resides: how memory of the past is often "filtered through the lens of the present" or how "history is always told from the perspective of whatever group . . . is fortunate enough to . . . become the documentarians."[29] Genre helps mediate the relationship between such theoretical ideas. So, while Ruppersburg argues that the film is "historical fantasy rather than a realistic portrayal of history,"[30] Toscano contends that, through humor, the Coens "keep putting new mustaches on the past, thus creating an on-going dialogue between the past and the present . . . to keep us questioning what is good and real . . . [in a way] that we hardly realize the questions have been asked."[31] Noting the scholarly disagreements above concerning the complexities of public memory, alongside all that the Coens attempt to accomplish and the role of the soundtrack within the film, parody seems the only vehicle by which the narrative can be loosened from the constraints of linear "truth" enough to accomplish its intended goals—however debatable the aims may be. Furthermore, in reference to implied issues of class consciousness and notions of culture, it is ironic that the success of the Coens' use of the sophisticated, high-culture tool of satire is notably dependent on so-called low-culture vernacular music. Without the soundtrack, the film stands as slapstick comedy only. With it, the comedic satire can become a vehicle by which Americans are willing to have uncomfortable conversations regarding the history and contemporary ramifications of Jim Crow in the Depression South. Or perhaps satire affords simply another mechanism for avoiding it altogether.

As such, the music potentially alters consumer perceptions of those historical dichotomies, reimagining them within the Coens' sepia-toned, roots-music-scored Mississippi. Smith and Leiter's readings argue that, through ahistorical nostalgia, the film and music take away the music's political power and radical potential. If so, is the film's legacy merely a successful corporate marketing of old-timey American music rather than anything approaching active countercultural possibilities for those without direct access to power? Could the film's use of music be providing what theorist Fredric Jameson called "utopian longing" for how things "ought to be?" Does the film's use of music play on consumers' "utopian longings" with "fantasy bribes" in order to emotionally manipulate viewers and garner enough cultural capital to commodify an ideal?[32] Furthermore, if musical artists inspired by O Brother's re-presentation of traditional American music adopt the roots stylings, could they miss the original music's cultural context? If so, will the new music be mere stylistic mimicry and not an avenue to explore contemporary issues of race, class, gender, place, and identity in the light of that historic context?

A good illustration of the points Smith and Leiter make are the white-class struggles presented throughout. As the three men leave the radio station, having recorded their song, they pass Pappy O'Daniel. Delmar, unaware of O'Daniel's prominence, cordially tells the governor about how he could get paid for recording. The governor calls him a "dumb cracker" and, after refusing to "press the flesh" for their votes, states that he is interested in "mass communicatin'," not "one at a timin.'" Later, by the night's campfire, the men dream of how they will spend their share of the fortune they're seeking. Pete dreams of opening a five-star restaurant, wearing a tuxedo, and never having to "say 'yes sir' and 'nah sir'" again. Delmar wants to buy back the family farm from the savings and loan because "you ain't no kind of man if you ain't got land."[33] These remarks foreground the class conflict indicative of the Depression-Era South. Yet, arguably, this message may be overlooked in light of how the music ironically reconciles O'Daniel and the Soggy Bottom Boys in the end, literally liberating them.

Still, the music also functions as a mediator of those harsh realities. Perhaps the closest the Coens come to realizing the violent reality of Jim Crow Mississippi is in the near-lynching of Tommy Johnson at a Ku Klux Klan rally. Johnson's character, a guitar-toting bluesman and purposeful conflation of historical blues legends Tommy Johnson and Robert Johnson, has been seized by the clan under suspicion that he sold his soul to the devil. Using the hate-filled vestiges of the era—a towering, burning cross, a rebel flag, and the hooded and outfitted Klansmen—the Coens create a *Wizard of Oz*–like choreographed routine with comedically ominous chants and movements. Yet, they marry these seeming incongruences with legendary bluegrass musician Ralph Stanley's haunting a cappella version of the century-old folk song "O Death," whose panicking narrator begs death for reprieve. Gubernatorial candidate Homer Stokes, decked and hooded in bright-red regalia as the KKK's Grand Kleagle, then leads the gathering with a speech indicative of the time:

> Brothers! Oh, brothers! We have all gathered here to preserve our hallowed culture and heritage! We aim to pull evil up by the root, before it chokes out the flower of our culture and heritage! And our women, let's not forget those ladies, y'all. Looking to us for protection! From darkies, from Jews, from papists, and from all those smart-ass folks say we come descended from monkeys![34]

The scene is indicative of the ways in which the Coens deftly weave satirical pastiche with historical poignancy to make a multifaceted imprint. In the scene, the music provides the necessary conduit between the absurd and the harsh realities. Yet, by depicting the racists of yore as *Wizard of Oz*–like munchkins, exotic and absurd, rather than the mundane, run-of-the-mill people such men and women were, does it rob the contemporary audience of an opportunity to judge Southern racial dynamics? Does the fantastical prevent the music from asserting its role as cultural spotlight, as voices and sounds from the margins, as a reminder of the lingering effects of a reprehensible past?

The music is not as cleanly resolved as Smith and Leiter suggest. Instead, the irony can also complicate attempts to neatly categorize. Arguably, the music can both serve as a moderator for the slapstick irony while in other ways offering a utopian escape vessel for historical memory. By tuning consumer ears back to America's musical past, is Burnett conjuring the ghosts of the music's context, Robert Johnson walking out of a juke joint in Greenwood, Mississippi, in the 1930s with only a guitar, or at the intersection of Highways 61 and 49 right outside Clarksdale, ready to conquer the world? The music's setting grounds the songs in a sense of place. The Mississippi Delta, called by James C. Cobb "the most Southern place on earth," with its alluvial soil and legendary stories of excess and hardships, has its own mythologies born out of its many paradoxes. The Delta has the richest soil and the poorest people, the closest proximity of races yet the most violent racial oppression, and it is arguably the source of some of America's greatest literature while maintaining the country's most uneducated populace.[35]

These contradictions come to full fruition in the region's rich musical tradition. Bill C. Malone argues that in "a social context of poverty, slavery, suffering, deprivation, religious extremism, and cultural isolation," music afforded Southerners "a form of self-expression that required neither power, status, nor affluence."[36] Indeed, as Charles Roland notes, poor Southerners "responded by preserving and developing a folk tradition of ballads and spirituals, of blues and jazz, and of hillbilly, country, and gospel music."[37]

The *O Brother, Where Art Thou?* soundtrack, incorporating several Southern musical genres, offers songs filled with the contradictions that epitomize the South: religion and debauchery, nostalgia and development, home and adventure—the very ideals by which the blues, country, and, by association, rock music were born. By doing so, Burnett participates in a long tradition of Southern cultural commentary that Hollywood and television producers, authors, and musicians have been expanding upon for a century. Burnett re-presents standard Southern archetypes, symbols, and themes for a contemporary audience. By intermingling the genres, Burnett shows the complexities imbued within music that has historically been characterized by racial collaboration and contestation, while also directing a chorus of voices responding to the harsh realities of Delta life. Does Burnett's musical colloquy then offer a historical window to understanding poor whites and African Americans in the Delta? Does it potentially further longstanding stereotypes? Does it romanticize the people, the time period, and the South? Or does it resist either-or fallacies and instead, like a kaleidoscope, offer concentric circles of romance, memory, history, and poetry, doubling back and grafting other bright colors, weaving and clashing together, offering a philosophy for the present?

Reading the soundtrack, examining form as well as themes and symbols, helps illuminate how the music functions culturally, potentially adding to the historic context for African American Delta life while also supporting the mythic properties in contemporary presentation and consumption. "Po' Lazarus" is a chain-gang chant, using call and response and conjuring images of African Americans in notorious Delta prison work camps like Parchman. In fact, the soundtrack version, credited to James Carter and the Prisoners, was recorded in 1959 by Alan Lomax at Parchman's Camp B of the Mississippi State Penitentiary at Lambert. Delta prisons themselves are mythic symbols, carrying connotations of unjust suffering and social control, as men were often sentenced to labor camps or prisons for breaking social-conduct laws, like running away from tenant duties or work camps or not conforming to the rigid social demands that came with interactions between whites and blacks, particularly black men and white women. Writing on his observations at Parchman, Lomax noted that "everywhere we heard of men working till they dropped dead or burnt out with sunstroke." Some prisoners chose other methods of beating back against the oppressive labor conditions: "The sight of a one-legged or one-armed man who had chopped off his own foot or hand with an ax or a hoe was a common one."[38]

The prison chants not only broke up the drudgery of work, but they were one of the few accepted means by which black people could publicly voice their dissatisfaction with the social structure. The songs could function as public lamentations with implied social critique, in the tradition of slave field hollers and gospel songs. The connections between slavery and the prison chants are unmistakable and suggest the thousands of daily indignities, the rampant violence and intimidation, and the rigid social structure which left African Americans struggling to assert their humanity, individually or collectively, in the midst of a majority white culture bent on stamping out black agency.

"Po' Lazarus" uses religion and violent imagery, with Lazarus and the sheriff serving as archetypes. The Delta sheriff figure is a myth type in any study of turn-of-the-century Delta communities. Sheriffs were notoriously corrupt and ruthless, sanctioning violence as a means of social control. In her autobiography *I Know Why the Caged Bird Sings*, Maya Angelou describes a childhood encounter in the Delta town of Stamps, Arkansas, with such a sheriff who, straddling his horse, had come to warn her family of a looming lynching that night, because a "crazy nigger messed with a white lady." Angelou was struck by how "his nonchalance was meant to convey his authority and power over even dumb animals. How much more capable he would be with Negroes. It went without saying." Commenting on the faces of the nightriders the sheriff would lead in pursuit of the black man they intended to lynch, Angelou describes their "cement faces and eyes of hate that burned the clothes off you if they happened to see you lounging on the main street downtown on Sunday."[39]

In "Po' Lazarus," the high deputy is too afraid to go after the notorious Lazarus, who has never been apprehended and is hiding out in the mountains. Hunted by the sheriff instead, Lazarus is shot down with a .45, with the lawman laying the dead man's body on the commissary gallery, itself a symbol of the corruption and persecution of poor Delta workers, as many were oppressed by crooked owners charging exorbitant prices. The body's placement is no coincidence; it is a warning for all to see.

The name Lazarus conveys theological significance as well. In the gospel of Luke, Jesus tells the parable of the rich man and Lazarus—a beggar "covered with sores, who desired to be fed with what fell from the rich man's table. Moreover, even the dogs came and licked his sores." Yet, when Lazarus dies, he is "carried by the angels to Abraham's side," while the rich man when he dies is sent to Hades. After begging Abraham for relief and for the prophet to send Lazarus to his brothers to warn them, Abraham refuses: "They have Moses and the Prophets; let them hear them."[40] Therefore, though a sense of fatalism drapes over the story, leaving the message, sung by the prisoners, that the black man's only agency is martyrdom, the song's lament hopes for a day when the poor will be in heaven and the rich oppressors will finally get what they deserve. The character Lazarus thus stands as a mythic antihero fugitive trying to assert individuality and self-actualization in the face of legal structures hell-bent on keeping social order.

The gospel, country-blues, and prison chants Burnett positions in the soundtrack take the listeners on their own journey through African American musical expressions, highlighting the similarities of themes, sounds, and symbols which eventually evolve into what is cumulatively called the blues, a mythic term in its own right that is bathed in the contradictions and historic experiences of the South and of identity for African Americans, foreshadowing contemporary expression such as hip-hop. In the South at large, black people have historically had difficulty carving out cultural space for identity narratives. In fact, only until recent history has the term "Southern" implied more than whiteness.[41] As such, whites have often imposed identity on black people and black culture, negating its rich heritage, including music, foodways, religion, politics, art, and literature. An example of such a danger exists in the historical treatment of African American culture in the Delta and the South at large. There is a significant relationship between the repression of Southern African American culture and issues regarding identity today. How difficult is it for modern African American individuals and communities to have a distinctly Southern identity? When considering characteristics of Southern identity both historically and in modern contexts, have cultural narratives carved out space for African Americans to be the protagonists of the stories, creators of unique and vibrant culture—heirs to centuries' worth of culture that has reshaped and helped define American culture as we know it today? Or are black people and is black culture still something against which majority white culture judges itself? Are the blues and gospel singers alongside the slave hollers and prison chants viewed as exotic, subhuman historical figures who existed in a romanticized past? Are storylines simply remaking Huck and Tom's fascination with the exotic otherness of Jim? Is Southern identity still a markedly white enterprise in the American psyche? If so, the potential exists to merely further mythic archetypes like Sambo, Mammy, and the hypersexualized and violent Negro, or to perpetuate the myth that black life resonates with an overwhelming sense of fatalism, leaving few options for black agency. There is also the potential that, as in the *O Brother* soundtrack, certain groups, in this case black women, are left marginalized or voiceless.

Burnett's soundtrack seemingly takes dead aim at historical awareness. Emphasizing African American cultural heritage and agency further highlights how much white and black culture have intersected and how much they owe each other, that, indeed, so-called white culture has often been born out of the African American heritage. So, while the myths of African American music carry the potential to be more white marketing creations than black agency, the success of the *O Brother* soundtrack means that these myths and their historic connections are still vibrant and available for interpretation by contemporary audiences. Though the penchant for romanticism is still certainly possible, such interpretation is not the only avenue available. Ralph Ellison said that blues music is concerned with "an impulse to keep the painful details and episodes of a brutal experience alive in one's aching conscious-ness."[42] Thus, a song's context can provide a new lens by which to view an old problem. As African Americans in poor inner cities dogged with jobless-ness, poverty, and violence are continuously imprisoned at rates far greater than whites, as issues regarding police brutality and segregated schools still haunt American life, can Burnett's song choices accurately contextualize cur-rent social problems, helping contemporary cultural consumers recognize the long arm of American systemic racial injustice? Can "Po' Lazarus," "Hard Time Killing Floor Blues," and "Lonesome Valley" offer context for the various hip-hop artists, such as New Orleans's Lil Wayne, Atlanta's Outkast and Killer Mike, and Meridian, Mississippi's Big K.R.I.T., who comment on Southern identity and reality for contemporary African American communities? Lil Wayne's "God Bless Amerika" speaks to how "Po' Lazarus" has not atrophied, preserved only in the film's Mississippi amber.[43]

In Wayne's "God Bless Amerika," the artist's fate and distress loom. In the deadpanned, nasally slur for which he is known, the hip-hop star presents an eye-for-an-eye, dog-eat-dog worldview, where moments of beauty are caged within a future he fears will end with either premature death or incarceration. This is an America most citizens would not recognize. Here, Wayne's dirge engages Lazarus's ghost. It is alarming, confrontational, and heartbreaking in its resignation to systemic fatalism. The artist's narrative plays out in the song's video. The opening shot has Wayne in front of a giant American flag. In a sleeveless T-shirt that reads "Jesus Saves / I Spend" with a cross and dollar sign intertwined between the declarations, Wayne calmly, in the manner of spoken poetry, leads the viewer through the only America many from Hollygrove, the poverty-stricken New Orleans neighborhood in which Wayne grew up, know. Images of this America display a mosaic. African Americans who are young and old, including men, women, and children, both able-bodied and disa-bled, all with various facial expressions along a spectrum between the poles of happiness and sadness, are set in the context of communal symbols: barbe-cue, basketball, family, neighborhood supermarkets, music, and dilapidated homes. Wayne bounces around one dilapidated house with the words "They Don't Care" spray-painted on a collapsing wall. Interspersed are images of police in riot gear, on the march, with tear gas billowing. The message presents the difficult reality of inner-city life for many African Americans in similar contexts, the only America many of them know and an America many outside such places can hardly imagine. In the song, frustrations, joys, poverty, family, violence, the legal system, and a purposeful stab at the idealized white-picket-fence American mythology all swirl around in a present context rooted in a racial and cultural Southern past.

Even a cursory reading of the *O Brother* blues songs resurrects old spirits, the muses for Wayne's chillingly calm lament. Wayne's contemporary "Amerika" does not drop out of time and space, isolated and unique, and his audience is not incapable of reading his New Orleans context into the artist's lyrics. As the blues artists once assimilated themselves into mainstream popular culture, so, too, have Wayne and other hip-hop artists, whose global fame has much to do with the music moving to suburbs where the cultural messages embedded in hip-hop became accepted and often emulated by white middle-class Americans. As in the case with the blues, this platform offers a megaphone for African American cultural voices and messaging while simultaneously posing problematic questions regarding contemporary racial dynamics. Does the music's widespread dissemination across cultural, racial, and socioeconomic boundaries contribute to furthering racial stereotypes, or does it shine a spotlight on unique aspects of black culture and social problems affecting communities? The parallel cultural functions of the blues and hip-hop reinforce that the *O Brother* messages translate easily into the modern racial context. It is not a large leap to connect the dots between the consumption of Burnett's and the Coens' *O Brother* phenomenon and the middle-class consumers of artists like Wayne. The cultural space is not altogether foreign. Writing of blues legend Robert Johnson, rock critic Greil Marcus explains that "a critic's job is not only to define the context of an artist's work but to expand that context, and it seems more important to me that Johnson's music is vital enough to enter other contexts and create all over again."[44]

The mythic archetypes, symbols, and themes in African American song narratives play out similarly for poor whites in the soundtrack's roots country selections. The term "country" is used here in the literal sense, as a music born out of common, rural people across the South, in the Appalachian Mountains and Kentucky, the hills of Georgia and Alabama, and into the Mississippi Delta, Arkansas, and Texas, among other places. The music would eventually splinter into different genres such as bluegrass, yet the genres' wellspring lies in a similar source: the working-class, poor white. Bill Malone states that country music has traditionally dealt with the day-to-day problems encountered by average people, with primary characteristics including home, religion, rambling, frolic, humor, and politics.[45]

"Big Rock Candy Mountain," "Man of Constant Sorrow," and "In the Jailhouse Now" epitomize Malone's blue-collar paradoxes. "Big Rock Candy Mountain" presents a hobo utopia, with free cigarettes and whiskey and Edenic weather, where the legal authorities and their structures are stripped of real-world power. Far from the Southern agrarian's noble yeoman and the mythic Southern cavalier planter, the song presents the archetype of the shiftless, lazy, poor white cracker noted for his comical, drunken, harmless demeanor and lack of ambition. The song's context was not lost on Burnett: "There was a time in this country, and in country music, when the only poetry people heard in the country was the verses from the King James Version of the Bible. So there was a lot of Biblical poetry in country music. And this 'Big Rock Candy Mountain' was a country song that got into social commentary and satire."[46]

"Man of Constant Sorrow" picks up on the ramblin' loner motif, with the unsettled narrator's life dominated by trouble, loneliness, and discontent. This song and "In the Jailhouse Now" feature troublemaking wanderers. The latter song features a narrator telling the story of a ne'er-do-well rambler who finds himself in jail with no prospects. The song's raconteur fares no better—carousing with a gold-digging girl named Suzie and eventually landing in jail themselves.

The song was popularized by one of the first country music celebrities, Jimmie Rodgers, who Malone claims may have been the "first country singer who consciously cultivated the persona of rambler and built his reputation around that identity." By feeding quixotic imagery while downplaying the harsh realities, Rodgers "exploited the romance" and "contributed to country music a repertoire of songs about rogues, rascals, boasters, rounders, convicts, hoboes, railroadmen, cowboys, and other ramblers that still beguile us today."[47] Rodgers, along with Lazarus and bluesman Robert Johnson, shows the penchant for myths to create heroes and antiheroes that can serve as examples of certain behaviors or virtues or serve as stand-ins for the populace. Just as Homer's Odysseus was a mortal man with exaggerated gifts, these men become larger-than-life symbols, myths in their own right. Like Homer's characters, too, each culture needs its symbolic, mythological heroes, their virtues, motivations, and actions subject to idolatry and imitation. Rodgers' placement on the soundtrack, and the allusion to Johnson in Chris Thomas King's character, clearly modeled on the bluesman who legend has it sold his soul to the devil, is no accident. When Burnett told *Rolling Stone* that the story of the United States was Johnson's, a kid with only a guitar to his name walking down the road and changing the world, he followed by reminding of the regenerative power of music and narrative: "We've done that again, and again, and again— Johnny Cash, Hank Williams, Bob Dylan, Bruce Springsteen, Jimmy Rogers [*sic*], Howlin' Wolf, Muddy Waters."[48]

Those heroes withstanding, the country songs decidedly invoke a historic rural white context. In his seminal 1941 book *The Mind of the South*, W. J. Cash's "man at the center," the ordinary white Southerner, is characterized by the dominant trait of "intense individualism," of being "purely self-asserting." Yet this yearning is most often constrained by "the close-pressing throng of his fellow men, rigid class distinctions, the yoke of law and government, [and] economic imperatives—all these bear upon him with crushing weight and confine his individualistic activities to a very narrow space."[49] Cash's second "great Southern characteristic" was a penchant toward unreality and romanticism "in intimate relation to hedonism."[50] Violence was often a "channel of discharge."[51] Cash offers descriptions of a man who loves to dance and drink and who "fight[s] harder and love[s] harder than the next man."[52]

"Big Rock Candy Mountain," "Man of Constant Sorrow," and "In the Jailhouse Now" further the outside-the-law romantic myth of the travelling troubadour and rambler. However, while hedonism offered a respite from the realities of working-class life, the humor and bravado ultimately mask the violence, unemployment, heartbreak, isolation, and sometimes death that were both cause and consequence of such a lifestyle. The songs also connote a loss of community and familial attachment, and offer a critique of capitalism with its low wages, loss of work, worker separation from the spoils of labor, and the detrimental trappings of materialism.

The different approaches in these songs all speak to the difficult reality for working-class Delta whites. Such certainties counter the rich, white, *Gone with the Wind* fantasy so often associated with the South. Implicit within these narratives is the idea that fatalism and escapism infuse poor white realities. The songs speak to the contradictions and conflicts omnipresent in the Delta poor white's life. However, as was the case with the treatment of African American archetypes, these narratives can further perpetuate longstanding mythologies surrounding rural whites—the cracker-barrel peckerwood, drunk on whiskey, jobless, and homeless, who is often presented in comedic, violent, or sexualized terms. Or, the myths can whitewash their harsh economic and social existence. The songs also do little to present the omnipresent racial conflicts present in the South, and they arguably do not come to terms with the advantages poor whites held culturally, materially, and psychologically over African Americans. Yet, when placed side-by-side in shared cultural space and studied in tandem, common themes of fate, escapism, isolation, and unrequited love, along with a yearning for self-actualization, speak to the similar gene pool from which both musical genres were born—highlighting their commonalities as much as their contentions.

Perhaps no song on the soundtrack so clearly connects the races and the genres as "Didn't Leave Nobody But the Baby." Originally an African American field holler and lullaby once recorded by Lomax on a 1959 trip to Senatobia, Mississippi, Burnett remakes the song into a haunting, sexualized song, sung by Gillian Welch, Emmylou Harris, and Alison Krauss. Welch called the song "an Appalachian siren-song-seduction-lullaby-death-chant."[53] The ambiguous message throughout the lullaby has a baby apparently abandoned, perhaps by his father to work the fields, and by a mother who left some time ago under possibly inauspicious circumstances, with intimations of promiscuity. The song has a macabre tone with its insinuation of infanticide and the evocation of grave imagery. Genre-bending, the narrative combines themes of innocence and death, agrarian responsibility and sexuality, and an overarching sense of spirituality and violence simultaneously.

In addition, religion permeates all the aforementioned genres—either directly or indirectly. Religion in the South is an enigmatic and mercurial topic, carrying the weight of heritage layered with political, racial, cultural, and theological contradictions. In the soundtrack, the gospel staples presented offer themes of earthly piety and examples of believers working out their salvation alongside narratives of the Christian's response to death and the afterlife. "Down to the River to Pray" combines familial ties with the broader Christian community, while giving a recipe for finding favor with the Lord. The message is a prescription of communal history and spiritual disciplines—prayer, study, and baptism—which are staples of evangelical salvation. Indeed, the scene in the movie is a mass river baptism in which Pete and Delmar "warsh their sins away." Furthermore, roots heroine Alison Krauss's version of the folk staple is one of the more angelic, restrained, and beautiful songs on the soundtrack.

When the singer questions, "Who shall wear the robe and crown," and begs the "Good Lord [to] show me the way," the prescription is laid out clearly.

Concerning the Christian response to death and eternity, "I'll Fly Away," "Angel Band," and "O Death" offer differing perspectives. The gospel classic "I'll Fly Away" uses prison imagery to call for a celestial escape from the weariness of life. Similarly, "Angel Band" presents a spiritual hopefulness in death, a victory over the toils of life's struggles. In contrast, in Ralph Stanley's version of "O Death," the most haunting track on the album, Death is gatekeeper to heaven and hell and is personified in a more unwelcome and graphically realistic light, taking the soul and leaving the body to decompose. With his mother offering comfort at his deathbed, the singer begs for Death to consider his youth. Highlighting the conflict between materialism and spiritualism, the singer offers all the wealth at his command, to no avail. Implicitly, instead of the seemingly blind hopefulness of the pious, the singer clings to life, either doubting his own soul's destination or the eternal promises offered by religion.

The struggle between devout faith and doubt is one example of other conflicts and contradictions in the South's religious mythologies. Cash's observations on Southern religion in the 1930s speak to this myth. Cash talks about the faith of the Southerner as "simple and emotional as himself." This faith drew men together with fire-and-brimstone apocalyptic imagery, "cast[ing] them into the pit, rescu[ing] them, and at last bring[ing] them shouting into the fold of Grace." This was a faith "not of liturgy and prayer book, but of primitive frenzy," worshipping a personal deity, "a God for the individualist . . . whose representatives were not silken priests but preachers risen from the people themselves."[54]

Such emotionalism gave the church, and her representatives, significant authority over the faithful. Similarly, religion was used by many, including planters and politicians—most of whom were segregationists and white supremacists, and some of whom saw themselves as the pious seeking to do God's will on this earth—to feed people's hopes of spending eternity in Heaven, further complicating the myths, archetypes, and symbols born out of Southern religious tradition. Certainly, the negative social aspects of religion are what critics like H. L. Mencken had in mind, lampooning the South as a place of religious zealots, bigotry, racism, and anti-intellectualism, connotations which carry significant cultural currency in today's South as well. But Mencken and Cash's conclusions, as in the case of mythic representations of

African Americans and poor whites, do not give justice to the complexities of religious life in the South. Religion, too, is filled with the contradictions of the Southern human situation, yet many of the same negative archetypes have been perpetuated in contemporary Southern narratives, as bible-belt fundamentalism and conservative politics have increasingly become insep- arable bedfellows, which can come with unspoken racial undercurrents. As such, the soundtrack's gospel songs participate in a longstanding religious her- itage, mapping current political, social, racial, gender, and class issues onto age-old Southern spiritual mythologies. The songs remind us that religion in the South continues to carry loaded signifiers, particularly of social class and political affiliation. Yet the soundtrack complicates a myopic understanding of the region's religious impulse. The songs' lyrics address a people hoping for a better reality. They are eager for prescriptions on how to live, and they long for moral clarity and courage. They are a hope-filled people looking for a world- view by which to filter through and manage life's troubles.

In a biographical treatment, Bradley Hanson shrewdly argues that Burnett's Christian background should be read in to the O Brother creation and mes- sage. Having a shaky relationship with the Episcopalian religion of his youth, Burnett seemingly regained religious devotion during the 1975–1976 Bob Dylan–led Rolling Thunder tour.[55] In Bob Spitz's biography of Dylan, he notes Burnett's Christian impulses during this time: "T-Bone moonlighted in the service of the Lord. He was an early disciple of born-again fundamentalism" possessing "all the spooky religious rhetoric of a Christian missionary."[56] Yet, Burnett's religion was not without a questioning spirit. His was not the thoughtless crutch, fever-pitched and blindly devoted, so often ascribed to the South's religious. A couple of years removed from the Rolling Thunder tour, Burnett argued that, without fully understanding what they believe and why they believe it, Christians will never progress from a "safe, bourgeois" state, arguing, "let's be in the world, but not on the terms of the world."[57]

This allusion to the apostle Paul's message to the Roman Church to not con- form to the pattern of the world, along with the Christian ethic of being disci- ples, influenced Burnett's vision of music's role in culture: "If Jesus is the Light of the World, there are two kinds of songs you can write. You can write songs about the light, or you can write songs about what you can see from the light. That's what I try to do."[58] In regards to his craft, seven years after the Rolling Thunder tour he articulated his purposeful philosophy regarding music: it "touches people deeply, and therefore the question it raises is, what are you going to do with that responsibility?"[59]

Undoubtedly, modern consumer perceptions of the religious South were grafted into the *O Brother* reception. In the chapter "Jesusland" in her book *The New Mind of the South*, Tracy Thompson summarizes the South's religious tradition in the modern imagination. Beginning in the 1950s and '60s and reaching its zenith in the 1970s and 1980s, led by Jerry Falwell's Moral Majority and Christian media mogul Pat Robertson, the contemporary South's evangelical alliance with conservative politics began to solidify. As Thompson notes, particularly in the South, this religious-political alliance made up of white middle-class Southerners became increasingly "fundamentalist in tone, more political, and overall less hospitable to so-called 'moderates' or 'liberals.'"[60] Such fundamentalism has continued to be influential in the region's political dynamics, characterizing the South politically and religiously as conservative and intolerant. Yet, as Thompson notes, the region is not homogeneous in these regards: "Evangelical religion had once been a big tent that all Southerners could live under, but once it was divided into 'liberal' and 'conservative' camps, it divided Southerners, too."[61]

Responding to this division, and channeling the frustrations of many contemporary Southerners concerning the capitalism-modeled megachurches and their health-and-wealth prosperity gospel, the television evangelists' emotional manipulations for profits, and the fearmongering about and othering of those who dare disagree, Burnett, in the summer of 1992, lashed out: "Pat Robertson and all those people should be horsewhipped. . . . They're smug, self-righteous, pretentious. . . . Jesus was the exact opposite. . . . He was powerless, He emptied himself of all power. He was accepting."[62] Eight years prior to *O Brother* and twenty-one years before Thompson's *The New Mind of the South*, Burnett prophesies the ethos of the next generation of religious-minded Southerners. Thompson contends that the generation of Falwell, Robertson, and Billy Graham will be replaced with a "more global, socially conscious evangelicalism . . . tired of the culture wars, disillusioned with Republicans and Democrats."[63] As Bradley Hanson argues, T Bone uses *O Brother* as "a transport for a social, aesthetic, and religious message."[64] It's a narrative that, when viewed through contemporary Southern identity, serves as a corrective, an attempt to wrestle religion and music back from those who seek to misrepresent. It's a philosophy at the heart of the movement he heads, and it plays out in contemporary culture and an increasingly diversified Southern populace.

The album's success speaks to how the music of the South still captures the imagination of the world, and perhaps to how its history is still interpreted and presented in a collage of facts and misrepresentations, producing misplaced feelings of nostalgia and romance, simultaneously mythologizing and stereotyping the South and her occupants. The *O Brother* soundtrack, with its themes of poverty and racism, family, quest for independence, personal dignity, and self-definition, and freedom from life's hardships, whether in this world or the next, offers a different myth of the South than the Old South planter utopia. Indeed, the once-typical mythological treatment of the South's antebellum history was centered on wealthy white fantasies of a pastoral Eden, a sea of cotton fields and plantations where affluent gentlemen and genteel white women ruled a world in which blacks and poor white trash, lacking the intellectual ability and moral fiber to navigate the political and social realities of American life, knew their place. The myths in the *O Brother* soundtrack complicate the Delta's story and offer a lens by which to view the contemporary Southern condition.

The soundtrack proves that there still exists great value in reimagining Southern myths in popular culture for a new generation of consumers. By March 2002, the album reached number one on the pop charts, beating out pop star Brandy's *Full Moon*, Canadian rocker Alanis Morissette's *Under Rug Swept*, alternative band Linkin Park's *Hybrid Theory*, Top 40 Nashville darling Alan Jackson's *Drive*, Atlanta hip-hop artist Ludacris's *Word of Mouf*, R&B singer Alicia Keys's *Songs in A Minor*, and Jennifer Lopez's *J to tha L–O!*, Kylie Minogue's *Fever*, and Pink's *Missundaztood*.[65] With such consumption comes an essential question: do the songs and artists help contextualize contemporary Southern life? For music consumers in the twenty-first century, such myths— with their themes, symbols, and archetypes—get grafted into post-Depression mythologies surrounding the civil rights movement and industrialization. Furthermore, mythologies involving musicians like Johnny Cash and Elvis Presley have been born alongside myths surrounding new genres of music like hip-hop and the growing lore surrounding athletics, particularly college football, in the South. With such expansion, Burnett's *O Brother* soundtrack helps reinvigorate the layered and complex mythologies surrounding the South as a new generation adds its own narrative interpretation to the culture's past, present, and future. Yet, with such presentation comes further debate and potential for unintended consequences, both for good and ill, as bands like Mumford & Sons and the Avett Brothers build on the *O Brother* momentum with decidedly roots-based aesthetics and sounds, purposefully curated for contemporary popular audiences.

CHAPTER 2

THE MUMFORD MOMENT

O *Brother*, the Folk Fad, and the Roots
of a Southern Renaissance

I don't really know what an Okie is, but I feel like one.
— **TED DWANE,** Mumford & Sons

History, memory, and identity swirl around in music, in which meaning creation is further complicated by the engagement consumers have with the sound,
aesthetics, and text. Despite the debatable cultural and historical messaging
throughout the O *Brother* soundtrack, the possibility of consumer whitewashing, nostalgia, and oversimplification—perhaps fueled by the perceived
authenticity of the music—is evident in some of the nonprofessional movie
reviews on the Internet Movie Database. For example, one reviewer, who states
she lived through the Depression, found the music "originally American" and
"authentic" and was "amazed that someone not of our generation could have
captured the essence of that period of United States history."[1] Another argued
that the "movie grabs and clutches at raw truth of the Southern mind-set" and
that it "beautifully depicts history and tradition" that are "intractable to a certain way of life." The reviewer comments that the music is both "haunting" and
"cleansing" and that, overall, the movie represents "the raw truth of the Deep
South and its culture for an era gone by."[2] Lastly, one reviewer particularly sin-
gled out the soundtrack, calling it "the real star of the film," which "gives you an
impression of a magical land where everything was perfect and everyone was
happy, far from what was actually happening at the time. But somehow the situations don't seem all that unrealistic and you end up loving the characters all
the more. You just want to keep singing that song again and again."[3] *Los Angeles
Times* film critic Kenneth Turan substantiates these reviewers' attraction to the

film's soundtrack: "*O Brother*'s music is more than pleasant background; it is a living presence, and with apologies to an excellent cast, just about the star of the picture."[4]

I identify with the reviewers' honest reactions to the film's evocation of the past through music. My grandparents, Carthel and Mary Eveyln (Pruitt) Jones, grew up during the Great Depression. As a child, I heard their stories of working cotton fields and of my great-grandfather walking miles down dirt roads each Sunday to preach for a small Baptist congregation. There was a legendary story of my grandfather, Pop, accidentally cutting off the top part of his big toe as a boy while chopping firewood, only to be sent back to the fields a day or so later. They spoke of neighbors gathering to listen to the St. Louis Cardinals baseball games on the radio, of growing their own food and tailoring their own clothes. In their isolation on Joy Mountain and in Romance, Arkansas, they were largely sheltered from the racial conflicts so prevalent in other parts of the South. Furthermore, like many Southerners of their age, they moved from rural areas to, in their case, the county seat, looking for better-paying jobs and an easier life. They had two daughters and bought a little white house. Every time we spent the night with them, Pop sang the old folk staple "Down in the Valley" at bedtime. In his colloquial version, he would trill the *L*'s over and again:

> Down in the val-l-l-l-ley, the valley so l-l-l-low
> Hang your head over, hear the wind blow,
> Hear the wind blow, dear, hear the wind blow.
> Roses love sunshine, violets love dew,
> Angels in Heaven know I love you,
> Know I love you, dear, know I love you.

My understanding of the Depression Era was filtered through those stories which were told to the soundtrack of that song, and my notions of class, race, and poverty were mapped in with them. These reactions show the complex relationship viewers have in reconciling *O Brother*'s music-filled irony with the harsh realities of the Depression-Era South. These reactions mirror what seminal folklorist Alan Lomax saw in folk music and its reception in his day. Writing in 1947, he notes with approval the "spring freshet of enthusiasm for native balladry and folklore that is running through the country from coast to coast." While he admits that "there may be an element of escapism in this trend," he finds that it speaks to "our hankering after art that mirrors the unique life of this western continent."[5]

Thus, the nostalgic impulse created by the Depression setting and the re-presenting of "old-timey" music come into direct conflict with the film's treatment of modernity and the idea of the South in transition. As the three men survive the flood at the end of the movie, Everett comments on the impending modernization that is to come:

> The fact is, they're flooding this valley so they can hydroelectric up the whole durn state. Yes, sir, the South is gonna change. Everything's gonna be put on electricity and run on a paying basis. Out with the old spiritual mumbo-jumbo, the superstitions and the backward ways. We're gonna see a brave new world where they run everybody a wire and hook us all up to a grid. Yes, sir, a veritable age of reason. Like the one they had in France. Not a moment too soon.[6]

As shown, whether the film and soundtrack are "authentic"—and the subsequent effect for interpreting the film and concerning the ideas of tradition and public memory—is debatable. Yet, looking at the separate success of the soundtrack may give unique cultural insight. The T Bone Burnett–produced soundtrack won multiple Grammy Awards and sold millions of albums. It even spawned a Nashville concert, documented by D. A. Pennebaker in *Down from the Mountain* (2000), and a subsequent tour. Burnett's formula for creating the soundtrack ties history and the modern world together, showing the relevance of roots music and tradition in contemporary cultural consciousness. As he has done with other soundtracks, notably for *Cold Mountain* and *Crazy Heart*, Burnett uses original artists such as Harry McClintock and the Lomax prisoner field recording alongside contemporary artists reimagining roots classics, in this case Emmylou Harris, John Hartford, Alison Krauss, and Chris Thomas King, among others. Sometimes the actors sing on camera, as in Tim Blake Nelson's version of the Jimmie Rodgers hit "In the Jailhouse Now," and sometimes they don't, such as when Clooney lip-syncs Dan Tyminski singing "Man of Constant Sorrow." Other times the musicians appear in the film, as do the Cox Family and the Fairfield Four.

So, while some "purists" took exception to Burnett's presentation, ultimately he makes a harmonious argument consistent with the history of roots music and the notion of tradition. Burnett clearly places his soundtrack within a historical, regenerative process, a practice that is itself a part of the history of folk music and one which clearly plays a role in cultural identity and memory. By reviving the music, Burnett summons the past seen as "traditional"—as Richard Middleton puts it, "a home that has been lost."[7] Furthermore, by using modern musicians and offering the music to a contemporary audience, the soundtrack and the musical reinterpretations participate in tradition while allowing consumers a participatory role in tradition-creating as well. Highlighting the music's historical context is essential for such interpretative effort. Without context, the voices from the music's background are silenced, undermining the community necessary for widespread participation and hushing the music's creative activist potential.

Bearing these thoughts in mind, two questions resonate: why was the music so successful, and what have been the effects since? Coming out at the beginning of the twenty-first century, in the middle of the tech boom and Y2K hysterics, the soundtrack serves as a counter to the impulses and demands of the modern world. The collection certainly stood in stark contrast to the music dominating the late-nineties charts. The nineties saw the rise of grunge, alternative, and teen pop with iconic bands like Nirvana and the Red Hot Chili Peppers sharing cultural space with Britney Spears, the Backstreet Boys, and Latin heartthrob Ricky Martin. In contrast, the success of the soundtrack altered the popular music landscape over the next decade, reintroducing banjos, stand-up basses, and stripped-down singer-songwriter harmonies to a new generation of popular-culture consumers.

Though the soundtrack was a surprising success, Burnett admits he foresaw a great opportunity. Growing up in Fort Worth, Texas, in the 1950s, Burnett consumed the eclecticism of local radio where "there was no artificial separation according to whether a song was rock, or country, or blues—just music . . . here's the Beatles, then something by Peggy Lee. Then, a Hank Williams favorite, and then something from Little Tommy Tucker, four songs in a row, no categories."[8] Not surprisingly, with both the B-52 Band and the Alpha Band in the 1970s, Burnett would continue to produce art that mirrored his upbringing, mixing rock and roll, blues, soul, and country, foregrounding his twenty-first-century ethos. Though not commercially successful, the Alpha Band's critical acclaim—a yin and yang recipe Burnett would endure throughout his solo career as well—gave the producer a glimpse of what this eclectic formula could offer contemporary culture. For O Brother, he recognized that this type of music "had gone away" from popular culture, that it "wasn't trending." Yet, with a George Clooney movie, with incredible musicians playing these beautiful songs, and with the benefits of the promotional budget for the film, Burnett "knew we were going to be able to shine a light on the music that had not been shone for decades. I knew that if someone heard Ralph Stanley singing 'O Death,' it was going to be arresting, and it turns out it was."[9] More than just reintroducing a forgotten sound and one of its heroes to a popular audience, Stanley's presence on the soundtrack carries weighted significance. To understand this implication, Stanley's participation must be read with pre–*O Brother* eyes, before the millions of albums sold, awards, and widespread acclaim, and prior to debates surrounding whether the film and soundtrack are "authentic" or whether they further stereotype and commodify Southern heritage. There must have been a glimmer of uncertainty in the bluegrass musician's mind: how would the Coens interpret the music and its Southern context? Would they do the music justice, or would it be used to further isolate the sounds and the people with whom such music was associated?

Such doubts foreground the debates surrounding the effects of the film's soundtrack on popular music since. Stanley's agreement to be a part of this experiment gave ethical and sonic stimulus and a cloak of legitimacy in the beginning, while continuing to serve as moral cover in the following years. Not surprisingly, the Virginia bluegrass don's spiritual gravitas was never lost on Burnett. To him, Stanley seemed to be a "mythical, legendary character . . . like Paul Bunyan," living in another century and removed from mortal man.[10] Burnett concedes that Stanley's endorsement was the "linchpin." He describes a session at Ocean Way Studios in Nashville with "the whole community," Emmylou Harris, Norman Blake, and the like, where the producer claims that he and the musicians were "feeling our way through it." When Stanley walked in, Burnett recalled the place going silent in reverent awe.

Was the reverence also laced with fear, as the questions of authenticity, motive, and depiction were being tested? Without Stanley's approval, would any of them continue? Would the soundtrack exist as it does now? Speaking of Stanley like an Old Testament prophet, Burnett believed that the venerable bluegrass myth-man's blessing was "the moment the spirit of the thing began."[11] Perhaps the same can be said of the consumer response referred to earlier. Whether consumers knew of Stanley's past or not, whether they understood the implications of his participation, Burnett knew that, for the contemporary generation of music consumers coming off a decade of postmodern ironic grunge and boy bands, to hear Ralph Stanley sing a cappella would be "arresting." And for the musicians to come in the years following, could there be any better living man from whom they should take cues?

Yet, the very idea of the mainstreaming of Americana music leaves some with a bitter taste in their mouths. Benjamin Filene is one of them. Asserting that he is neither a "purist," a "protector," nor a "hoarder," Filene still concedes that the so-called folk fad has left him, to use his word, "grumpy."[12] Questioning whether the *O Brother*–inspired revival was what the 1930s Americana tastemakers had in mind, Filene compares the two.

In the thirties, revivalists were keen on communicating how American folk songs were not a remnant of the past, but "vital parts of living social systems"—a point some could argue is similar in today's movement, only with different demographics and dynamics along with imagined and real communities. Noting the role of "hybridity," the in-between state connecting so-called "genuine" or "pure" folk elements and popular culture, Filene argues that, like Lomax, Harry Smith, and others before him, Burnett's eclectic soundtrack mirrors the thirties folk thesis of an adaptable and dynamic music. Yet, Filene's primary concern is that the music's countercultural agency in the thirties, its ability to be seen as "an alternate source of strength in a time of crisis in America," will be lost on the new generation of consumers.[13] Filene believes that *O Brother*, most notably through its marketing (album liner notes conjuring a tattered scrapbook, the CD disc's display of prison stripes, and the *Down From the Mountain* documentary title and subsequent tour being three examples used), isolates the music from contemporary reality and that modern consumers look back on this music with "the idealism and the exoticism . . . [of viewing] another world, and we watch . . . with the detached fascination we might give a carnival sideshow." He fears that such "folk chic" becomes a fad only, not a profound, satisfying, and long-lived cultural force.[14]

Filene's folk-fad fear is warranted, and, as my interviews with producer Jason Weinheimer and artists Bonnie Montgomery and the Burnett-produced the Secret Sisters will confirm, the cultural scholar has company. In the years since his 2003 essay, so-called folk culture has been further commodified as the sounds and aesthetics of roots music merged with hipster culture, creating folk-inspired throngs in designer selvedge denim, bearded and mustachioed, with omnipresent banjos, calcifying roots as product. No band symbolizes folk mania more than England's Mumford & Sons, who fill stadiums with the

sounds of guitar, banjo, fiddle, piano, and stand-up bass acoustic instrumentation, ushering in what some have dubbed "arena folk." The band points to the
O Brother soundtrack as the cornerstone for their early sound: "I feel slightly
embarrassed saying how much of an influence *O Brother* was," admits Marcus
Mumford, who was thirteen when the film came out.[15] Burnett would later tap
Mumford to help produce and sing on the soundtrack for *Inside Llewyn Davis*,
another Coen film set in the Greenwich Village 1960s folk scene. From 2009
to 2012, the band's *Sigh No More* and *Babel* albums were omnipresent on radio
airwaves, Spotify playlists, and YouTube. To put it in context, as of this writing,
two of the band's singles from these albums, "Little Lion Man" and "I Will
Wait," have 103,293,560 and 124,840,267 plays on Spotify. Babel, which debuted
at number one on the Billboard 200 charts and became the fastest-selling rock
album of the decade, also won the 2013 Grammy for Album of the Year.[16]

Banjo player Winston Marshall's reaction to the film was more emphatic:
"Watching it [*O Brother*] was . . . the end of me. It was like, 'That is the music
I want to make.'"[17] In a *Rolling Stone* article subtitled "How Four Brits Turned
Old-Timey Roots Music into the Future of Rock," Mumford spoke of the
band's original attraction to the countercultural music, recalling "blaring the
O Brother soundtrack and Flatt and Scruggs" while driving around London,
"getting really funny looks and enjoying it . . . in a kind of fuck-you way."

Yet, the article's author, Brian Hiatt, notes a concern many consumers may
have: "The idea of four privately educated young British guys drawing on antediluvian American styles—and sometimes seeming to dress up like the 1930s
Okies they've been known to sing about—has raised its own questions about
authenticity." Stand-up bassist Ted Dwane reveals a bit of the tension involved
when he first claims, "We kind of are Okies at heart," and then follows up by
admitting, with a grin, "I don't really know what an Okie is, but I feel like one."

In an emblematic cultural moment, the band shared the stage with the Avett
Brothers and Bob Dylan at the 2011 Grammys. The foursome, in their standard folk-signifying apparel—Mumford in a waistcoat, Marshall with a bright
yellow trucker's hat and a Colonel Sanders–looking western tie—opens the
set with an energized sprint, Marshall head-banging his way through spirited
banjo playing on their wildly popular song "The Cave," a philosophical number that is a call to live freely and intentionally, evoking perhaps the conversion
of Francis of Assisi, Plato's allegory of the cave, and the poet Homer.

The curtain then opens to reveal North Carolina–reared roots-rock band the Avett Brothers, whose "Head Full of Doubt" equals Mumford in its philosophical questioning. On piano, Seth Avett, dressed in black, sings of an intellectually transcendent reckoning, embracing doubt, encouraging the pursuit of a life well-lived, and challenging an overly simplistic and tethered worldview.

As the song fades, a woman's voice comes over the PA system: "Ladies and gentlemen, Bob Dylan." To applause, Dylan coolly saunters out in a black suit with an open-collar gold silk shirt and matching kerchief tied around his neck, harmonica in hand. With Mumford & Sons, the Avett Brothers, and his own band backing, Dylan presides as man-legend over the medley. In his unmistakable gravelly singing voice, the enigmatic performer slides, as he had done for over four decades, effortlessly into his electric blues-based 1965 tune, "Maggie's Farm." Never one for leaving things to chance, Dylan's song choice is worth analyzing. Structurally, the blues-inspired repetitions, sung twice at the beginning and once at the end of each verse with explanations of the protest in between, is perfect for the call-and-response, pop-culture hootenanny playing out on stage. Naturally, the bands respond to their muse's call. The song's messaging is equally appropriate. Coming during Dylan's transition from 1960s folk music hero to inventive rock star and cultural philosopher-king for an entire generation, "Maggie's Farm" has often been considered his break from the folk movement that had defined him up until that point.

Clearly in his element—smiling, gesticulating, and acknowledging the English band over his right shoulder and the North Carolina foursome over his left—Dylan stands in the middle as the ocean between this centuries-old transatlantic musical exchange and as cultural conduit between the past, present, and future. Behind him, the camera shows both bands unmistakably reveling in the affair. They relish the moment without pretense, abandoned to shouting, smiling, singing, and playing along with their heads thrown back. It's clear we're watching a story they will all tell their grandchildren.

The audience is moved to a standing ovation as the cameras cut to a visibly enthused Neil Young waving at the stage, behind him John Mayer and the rapper Drake, before cutting to Jennifer Lopez and her then-husband the Latin pop star Marc Anthony. On a night when the music community participants included the Canadian indie band Arcade Fire, Mick Jagger and R&B artist Raphael Saadiq, pop-country singers Miranda Lambert and Lady Antebellum, hip-hop and pop singer and sometimes host of the television show *The Voice*

CeeLo Green, hip-hop megastar Eminem, pop stars Lady Gaga, Katy Perry, and Janelle Monáe, and legendary actress and singer Barbara Streisand, among others, this performance solidified the roots-based rock imprint as a legitimate musical and cultural twenty-first-century movement. Like Stanley had with the *O Brother* soundtrack, Dylan's participation serves as stamp of approval. It's impossible to read the exchange as a passing of the torch, as Dylan's myth and music catalogue are too culturally entrenched and eclectic for such a declaration, but his presence there is significant. Though the bands share a common muse, a purposeful glance backward into the American roots catalogue for reinterpretation, the commonality is less based on folk stylings and more on the power of songwriting set in context. For the Avett Brothers, Dylan's blessing substantiates their leadership in a neo-Southern roots renaissance. Yet, for Mumford & Sons, one cannot know if the exultation on stage was equally fed by their own desire to not play the "folk" role any longer. As their fame had grown, the band began to distance themselves from the folk-inspired sounds and stylings that had made them world-famous.

As Filene notes, with musicians such as Wilco's Jeff Tweedy and rocker Jack White, attempting to play music that is so rooted in context and being pigeonholed as such an artist has always been a problematic tightrope to walk.[18] By implication, the image-versus-substance debate has always been a core element surrounding judgments of "authenticity," and Mumford is clearly no exception. This was not lost on the band. Two years after shouting backing vocals to "Maggie's Farm," the band's 2013 video for "Hopeless Wanderer" was a full-on parody of folk clichés. The video opens with an old-timey sepia-toned title card and the band playing in an overgrown, pastoral, Edenic field, dressed like Ray-Band indie farmers. The scene cuts to the foursome walking down a gravel road like travelling troubadours playing for their supper, carrying all their instruments: tambourine around the bassist's neck, mandolin on his hip. Only then does the viewer realize that it's not Mumford & Sons but actors and comedians Jason Bateman, Jason Sudeikis (an accomplished folk musician in his own right), Ed Helms, and Will Forte (with chest-long fake beard flowing in the wind). With its emotional lip quivers and full-on cry shots, obligatory barn and ribbon mics, a bandmate make-out session, shots of the "band" on a small boat in an apparent bog, a four-banjo'd barbershop quartet with synchronized gyrations, the message of the video was clear: Mumford & Sons had folk fatigue, and they wanted their fans to know. In the process of commodifying roots sounds and aesthetics, they had, in a circuitous irony, commodified themselves.

The video ends with an unambiguous scene where the band destroys all their instruments, except for Forte's character, who simulates sex with his stand-up bass. The images are telling. The band had, as represented by Forte's copulation, satisfied itself. They had taken what they wanted from Americana sound and aesthetics and were moving on, connoting that perhaps they had been role-playing all along. The band realized they were in danger of becoming or had already lapsed into being cultural schmaltz, and they were keen to get ahead of the narrative. Not surprisingly, their 2015 album *Wilder Mind* would be a synthesizer and electric rock album. Articles titled "Even Mumford and Sons Are Sick of Mumford and Sons, the Banjo Is So Last Year" and "RIP Mumford and Sons' Banjo, 2007–2015" mirrored the band's own feelings. When asked about the banjo for future albums, Marshall was blunt: "Fuck the banjo. I fucking hate the banjo."[19]

Marshall's reaction is understandable. Popularity breeds contempt, even self-loathing, and with bands like the Colorado-based Lumineers taking cues from Mumford and further branding folk stylings, the band's transition in musical taste was inevitable. To be fair, it is only natural for bands to experiment with new sounds and stylings. Mumford & Sons were never a quaint folk band; they are, and have always been, a pop band that has relied on folk, roots, or Americana stylings. Commenting on the "Americana" label, Burnett contends, "I think it's just pop music . . . really. If you look at the Lumineers, Mumford & Sons or Adele—it's in the same stream as that music. . . . I mean, Marcus Mumford is a genius songwriter. . . . [T]hey're a killer band, but the fact that he's such a genius songwriter is what's pushing them through."[20] And if Mumford plugging in and "murdering" the banjo, as Marshall put it in the same interview, were the end of Burnett's influence on contemporary culture, we could declare Filene somewhat of a prophet. But Mumford's abandonment of Americana sounds could have been predicted, perhaps in part due to the band's lack of context. Perhaps it's not enough to "feel like an Okie"—and this is where Filene's fears potentially falter. The key to the music and the roots of Burnett's philosophy, soundtracks, and cultural imprint are grounded in place. To understand this is therefore to have to place the cultural moment in the context of the American South.

Filene is correct in identifying that "redeploying America's musical heritage is at the core of the current revival" and that this revival is "reinforcing for a new generation the idea that the building blocks of today's global pop culture lie back in seemingly forgotten corners of American culture."[21] However, implied yet unstated in this cultural glance backward is the role of the American South in shaping popular American and global culture. The lineage leading from Robert Johnson, Muddy Waters, and Chuck Berry to the Rolling Stones, from Harry Smith and Woody Guthrie to Bob Dylan, is without question. The *O Brother*–inspired cultural movement, including the soundtracks Burnett has produced with the cultural capital they afforded, must be grounded in light of the past, present, and future of Southern cultural identity. Filene's admitted grumpiness indicates a potentially emotional blind spot in his reaction to the folk fad. This same reaction is one with which country music scholar Bill C. Malone has admittedly wrestled. The context of the consumer has changed since the thirties- and sixties-inspired movements. Commenting on the state of contemporary country music, and particularly on the fact that it has, in his estimation, abandoned its working-class roots in favor of blue-collar posturing, Malone provides his "most sobering admission—the suspicion that Top 40 songs may be more 'realistic' than any other form of country music, in that they more completely meet the needs of a majority of today's fans," by which he means consumers who see "blue-collar" through a middle-class, suburban lens.[22]

The Southern consumers of *O Brother, Crazy Heart, Inside Llewyn Davis, Walk the Line, True Detective, Nashville,* and *Cold Mountain,* as well as musicians like the Carolina Chocolate Drops, the Avett Brothers, and the Secret Sisters, are the great-grandchildren of this music's 1930s context. The new Southern contributor—and artists and producers as well as consumers are all contributors here—has direct lineage to the South's cultural framework. Yet, as demographic studies continue to show, by and large these young people's parents or even grandparents left rural areas in search of jobs and opportunity. The new consumers and producers in this Burnett-inspired Southern community are typically college educated. They have been schooled in Wright, Faulkner, Welty, O'Connor, and Angelou more than *Gone with the Wind*. While direct familial ties to music remain strong, they are as likely to be trained at music conservatories as by family. Their musical stylings are a constellation of genres—hip-hop, indie, punk, heavy metal, American roots, alongside variations of country and rock. They have been raised on Southern typecasts, Jeff Foxworthy jokes, and stereotype-filled television and film representations. Yet they know from awkward family reunions and Thanksgiving dinners that some stereotypes are earned, but not all. As such, they grew up simultaneously proud, embarrassed, confused, and ultimately conflicted about their Southern identity. Many have left the South only to return later. They grew up hearing stories relating their Southern past in the context of their present, tales without beginnings or endings, of truths bred with folklore and sacred pageant rites; they just were, or are, in a concoction of present-tensed past. They grew up in towns named after old ghosts of a mythologized past, where county court-houses that escaped a burning censure stand as gothic symbols of a hurtful past and a hopeful future. In their South, you're just as likely to hear country music as you are hip-hop blaring from car speakers at the local Walmart. Their South is as much Johnny Cash as it is Lil Wayne, as much Billy Reid and Sid Mashburn as it is Uncle Si or the Blue Collar Comedy Tour. And they have friends of several different ethnic backgrounds. They're likely to be of Asian, Hispanic, or Indian descent and to enjoy marrying Southern traditions, sounds, and foodways with a host of imported customs.

Greil Marcus contends that "it is a sure sign that a culture has reached a dead end when it is no longer intrigued by its myths."[23] Clearly, some consumers did not or could not see through *O Brother*'s parodic, myth-provoking façade. Certainly, some of the music and styling inspired by the soundtrack lacked the depth of context for long-term sustainability. Yet, when viewed in light of Burnett's soundtracks and the group of artists he has associated with since, a vibrant, sophisticated community is present, wholly capable of translating those soundtracks, filtering the parody of the *O Brother* film out of the music, and engaging the myths with critical awareness. In fact, many weaponize the parody against the tired monuments of the South's past. As contemporary Southern authors like Barry Hannah, Bobbie Ann Mason, and Clyde Edgerton show, parody, with historical awareness in mind, is available to "deconstruct dead structures, revaluate regional values, [and] recode paralyzed cultural codes."[24] It is no coincidence that the Coens base *O Brother* partly on the 1941 Preston Sturges film *Sullivan's Travels*, a story about a disgruntled yet successful Hollywood comedy director's attempt to work on a socially conscientious project—adapting the novel *O Brother, Where Art Thou?* to film—despite the studio boss's protest. To better understand his stated subject, Sullivan hits the road as a penniless hobo and much hilarity and mistaken identity ensue.

Sullivan's Travels in turn references Jonathan Swift's famous satire, in which Gulliver pursues self-discovery and Swift pronounces judgments on his contemporary culture. Sullivan, too, pursues self-discovery through his artistic experiment, yet there is more at work in the film. *New Yorker* writer Nicholas Lemann, a self-proclaimed fifth-generation, though "long expatriated" Southerner, observes another message in the film. During the 1930s a host of New Deal liberals—photographers, sociologists, journalists, and the like— came to the South to study and document life. Lemann argues that Sturges's film "manages the nearly impossible feat of poking fun at such visitors while also making it clear that their mission had a powerful moral justification."[25]

Perhaps in the vein of Sturges and Swift, the Coens' film is an episodic self-discovery of an entire region through satire. And perhaps Burnett's community of Southerners are sophisticated enough to translate the satire while clueing in to the music's context. If so, their interaction with *O Brother* and the music and movement that precede it reads as an attempt to translate that sound's complex relationship to time and place to their generation, using its ethos to combat the issues of their day. If this weren't the case, Burnett's work would read more like the Blue Collar Comedy Tour than regenerative, context-driven art. As scripture tells us, you can judge a tree by its fruit.

Writing for the *Atlantic*, Paul Elie examines Burnett's role in this cultural negotiation. Speaking of traditional music's "collective" ethos, Elie believes Burnett's success resides in "taking the hootenanny to the movies—using Hollywood cash and clout to get people with old-school wooden instruments to make music together . . . [making] the roots soundtrack . . . generative rather than retrospective." Unsurprisingly, Elie connects the contemporary cultural influence of Burnett's catalogue with Harry Smith's *Anthology of Folk Music* and the sixties Dylan-led revival.[26]

In his thorough and poetic tour, *The History of Rock 'n' Roll in Ten Songs*, rock music's philosopher emeritus Greil Marcus notes the "omnivorous assemblage artist" Christian Marclay's penchant for breaking various albums and then piecing the shuffled assortment back together so they could play. Marcus argues that by "recognizing the way in which an object has lost its original, seemingly defining context and occupied another . . . [the] construction, or deconstruction, begins to tell a story it never told before."[27]

Positioning Burnett, with his 1930s-inspired recording philosophy, community of revivalist artists, and soundtrack productions, as a modern assemblage performance artist, purposefully plucking music out of one context and reassembling it in another while always paying homage to the former and inspiring regeneration in the latter, may help explain his role as cultural taste-maker. Once taken out of its original context, the music does not fully represent the original genesis, that primary source of sound and cultural milieu, but rather a new agency emerges out of this displacement for the contemporary moment.

Carrying this premise on into the following chapters, Filene's critique of the "folk fad" comes to mind: namely, that the contemporary audience is searching for nostalgia over agency, or, as he puts it, that an "idle demonstration of hip open-mindedness," undoubtedly affected by clever branding strategies and marketing campaigns, has replaced the music's countercultural potential to serve as an "alternate source of strength in a time of crisis."[28] This argument presupposes two characteristics regarding the contemporary scene: (1) that consumers are easily manipulated, passive receptacles, unable to decipher past context in light of present circumstances; and (2) that the music and its messaging lack cultural potency. In response, as will be shown over the following chapters, T Bone Burnett's soundtracks, the community of artists he has produced and worked with, and his ethic's extension into other cultural outlets stand in stark opposition to both of these presuppositions. Furthermore, the artists, particularly those with roots in the American South, have represented and continue to represent a music rooted in past context, a music whose messaging communicates a countercultural narrative regarding Southern identity along with a desire to participate in a sustainable, long-lasting community.

CHAPTER 3

SOUTHERN SPIRIT IN THE
T BONE SOUNDTRACK RECIPE

I used to be somebody, but now I am somebody else.

— BAD BLAKE

Critical theorist Walter Benjamin famously said, "Strength lies in improvisation. All the decisive blows are struck left-handed."[1] For Burnett, it must have been ironic that a film soundtrack offered him the popular-culture platform he had been fighting for yet had always just eluded him. Burnett's career has been artistically prolific. In the 1970s, his bands, the B-52 Band and the Alpha Band—the latter formed with Steven Soles and David Mansfield after their time touring with Bob Dylan's Rolling Thunder Revue—fused blues, country, soul, and rock and roll. Then came a string of critically acclaimed yet commercially less successful solo albums, most notably *Truth Decay* (1980), *Proof through the Night* (1983), *T Bone Burnett* (1986), *The Talking Animals* (1987), and *The Criminal under My Own Hat* (1992). In 1983, the *Rolling Stone* critics' poll tapped Burnett as songwriter of the year. Burnett had spent decades haggling with record companies, touring the country, and producing and recording music, yet his best shot to popularize his ethic and cement his legacy as cultural tastemaker seems to have come from an unexpected platform. In the decade following his *O Brother* success, Burnett made several more critically acclaimed film soundtracks using a similar formula carrying an explicit cultural message: contemporary culture should not just remember its musical heritage, it should create new music in the spirit of that inheritance and should regenerate it, both in the studio and in performance, with lyrics that speak to contemporary social dynamics. In the process, Burnett situates his musical presentations in the context of American recorded music's original muse: an ever-changing and expanding American South. In effect, Burnett's soundtracks reimagine the context of blues, soul, country, folk, gospel, and rock and roll music in the South. As such, he encourages consumers to readdress the Southern cultures and identities of the present in the light of the past.

In the wake of *O Brother*, T Bone's soundtrack formula crisscrosses Southern landscapes from North Carolina to Tennessee, Mississippi, Arkansas, Louisiana, and Texas, and to the Southern diaspora in California and New York, with a rich variety of sounds of the South: in *Cold Mountain* (2003), Appalachian mountain music; in *The Ladykillers* (2004), gospel; in *Walk the Line* (2005), Johnny Cash's folk, rockabilly, and country beginnings; in *Crazy Heart* (2010), outlaw country-western; and in *Inside Llewyn Davis* (2013), the sixties folk movement. He uses the same formula in his work for television and theater: in season one of *Nashville* (2012), modern Top 40 pop country; in seasons one and two of *True Detective* (2014–2015), an eclectic blending of genres that defies simple categorization; in a joint effort with the folk duo the Civil Wars, on the soundtrack for *A Place at the Table* (2013), a social-justice documentary film on hunger in America; in a venture into theater on a John Mellencamp and Stephen King collaboration, *Ghost Brothers of Darkland County* (2012), country, folk, and rock; and in *American Epic* (2016), a PBS documentary detailing the history of early American recorded music, a variety of genres.

With his Texas background and roots music ethos and philosophy, it is not surprising that much of Burnett's work resides within or has direct connection to the South. Regarding his soundtracks, Burnett's work falls into a long tradition, as the South is a particularly fertile film setting. In fact, cinematic portrayals of the South have carried significant weight in historical interpretation and cultural understanding, for good and ill. Furthermore, much of what modern man knows of history comes from media portrayals, and often perception is more important than reality when it comes to historical memory. Indeed, perception frequently *becomes* reality. Therefore, how historical events and people are presented matters a great deal, particularly in mediums reaching large numbers of people who often lack the encouragement to decipher in-depth historical nuance. As Andrew B. Leiter contends, "even the films which no one takes seriously as representative may still have serious cultural . . . implications."[2]

These portrayals most often incorporate stock characters, helping cement and exaggerate long-standing stereotypes into Hollywood archetypes: the Confederate colonel, the mammy, the Southern belle, the violent black man, the shiftless hillbilly, to name a few of the more prominent. Jack Temple Kirby claims that in surveying imagery in mass media—from films, best-selling fiction, music, television, and more—"whatever the artistic or scholarly merit" of these mediums, they are "significant in representing mass taste, perception, and understanding."[3] Arguments surrounding the parody in *O Brother* aside, Burnett's soundtracks stand as a counterpoint to the oversimplified and stereotyped South and provide an avenue by which Southerners can assert contemporary Southern identity in light of the past, rediscovering and promoting the good, addressing the bad, and carving out a potential ground for the future. Burnett's soundtracks, created for the present while addressing the past, speak to a Southern cultural identity that is shifting and on the move, and with such movement comes great opportunity. As historian George Brown Tindall reasons, "to change is not necessarily to lose one's identity, to change sometimes is to find it."[4]

In addition to Southern identity, Burnett's soundtracks read as rebellion against what pop culture wanted, or thought it wanted, to consume. The critical and commercial success of his albums have seemingly reminded consumers of music they had either forgotten or had missed in its first go-round. With questions of identity and cultural consumption and production in mind, Burnett's soundtracks should be analyzed both according to how they function as narrative within the films and how they participate as generative art in culture outside the film's text.

The soundtracks function within the films as a means of complicating tired stereotypes, while carving out cultural space for rejuvenating questions of Southern identity through the music's context. For example, one archetype that has consistently been presented in media is that of poor white folks, most often called hillbillies or rednecks. Leiter states, "more than any other medium . . . movies have shaped popular perceptions of the redneck South," citing "backwards mountain men, moonshine, and feuds" and going on to claim that these stereotypes are "presented with the least acumen . . . [and are] unapologetically exploitative while making little or no claim to authenticity."[5] Leiter cites J. W. Williamson, who tallies seventy-one hillbilly films in 1914 alone. The hillbilly archetype has been consistently portrayed in movies set in and out of the South since, with examples such as *Easy Rider* (1969), *The Texas Chainsaw Massacre* (1974), and *Pulp Fiction* (1994). Even the cartoon series *The Simpsons*, set in a fictionalized Springfield meant to represent every-town America, had its stock "hillbilly" character: Cletus the Slack-Jawed Yokel.[6] While such portrayals indicate that the stereotype transcends the South (*Pulp Fiction* was set in Los Angeles), the archetypal figure is distinctly associated.

The portrayal of rural white folks has long suffered from oversimplified typecasting in film and media, intensifying broad misunderstanding of a group not well understood and with little intellectual and cultural agency of its own. This cultural misunderstanding of rural whites often produced easily packaged dichotomies: planters and white trash, or romanticized yeoman and redneck. This left little middle ground for complex truth. As Kirby asserts, a cinematic dichotomy was born out of the clear distinctions between the wealthy elite and the poor working-class majority, just as portrayals of one group of poor Southern whites as sympathetic, hardworking, and dignified have contrasted with the redneck, poor "white trash" archetype.[7]

Regarding the now century-long affinity for appropriating and stereotyping poor white culture, Cobb tackles the assimilation of poor white identity into the national consumer culture. Summarizing Kirby and sociologist Richard Peterson, Cobb explains how redneck lifestyle displayed a "countercultural" and "anti-bourgeois attitude and lifestyle," thereby expanding redneck identity beyond "birth or occupational fate." Yet, the commodification of poor white Southern culture had the potential to move away from critical awareness toward a "'Hollywood' effect that leaves racial, sexual, and class exploitation on the cutting room floor while popular audiences are left to gorge themselves" on stereotypical imagery. From "redneck chic" music groups to the success of Jeff Foxworthy, Cobb notes that it became "obvious that those who were most enthusiastically buying (both figuratively and literally) into the redneck craze were the solidly middle-class folks who manicured the lawns and mangled the fairways of Southern suburbia."[8] Whether as romanticized yeoman farmers living in a utopian society or as a bunch of lazy drunkards who love to fight and fornicate, the historical plain white folk and his cousin the redneck or poor white trash have suffered from what Samuel Hyde calls "interpretative polarization."[9] Films have seemingly mirrored the scholarly conflicts. Karen Cox argues that, beginning in the 1930s, hillbillies represented a Southern type on radio, film, and cartoons. This popular cultural presentation stereotyped the "rural hick" as "poor, working-class, southern, barefoot, and ignorant," part of the "last vestiges of a premodern society."[10] A mirroring of O Brother's parodic approach, these characters were most often a source of comedy.

Benjamin Filene argues that the impulse feeding such caricatures was in part based on the early twentieth-century modernist obsession with primitivism, as audiences were interested in characters that were both "archetypal ancestor" and yet distinctly "other." Though often depicted in people of African descent, such as in Joseph Conrad's Heart of Darkness (1913), set in the Congo, a similar argument could be applied to the Southern poor. Filene contends that "the primitive" evolved into a "symbol that could encompass violence, sex, irrationality, and, at the same time, noble innocence and childlike naiveté."[11]

Music associated with Southern whites most often accompanied such cinematic stereotypes. Perhaps no film embodies the polarization of poor rural whites directly connected to music more than Deliverance. The film is the story of four urban white males who leave the comforts of Atlanta for a thrill-seeking canoeing adventure on the fictional Cahulawassee River in rural Georgia. In the process, the men enter into a series of deadly and horrific conflicts, primarily involving "hillbillies" and nature. The famous "Dueling Banjos" scene, which appears at the beginning of the film, sets the tone for the conflicts to come. The theme of class conflict is set in the opening credits, as the audience hears the Atlanta insurance salesman Bobby ask the group's macho leader, Lewis, whether there are any "hillbillies up there?"[12] Tensions between the rural and city people begin at a country gas station where the men stop to fill their tanks and find someone to drive their two cars to Aintry, Georgia. Bobby and Lewis repeatedly talk down to the old man filling their tanks, with the latter responding in kind to the city folks' condescension: "You don't know nothin.'" Furthermore, the images of the country folks presented are of a dirty, backward, sinister, threatening, and lazy people. Within this context, Drew begins playing his guitar. From outside of the shot, an apparently mentally disabled young boy named Lonnie, playing a banjo, begins mirroring Drew's guitar picking. The two echo each other back and forth with simple patterns before culminating in a complex and fast harmony between the two instruments: the two become one.

For a brief minute, the song serves as a cultural middle ground, connecting the two noticeably distinct groups who were each skeptical of one another. The old man is dancing; some of the rural people begin gathering, one whistling.

Everyone, even Lonnie, is smiling. Drew, symbolizing a bridge between the two worlds through his guitar, exclaims, "I could play all day with that guy!" Albeit briefly, the viewers can see the poor whites as humans, not as something "other"—as Bobby's initial question implied. Instead, the audience sees them asserting their agency through music while communing with the urbanite Drew. Though the boy is vocally silent, his banjo-picking prowess speaks for him and his community, giving voice to the marginalized.

Image is quickly shattered by reality, though. As Drew sticks out his hand for the young boy to shake, Lonnie turns his face away, refusing to shake the city man's hand. Despite the connection the two just shared, the music could not permanently bridge the cultural gap. The images of Lonnie and the poor rural folks and their dilapidated dwellings exist uneasily with the brilliance of the music, ultimately leaving an ambiguous haze over the encounter.

With the "Dueling Banjos" scene projecting an unresolved feeling, the city men continue on their adventure. They next encounter the Griner brothers— dirty, big, brutish men—and an old, furrowed woman tending to a severely disabled young girl. From this point, the images of rural country people continue along the stereotypically depraved and backward narrative, taking a decidedly violent turn in the woods. That night, having progressed on the river, Lewis gently picks the opening notes of the "Dueling Banjos" song from earlier in the day. This is the last time the song will be performed by a character in the film, seemingly putting to a close the potential for cross-cultural under-standing. This becomes evident in the next day's infamous "squeal like a pig" sodomy scene. Several times the director offers close-ups of the gun-toting mountain men, with teeth missing, adding a vicious, bestial quality to their stereotypically backward ways.

These two scenes, "Dueling Banjos" and the raping of Bobby, are what stand out most in the cultural memory of this film; therefore, the two are often lumped together in a haze of memory synthesis. While the film produces a certain overarching feeling through its key symbols, in this case a presumably inbred boy and his banjo and a violent hillbilly rape scene, consumers fuse them together, along with the flood of hillbilly iconography throughout, as they attempt to make sense out of the film's message and the people and place presented.

In the case of the ambiguous resolution of the dueling banjos scene, the audience reverts back to the visually unsettling portrayals of rural whites and the disabled boy expertly playing the banjo, thus coopting the song and the instrument as both become associated with the extreme violence by the mountain men—who look remarkably like the Griner brothers and the rural folks at the gas station. Basically, since rural people share a certain look and sound, they must *all* have the same ethics and values. They must all *be* the same. This idea is furthered when Ed kills a hunter who he mistakes for the escaped, gun-toting, would-be rapist. In essence, "Dueling Banjos" becomes the soundtrack fueling this stereotype.

Scott Combs shrewdly connects *Deliverance* to Quentin Tarantino's notorious "bring out the gimp" rape scene in *Pulp Fiction*, showing that even twenty years later white filmmakers are apt to "conjure up battered clichés of poor or regionally prideful whites." Tarantino essentially recreates the *Deliverance* rape scene in a Los Angeles pawn shop, filled with images of rebel flags, sodomy, and a mindless brute. The rape victim even refers to the Los Angelenos as "hillbillies."[13] Tarantino's "squeal like a pig remake" shows the cultural exportation of the stereotype, yet decidedly grounds it in its Southern, rural tradition, leaving movie audiences to make the not-so-subtle connection.

Lost among the domineering images of Lonnie and the sadistic rapists are any of the movie's representations of decent country people: the older folks at the lodge who feed and house Ed and Bobby toward the film's end, the rural family that helps Ed to a phone once they get back off the river, and the Griner brothers who delivered the cars in keeping with the agreement the two groups made. Such images should complicate the stereotype which the earlier scenes had reinforced. Yet, they all come after the viewer has been through the emotional upheaval of murder and sexual violence. Therefore, in popular culture's ultimate verdict, the movie and the "Dueling Banjos" song symbolize the worst stereotypes of poor white people, ultimately furthering the long-standing historical tradition previously noted.

Burnett's soundtracks complicate these stereotypes, reacting against cultural perceptions and carving out ground for the music and the people and places in which it was created for contemporary consumers. For example, many of the same themes from *Deliverance* exist in *Cold Mountain*, and music plays an equally important role both as narrative within the film and for Southern identity construction, though with decidedly different results. Set in a fictional North Carolina town nestled in the Blue Ridge Mountains during the Civil War, the film tells the love story of W. P. Inman, a Confederate deserter who escapes from a soldier's hospital in Virginia to walk home to his love, Ada Monroe. The journey is perilous, yet the chief antagonists of the film are not Northern soldiers but Confederate Home Guard agents who shoot or imprison deserters. As some critics have noted, the film also resembles a Homeric epic in form.[14] Like Odysseus, Inman encounters seemingly supernatural obstacles on a hazardous, contested terrain during his journey home. He is drugged and sexually enticed by the family of a Southern informant for the Guard, he aids a widow and her infant when she is threatened with sexual assault by starving Yankee soldiers, he is rescued and healed by a seemingly mythic old mountain woman, and he saves a drugged, pregnant African American woman from certain death at the hands of a hapless preacher.

Whereas *Deliverance* relies on "Dueling Banjos" exclusively, *Cold Mountain* employs a wide range of Appalachian and spiritual music remade mostly from traditional folk songs reinterpreted for the movie, though some, such as "The Scarlet Tide"—written by T Bone and Elvis Costello, performed by Alison Krauss, and nominated for an Academy Award—were written for the film. As in *Deliverance*, addressing the songs performed on film by the actors and how they function within the narrative structure speaks to perceptions concerning rural white people. By doing so, we can see how rural whites evoke a sense of purpose and a voice through music, in its role as an active part of the film's narrative, a generative quality on par with the actors' dialogue. This is particularly pertinent in *Cold Mountain*, as the actors often sing on camera rather than having songs play in the background. It also helps sets the stage for how the music can function culturally outside of the film.

Cold Mountain exists within a long tradition of Civil War cinematic depictions. As David Blight has argued well, three competing narratives "collided" over Civil War memory: the reconciliationist vision, which tried to make immediate sense of the devastation; the white supremacist vision, which essentially negated the role of slavery in the war; and the emancipationist vision, in which African Americans tried to evoke cultural efficacy.[15] In cultural memory, the white supremacist vision most often combined with the reconciliationist one to create a whitewashed public memory of the war.

The most notable film portrayals have often suffered from mythic nostalgia and oversimplification. Traditionally, such depictions have fed the trend of whitewashing the uglier parts of Southern history. Cultural anthropologist Ruth Landes asserts that such popular mediums depicted a South "gilded in sentimentality."[16] Karen Cox contends that Northerners and Southerners alike have viewed the South through a "magnolia-shaped lens."[17] She claims that advertisers and media makers of all types shaped national perceptions of the South as a region that "upheld its links to the rural past and [was] the one least spoiled by urbanization and industrialization."[18] Cox argues that between 1915 and 1945, with movies such as D. W. Griffith's *The Birth of a Nation* and Walt Disney's *Song of the South*, Hollywood engaged in cultural or historical mythmaking about the South with great success.[19] She believes that such imagery had negative effects that "in many ways kept it locked in the . . . past, hindering . . . progress."[20] Perhaps no film mythologized the South more than *Gone with the Wind*, pointedly so in the lines that appear before the opening scene:

> There was a land of Cavaliers and Cotton Fields called the Old South. Here in this pretty world Gallantry took its last bow. Here was the last ever to be seen of Knights and their Ladies Fair, of Master and of Slave. Look for it only in books, for it is no more than a dream remembered. A Civilization gone with the wind . . .[21]

The quote directly speaks to the film's modus operandi: a wealthy, white mythological treatment of the South's antebellum history centered on fantasies of the privileged few. *Gone with the Wind* exemplifies the systematic postwar public narrative that Lost Cause apostles preached: a pastoral Eden where wealthy gentleman and genteel white women ruled a world in which blacks and poor white trash knew their place.

Tara McPherson believes that those same mythmaking penchants exist presently: "The South today is as much a fiction, a story we tell and are told, as it is a fixed geographic space below the Mason-Dixon line."[22] She argues that in regards to the South, the nation at large suffers from "cultural schizophrenia." This region that has dark ghosts from the historical past (slavery, peonage, sharecropping, Jim Crow) has become a "mythic location of a vast nostalgia industry."[23] Such mythologies and oversimplified archetypes come at the expense of the cultural and historical nuances necessary for accurate understanding. McPherson maintains that "myths and narrative impact the real, shaping not only personal memory and perception but also our public and 'official' histories."[24] Nell Irvin Painter states a similar idea: "There is seldom a [single] 'the South,' for simple characterizations eliminate the reality of sharp conflicts over just about everything in Southern culture."[25] The devastating effects of blind allegiance to abstract racial and social myths still manifest in acts of hate in contemporary culture. After the senseless murder of nine African Americans inside the Emmanuel African Methodist Episcopal Church in Charleston, South Carolina, by the white supremacist Dylann Roof, many states began further debate surrounding Confederate monuments and in particular the Confederate flag. In response, the South Carolina legislature voted to remove the Confederate flag from its state capitol grounds, Alabama governor Robert Bentley had flags removed from a capitol monument, and Georgia governor Nathan Deal and Virginia governor Terry McAuliffe halted the use of specialty license plates that featured the flag. These actions were not taken without debate, however. For instance, around one thousand flag devotees showed up to rally against Bentley's decision, "flying hundreds of Confederate flags and claiming its removal is an affront to their southern heritage."[26] On December 17, 2015, the New Orleans City Council voted 6–1 in support of removing four Confederate monuments.[27] Meanwhile, Civil War reenactors, both "hardcores" and "farbs"—those who are perceived to be less concerned about historical authenticity— still flood battlefields each year.[28] In early 2015, the Arkansas state legislature voted to keep celebrating the Robert E. Lee and Martin Luther King Jr. holidays at the same time.[29] As mythologies merge with reality, David Blight argues, both "in real-life policies as well as in mysticism . . . [ideologies can take] hold on the American imagination,"[30] influencing generational societal ideals and public policy.

Studying film and other cultural mediums, such as music, can help break the habitual presentation of tired clichés and stereotypes too often associated with the Southern condition, both historically and in the present. Such studies can, as McPherson states, "help us retrieve this past and deploy it to new ends" by seeking out "livelier, less nostalgic Souths."[31] Such scholarship can aid in challenging a monolithic portrait of the region and its citizenry while giving voice to historic and contemporary groups who have been wrongfully maligned, oversimplified, or completely silenced. It is within such territory that Burnett's soundtracks reside.

There are some notable absences in Cold Mountain's portrayal of the Civil War, particularly the lack of African Americans. Yet, as Henry Louis Gates Jr. observes, both the novel and the film are "essentially a love story between two white people who live in a rural area where slavery was not a fundamental aspect of the economy."[32] Despite this, the film—aided by how the music functions throughout—presents a realistic portrayal of the harsh realities of the war and the multiple distinctions present within the rural white working class. The viewer sees several manifestations of rural Southern whites. Amidst the deviant power-grabbing and violence, there exist nobility and courage. Amidst the chaos of war, there stands community. As such, the film resists the polarities in which rural whites are traditionally presented: the exalted, noble yeoman and the hillbilly. Instead, at the very least the film complicates this oversimplification.

Cold Mountain somewhat muddies the revisionist mythological imagination regarding the Civil War by presenting the war from the perspective of rural, non-slave-owning, white Southerners who grapple with the environment and particularly with other Southerners—in this case, the Home Guard who are charged with catching deserters yet who also prey upon and bully the townspeople—as their lives are changed dramatically due to the effects of the war.[33] As Ruby exclaims about her fellow Southerners, "They call this war a cloud over the land, but they made the weather, and then they stand in the rain and say, 'Shit, it's rainin'!'"[34] *Cold Mountain*, the film adaptation of Charles Frazier's novel by the same name, attempts to reveal the perspective of rural white Southerners during the Civil War, and music has a purposefully important role in this portrayal. As John Cohen notes, the music of the time period was a motivating factor for Frazier while writing the novel, and as an advisor to the film's soundtrack Cohen maintains that "music would establish the atmosphere, setting the story in time and place."[35] Therefore, understanding how the music functions will serve as a guidepost for unraveling the harsh realities of Civil War life for a particular community.

Music was an integral part of Southern life during the nineteenth century. As Cohen notes, the mountains of western North Carolina depicted in the film "had been settled largely during the 1840s, and the prevalent music in this environment was old love songs, murder ballads, and church music."[36] Throughout the film, music, in several different forms, serves as a sort of narrative guide. Noted music historian Bill Malone states that "the songs chosen [during this era], whether religious or secular, may have been vehicles for social expression or complaint." Indeed, religion hovers over the film, as several figures, scenes, and songs contain spiritual imagery and themes. Malone argues that the South of this time period was a "stronghold of evangelical Protestantism . . . bequeathing to the plain folk a body of songs and performance styles . . . [that was] an integral part of southern life."[37] One such scene shows the small community at the announcement of impending war. The scene is set in a full church—presumably holding most of the citizens of Cold Mountain. This includes both Ada and Inman. In a cappella harmony, the congregants are singing "I'm Going Home." The exuberant singing by the congregation, welcoming the call to paradise and leaving the secular world behind, foreshadows the impending conflict and the clash over worldly versus spiritual matters. As men outside the church begin celebrating the news of the war's outbreak, the harmonies fade, and the sense of community afforded by the church singing ends. The two competing sounds overlap for a brief time, as the harmonies of the congregation are infiltrated by the men shouting outside, creating a dissonance in both sound and values. Eventually, as in the majority of the film, the war wins: "We got war! We got it! Ready to fight! Three cheers for North Carolina! Three cheers for the South!"[38] As presented in other scenes, the music—here symbolizing spirituality and community—often serves as the antithesis to the war and its agents.

In the next musical connection between Ada and Inman, they are separated by thousands of miles, as he is off fighting, getting gravely injured, and then struggling to return. Back in Cold Mountain, Ada's father has died, the Home Guard leader Captain Teague is preying on the community, and Ruby has moved in with Ada to help her survive. In this context, Ada plays the piano one last time, using the sheet music Inman gave her that had belonged to his father, before she is forced to trade the piano for supplies and food. This scene not only reinforces how music is passed down, forging a sense of intergenerational community, but also how, without someone to play the songs, it dies, and along with it an emotional, historical, interpersonal, and communal connection with the past. Ada plays the music not only in remembrance of Inman but also in mourning for the harsh realities of wartime, including the loss of family, community, innocence, and a way of life.

For the rest of the movie, most of the music is presented by Stobrod Thewes, Ruby's ne'er-do-well father, and his deserter travelling companions, the mentally handicapped Pangle and Georgia, played by contemporary rock star Jack White. These three present traditional folk songs using banjo, fiddle, and mandolin accompaniment.[39]

At first, Ruby is hesitant about her father reentering her life, as Ruby and Ada catch him trying to steal from them. Yet, the two eventually reconcile, with

Stobrod and Pangle serenading her with "Ruby with the Eyes That Sparkle." It is the Christmas scene, however, that most exemplifies music's role within the rural white community and its use within the film's narrative structure. Here, the group of friends, in a rare moment of levity, celebrate with a makeshift square dance, the quartet playing "Christmas Time Will Soon Be Over." Such seemingly simple fun is not without potential cost. The women can be shot for harboring outliers, yet the group has a brief respite from the harsh winter and the ever-watchful gaze of Captain Teague. However, the revelry soon gives way to Georgia pensively singing the folk classic "Wayfaring Stranger"—singing of heaven, where he will be settled, reunited with family, and have no more pain. As Ada listens to the words, she reflects, and the screen images cut between Inman—who is camped for one night with the widow and her child—and Ada, each thinking of one another. The music functions as expression of longing and hope while simultaneously giving voice to individual and communal lament. It also reinforces the yearning and isolation so prevalent throughout the film.

In a patriarchal society, music becomes especially important for women. Smithsonian folklorist and musicologist Alan Lomax contended that many times songs were "vehicles for fantasies, wishes, and norms of behavior which corresponded to the emotional needs of pioneer women in America."[40] Furthermore, Malone argues that in a society that generally "discouraged or repressed the articulation of private anguish, music . . . could exert a cathartic function, permitting the discharge of frustrations, pain, or rage."[41]

Shortly after the Ada and Inman montage, Captain Teague's group happens upon Stobrod and Pangle sleeping out in the open winter air. In a scene with grave tension, Captain Teague asks for a song. Stobrod plays the slow, soulful lamentation "I Wish My Baby Was Born," and Teague becomes visibly flustered. Standing and walking away from the group huddled around the fire, he begins to sing with them, staring off into the dark night. Clearly, the music here, as it does often throughout, functions on multiple levels. First, as the songs were often passed down in the oral tradition, they had historical messages about the way of life, values, and hopes of a particular people. David Heddendorf argues that the music preserved the memories of those who survived to play songs long since passed down. As the narrator in Frazier's novel states, the music "sums up a culture and is the true expression of its inner life."[42] Noticeably, the song touches an emotional nerve with the cruel captain. Secondly, the songs carry a message for the present as well, as suffering and longing are universal emotions in the human condition, not only in the war-torn South. Here, Captain Teague perhaps momentarily longs for a different time and laments the path he has chosen as tormentor of his own people.

Image is quickly shattered by reality, however, as Teague quickly wheels around and orders Stobrod and Pangle to stand away from the fire. The mentally challenged Pangle smiles, thinking they are going to have their picture taken. This visibly flusters the captain, who orders Pangle to put his hat over his face. As Teague shoots the two men, they symbolically hold their instruments in their hands. Indeed, later, when Ruby finds them, she picks up the abandoned fiddle first. Seemingly, by Teague shooting Stobrod and Pangle, the music will die. Music had often served the community as a respite from the harsh realities of war, yet upon the death of these two men, the stories of the past, the hope for the future, and the sense of community which the music so often symbolized would die too.

Stobrod, "whose passion for the fiddle redeems a misspent life,"[43] survives. Inman returns, only to be gunned down by one of Teague's men, but not before killing them all and purging Cold Mountain of the primary force oppressing the community. With these men dead and the war coming to a close, the community can begin to rebuild. The ending scene is Edenic, as Ada and her daughter Grace Inman are surrounded by Ruby—with child—Georgia, Stobrod, and Sally. The farm is vibrant, the weather no longer cold and icy, and the North Carolina mountains are filled with color. As such, it is fitting that Georgia and Stobrod sing the traditional song "Great High Mountain," delighting in progress through community, before they eat their meal. The dinner table and the music join to symbolize the familial community's restoration. Though individual families have been torn apart, the group stands together as a family in the end.

For the contemporary audience, the music is aided by the performance of Jack White. Undoubtedly, the audience will recognize White, and therefore the music and perceptions of rural whites are enhanced by his reputation and worth as a modern rock entertainer. Just as music contributed to the negative stereotyping in *Deliverance*, in *Cold Mountain*, by contrast, aided by modern musicians' reputations (the soundtrack features Alison Krauss, White, Elvis Costello, and Sting, among others), the perception of rural whites and traditional Appalachian music becomes enriched—perhaps inspiring a new generation of musicians such as Brooklyn's Punch Brothers and North Carolina's Carolina Chocolate Drops. Bluegrass music had never gone away, but arguably

White, Krauss, Burnett, and company help popularize and challenge the stereotypes often accompanying such music, carving out space for a new audience and a fresh way of imagining the music's context and Southern identity.
Burnett's soundtrack, therefore, re-presents banjo, fiddle, and mandolin music
for a contemporary audience, challenging the *Deliverance*-inspired stereotypes
fed by the instruments' sounds.

 Deliverance and *Cold Mountain* hold several commonalities. They are both
stories of class conflicts, primarily between white Southerners. They both have
characters who face extreme natural and manmade obstacles, fraught with
death, sexual violence, and breakdowns in community. In popular culture,
both movies and their soundtracks achieved acclaim. However, the portrayal
of rural whites in the cultural memory differs drastically. Its hyperbolized negative portrayal of rural whites, coupled with the horrific violence, remains the
lasting image of *Deliverance*. The nobility personified by Drew in the "Dueling
Banjos" scene evaporates when he dies, leaving the audience to associate the
music with a negative cultural stereotype of rural whites. *Cold Mountain*,
though filled with similar caricatures, uses music for its redemptive quality
as a voice for the oppressed. While many of the Southerners exhibit characteristics similar to the hillbillies in *Deliverance*, the lasting image from *Cold
Mountain* is of a rural community redeemed through song. Regarding the historic presentation of rural whites, the truth is a complex hybrid of both characterizations. That is the point of such a study: to break through the habit of
stereotyping groups and to offer a more nuanced portrayal. As Steven Knepper
claims, if we "choose to perceive the mountain folk as humans . . . [we can see
them] assert themselves from the margins . . . reclaiming their identities and
protesting their forced silence."[44]

 The most consistent and critical element in Burnett's soundtracks is how
the maestro roots the music in context: place, personal history, and the heritage of emotion and sound. This context-driven approach is an essential
component of Burnett's soundtrack ethic. The sense of place weighs heavy in
all interpretations of Southern culture, often becoming as much of a character as the characters themselves. Author Eudora Welty argues that place "is
the fountainhead of . . . knowledge and experience." Furthermore, she notes
that the South has "an inherited identification with place. It still matters. Life
changes, as it always will and should. But I think the heritage of place is too
important to let slide away."[45]

 The film *Crazy Heart* is a perfect example of Welty's sentiment and Burnett's intent. *Crazy Heart* is the story of down-on-his-luck former country-western star Otis "Bad" Blake, played by Jeff Bridges. Blake's self-destructive tendencies play out on screen from the bowling alleys and bars he plays to seedy hotels, one-night stands, excessive drinking and smoking, and the loss of relationships. The film is also rooted in the context of a country music in transition, represented in the contrast between Blake's outlaw ethos and his former protégé Tommy Sweet's (Colin Farrell) more contemporary pop country. *New York Times* film critic A. O. Scott speaks directly to the emotional terrain travelled by both the music and the character, in his beat-up Chevy Suburban: "Drinking, cheating, love gone wrong—a lot of country music expresses the weary stoicism of self-inflicted defeat. Loss and abjection are two of the chords that define the genre. A third is redemption."[46] The theme of redemption is certainly prevalent, as Bad is able to avoid total self-destruction and begin to attempt to repair his career, in the end more as a songwriter, and his relationships. Yet the theme of regional redemption prevails as Burnett continues in this soundtrack what has by this time become his norm, role, and modus operandi: to redeem America's musical heritage. That redemption begins with the role of place.

The soundtrack's bluesy western sound invokes the eclecticism of Burnett's Fort Worth musical upbringing, in many ways serving as homage to the context of his youth. In the late 1950s and early 1960s Burnett and musician-songwriter Stephen Bruton taught guitar lessons and worked together at a Fort Worth–area guitar shop: "We would sit around most of the day and look at guitar catalogues and dream about what we would get when we grew up."[47] Bruton's father, a jazz drummer, had a record store which served as a treasure trove of music where the two budding young music enthusiasts were introduced to Skip James, Robert Johnson, and the Stanley Brothers, alongside music from Folkways and the Library of Congress, records that weren't carried in mainstream record stores. From Bruton's father and his store, the two young men began seeing how certain principles could be attached to music and place. "Back in the day when stores were a reflection of the people who owned and ran them . . . they reflected their tastes and the things they thought were important about music,"[48] Burnett has reminisced. Reading Burnett's soundtracks through this lens opens up the producer's emotional and intellectual pursuit: recreating Stephen Bruton's father's record store for a popular music audience. He fills his soundtracks with the same wonder and sense of discovery he felt in

1950s Fort Worth: "We would hear all these beautiful old bands, records that just weren't on the Top 40 or anywhere close to it."[49] Burnett's placement of "O Death" as perhaps the "linchpin" moment of the *O Brother* soundtrack further solidifies the album's relationship to Burnett's past, as he recalls Bruton playing for him the Dock Boggs rendition from a Folkways recording in the same store where he discovered the Stanley Brothers. It is no large leap to connect the dots nearly a half-century later, when Burnett puts the song and Ralph Stanley together to alter the landscape of popular music for the next decade.

Jeff Bridges's character, too, is purposefully created with a hat-tip to Texas's Western heritage. Determined to create an authentic character grounded in the heritage of sound, culture, and place, for close to six months Burnett, Bruton, and the writers developed a backstory for Bad Blake, "who he was, what he had listened to, where he had grown up, what kind of stuff he'd liked and didn't like, who he wanted to be."[50] Those influences included Leonard Cohen, Townes Van Zandt, Hank Williams, Louis Armstrong, and Lightnin' Hopkins. Burnett and company even worked with Bridges to model Bad's singing voice after Don Williams. Furthermore, Bridges's characterization was based in large part on Bruton. Bruton had lived a musician's road life, first in Kris Kristofferson's band, then as a solo artist who eschewed the games artists had to play in Nashville. Living out the protest ethic that originally spawned the outlaw country movement, he opted instead to play in dives while driving around in a Suburban for weeks at a time, hundreds of miles, often coming back "with less money than he went out with." Bridges studied Bruton, down to his fashion and the way he held the guitar.[51]

The soundtrack's playlist reads as a primer to Burnett's context-driven ethos. While Bridges's character experiences redemption in the film, Burnett and company also redeem the music and its context. As with most of Burnett's soundtracks, *Crazy Heart* carries a particular formula with a clear-eyed message. Burnett takes traditional music and marries it with songs written for the film which either sound as though they were from another time or are an example of how new music is created through a direct lineage to the past. The result presents a work of art that is both steeped in historic context yet simultaneously regenerative and approachable for the present. It is no surprise, then, that *Crazy Heart*'s chorus of artists harmonize echoes of music past and present, featuring the blues, country-western, and contemporary country sounds of Buck Owens, the Louvin Brothers, Ryan Bingham, Lightnin' Hopkins,

Townes Van Zandt, Sam Phillips, and Waylon Jennings. Then there are the several noteworthy songs written for the film and sung by Bingham, Bridges, and Farrell: "Somebody Else" and "I Don't Know" by Bruton and Burnett; "Hold on You" by Bruton, Burnett, John Goodwin, and Bob Neuwirth; "Fallin' and Flyin'" by Bruton and Gary Nicholson; "Live Forever" by Billy Joe Shaver and Eddy Shaver, sung a cappella by Robert Duvall; "Brand New Angel" by Greg Brown; and "The Weary Kind" by Bingham and Burnett, which went on to win a Golden Globe, Academy Award, and Grammy.

At the heart of the soundtrack exists a tension between the past and the present. The character Sweet represents the new breed of country music. He eagerly pays tribute to the past, regularly giving Bad Blake credit and offering his popularity to help the aging country legend. Yet, Sweet purposefully distances himself from Blake's outlaw ethos, and when the two sing the duet "Fallin' and Flyin'," it is culturally significant on-screen and off. On-screen we see the metaphorical passing of the torch from Blake to his protégé. Off, the consumer is reminded of the essential nature of place and the music's context. It's a prescription for how music transitions with context in mind, with regenerative evolution, not abandonment. Interviewing Blake for a Sante Fe newspaper, Maggie Gyllenhaal's character Jean asks, "In today's world of artificial country music, who's real country?" Blake smirks, scratches his head and fidgets. Self-conscious, she asks, "What? Is that a stupid question? Is Tommy Sweet real country?" "Tommy, he tries covering it up. I taught him country. . . . He's got to compete with what's coming out of Nashville today. But, yeah, he's real country," Blake reluctantly, quietly, admits.[52]

This is at the heart of the film's creation and its purpose. Artificially, it might be about generational divide and authenticity. Waylon Jennings's song "Are You Sure Hank Done It This Way," which questions country's practice and progression and which plays as Blake pulls in to the Phoenix pavilion to open for Tommy, speaks to the insecurity of country artists' relationship to the past.

But with Burnett, it's never that simple. Tommy's Cadillac Escalade looks pretentious compared to Blake's "Old Bessie," but his songs are an extension of his mentor's. Sweet is not as raw, he drinks water rather than whiskey to save his voice, but we are let in on his own relationship troubles, and the tension between the two musicians connotes more than just a mentee stepping out on his own. We see Sweet wrestling with making contemporary country music for a new audience, rooted in what he learned from Blake, which does not bastardize the genre. We see him grappling with what each generation attempts: to make its own mark, carve its own path. Sweet's music is rooted in Blake's context, but it speaks to a new audience. Hank may have not done it this way, but Burnett's soundtrack lays out the producer's preference for how contemporary artists should create new music. Through the songs created for Tommy and sung both by Farrell and Ryan Bingham on the soundtrack, Burnett shows that contemporary music rooted in telling stories of people and their relationships to each other and to particular places can honor the past in the same way that Bad Blake's and, by comparison, Hank Williams's music did, while still being original and relevant in the present.

Yet the film and soundtrack's message is not only about a new generation. In many ways, like *Cold Mountain*, *Crazy Heart* complicates mythologies surrounding country music and working-class whites. The first lines we hear Blake sing in the film are "I used to be somebody, but now I am somebody else."[53] We've followed his 1978 Chevy Suburban briefly through the New Mexico mountain-lined desert, the highway carved into ancient rock formations. Blake has pulled in to the Spare Room bowling alley, argued with his manager and the bowling alley's owner (who refuses him a tab on Blake's manager's instructions), checked in to the Starlight Inn where he watches porn and gets drunk on his preferred whiskey (McClure's), and finally shown up late for his show. The song's words offer a telling contrast between the life he has lived and the depths to which he feels he has now sunk. They are laced with irony as they spill out in Bridges's gravelly voice. By the end of the film, the same words become more optimistic. That's how music, people, and places evolve. In the end, he is no longer what he was. He is not a music star in the present. He is a legend. He is no longer self-destructive. He is carving out a new path. We see a bittersweet transition unfold, and the music connects the past and present, telling the story of evolving sounds, places, people, and communities. The film takes us behind the scenes of Blake's pain: the loss of his relationship with Jean, the refusal of his estranged son to reconcile, and the loneliness and heartache prompting his alcoholism and his sobriety, all fueling his songwriting. We see the birth of the context of a song. The fact that Blake's new material, particularly the ending "The Weary Kind," will be sung outside of *his* context casts a somewhat enigmatic haze over the narrative. When Sweet sings Blake's song of days and nights filled with lost love, addiction, pain, and mental and physical distress, the music and message are pure, even if its popular-culture medium is not the direct lifeline to the song's genesis.

Bad Blake complicates Southern stereotypes. His character does not allow for whitewashing or mythologizing a music hero in the way culture often does. There are terrible consequences for his actions. We see this in the heartrending, poignant ending. Jean is engaged to someone else. "He's a good guy," she promises.[54] Blake gives Jean one of his royalty checks for her son Buddy's eighteenth birthday. Sober and productive again, he still has not reconciled with his estranged son, but he is no longer self-sabotaging his life away. Reconciling his past, present, and future is complex. There are no simple answers. The film's music is the soundtrack for that ambiguous and enigmatic emotional dissonance, reminding us that the most influential music of the past and present is always born out of raw emotions and the complexities of life. The soundtrack of Blake's evolution mirrors the film's message regarding the South in transition as well. *Cold Mountain* and *Crazy Heart* are two sides of the same coin, wrestling stereotypes away from mythology and oversimplification by using music rooted in the past yet charged with creation in the present. Just as Ryan Bingham and a generation of country musicians continue to make music inspired by their outlaw predecessors, Burnett continues to work with contemporary artists who reinterpret traditional bluegrass music, like the Punch Brothers and Rhiannon Giddens of the Carolina Chocolate Drops. Blake's story and Burnett's soundtrack confront a generation born into a culture that has commodified rural Southern whites and country music into a simple marketing package.

Much of Burnett's philosophy plays out in his selection and arrangement of his material. The *Crazy Heart* soundtrack formula mimics his approach to the *O Brother* and *Cold Mountain* repertoire, indicating Burnett's intent. In *O Brother*, the producer most notably took traditional songs and either let stars of the past sing them or had contemporary artists reinterpret them. On *Cold Mountain*, like in *Crazy Heart*, he took this one step further. The traditional songs are still there, such as when Jack White sings "Wayfaring Stranger" and "Great High Mountain," but he generates new content that a casual listener could easily mistake for traditional, for example "The Scarlet Tide," written by Burnett and Elvis Costello and performed by Alison Krauss; "You Will Be My Ain True Love," written by Sting and performed by Krauss; and

"Never Far Away," written and performed by White. It is a formula he retains in *Inside Llewyn Davis* and *The Ladykillers* along with his forays into television and theater, using contemporary artists like the Punch Brothers, Marcus Mumford, and the Nappy Roots alongside revered performers of old, mixing in traditional songs, reinterpretations, and original material. Writing for the *Atlantic*, Paul Elie argues for a reimagining of Burnett's methods as "mix[ing] old legends with new artists, movie stars with masters of the Dobro," particularly highlighting how the producer promotes his purpose using Hollywood's tools. Elie contends that Burnett offers his productions as "an act of discovery, a wpa-style effort to set a levee of traditional music against the rising tide of hits radio."[55]

Burnett uses his soundtracks as discourses on the relationship of music's past to its present, while decidedly grounding the sounds in a Southern context as complex as the men, women, and communities out of which such music is born. In the progressive unfolding of the relationship between the character Bad Blake and the soundtrack of his story, as created by Burnett and Bruton, the contextual process is as important as the sound. When questioned by *Rolling Stone* regarding season one of the television show *Nashville* and the atmosphere he strives for with his music, Burnett explained, "The idea is to create a universe of music unto itself." Referencing the performance at the end of episode one, Burnett maintained that "when the song is part of the story and it all comes together in a performance, and in a rehearsal, and in a recording session and you see the process of what people go through and how it comes together: That's the thing that I think is thrilling."[56]

Concerning season one of *True Detective*, the show's creator Nic Pizzolatto admits that Burnett's "music is one of the main leads of the show, and I consider it as essential a part of the vocabulary of *True Detective* as my writing." Burnett recalls being charged with avoiding "the typical Louisiana Cajun sound," instead focusing on "creating an alternate reality, where it's not a kind of Louisiana that we've heard before."[57] As such, the soundtrack for the first season represents the eclectic sounds of the 1990s and present-day Louisiana combined with Americana and rock staples, featuring a diversity of artists, with some you might expect to hear, such as the sounds of country, gospel, and the blues with artists like Buddy Miller, Bo Diddley, Slim Harpo, C. J. Johnson, Dwight Yoakam, John Lee Hooker, the Staple Singers, Steve Earle,

Kris Kristofferson, the McIntosh County Shouters, Blind Uncle Gaspard, Emmylou Harris, Waylon Jennings, and Lucinda Williams. Others more accurately represent the South in transition. Not wholly isolated from the rest of America, these Southerners reflect generic traits comparable to those of other Americans, shopping at Dollar Generals, making their living in similar ways, and suffering and rejoicing from the same joys and pains. Thus, the inclusion of hip-hop, metal, and alternative bands with little or no direct regional connections and whose sounds do not evoke stereotypically Southern identity, such as Wu-Tang Clan, Boogie Down Productions, Primus, Grinderman, the Handsome Family, the Melvins, Sleep, and the Black Angels, accurately portrays the South as well. Yet, there still remains a cultural quality unique to particular Southern contexts. Pizzolatto was looking for a sound that "comes more from the psychology of the place, rather than its exact musical history . . . a Louisiana of the mind," or what Burnett calls a "psychosphere."[58]

The series' closing song, a Burnett original featuring Father John Misty and S. I. Istwa, evokes the enigmatic feeling Pizzolatto wanted for the dark, psychological crime drama. Here, Burnett presents a town that has, through its inaction, complicity, and resignation, traded away its intentional community and creative individuality. Inspired by the brooding Louisiana swamps and backdrop and the degradation of humanity unfolding throughout the series, Burnett's philosophical existentialism reads as a challenge. The song's title, "The Angry River," implies that the culture has created the river's channel and there is a price to pay. Clearly philosophical, this also reads as a metaphorical continuation of his ethic of purposefully and decidedly resisting the temptations of the contemporary world by grounding music in place and connecting it to a purpose.

The song was foreshadowed years earlier in "Tear This Building Down," from his 1992 album *The Criminal under My Own Hat*, in which Burnett plays the role of destroyer. As forest fires are good for forests, Burnett suggests destruction as a means of cultural rejuvenation, breaking down the entire infrastructure and motivations of contemporary culture to get back to the original inspiration. There is pain in the futility, distress in his longing for the purity of starting over at the beginning. Perhaps his soundtracks serve as the fire, ironically using Hollywood's tools to build something regenerative from the ashes.

When songs are part of the ongoing story of particular places and they are rehearsed, recorded, played and performed on the big screen, in concert halls, in online playlists, and on car stereos, we can see the South and her people both in their historic context and as they transition and evolve. We hear the South on the move, as the texts of the present echo the texts of the past, offering contemporary Southerners a means by which to process their present in light of their shared cultural past while shedding light on what theorist Julia Kristeva terms a "mosaic of quotations" arising from the fact that "any text is the absorption and transformation of another."[59] Furthermore, beyond the sounds and presentation, texts' meanings undoubtedly splinter as new understanding emerges from consumer engagement.

It is fitting that Blake's opening song lyrics, "I used to be somebody, but now I am somebody else," were penned by Burnett.[60] Burnett is no longer the countercultural singer-songwriter arguing his case from the margins. He is now a philosopher-king, tastemaker, gatekeeper, and preservationist, far removed from yet intimately connected to his first recording studio, where at age seventeen he and some friends recorded Fort Worth–area bands and musicians travelling through.[61]

Now, Burnett resurrects for a popular audience music—and, by extension, social contexts—often only consumed and thought about by musicologists, historians, audiophiles, college professors, record collectors, and the like. Burnett takes a popular audience inside Stephen Bruton's Fort Worth record store, inside the mind of Bruton's father, as he teaches us what matters about music. Burnett is as much Harry Smith as he is William Wordsworth, who believed his role as poet was to translate the mysterious qualities of the natural world and memory to the common man. For Wordsworth, where most people saw only a meadow, sunset, or city, the poet saw his childhood, his life's calling, and his God. Burnett attempts something similar: to translate why context, history, and the process by which music is conceived, created, produced, and performed matter and to position the music for consumption using the very tools that are perceived to be at odds with the music's folk origins. Burnett's soundtracks are a mode of storytelling rising out of the actual film narratives, engaging consumers with how music can serve as the vehicle to understand ways of living, thinking, and behaving, and how such mediums permeate cultures both consciously and subconsciously, serving as compelling guides to the identities of places and people. He is now T Bone *Agonistes*, engaged in a decades-long struggle. *O Brother* gave him the spotlight. Subsequent soundtracks became his fiat, the crucible furthering his ethic and illuminating the process and places in which sounds and identities are created. Turning the page, we see how his countercultural community of artists take hold of the zeitgeist, helping galvanize Burnett's principles for the present and the future.

CHAPTER 4

T BONE'S INNER CIRCLE AND
THE SECRET SISTERS' SOUTHERN CHARACTER

The South is the only place we play where
everybody can clap on the off-beat.[1]
— **ROBBIE ROBERTSON**
When they sing, it sounds like music.
— **T BONE BURNETT**

If popular music as we know it is the great-great-great-grandchild of sounds created in Southern contexts, then can music produced or performed in the South, either by Southerners still living there or by those who through ancestry or birth belong to the Southern diaspora, ever just be music? No, and perhaps even more so when a harmony-singing sister duo from rural Alabama were discovered the first time they publicly sang together at a Nashville tryout by a panel from Los Angeles associated with Interscope.[2] Before they could blink, Laura and Lydia Rogers, then twenty-three and twenty-one, were on a plane—the eldest sister's first flight—to Los Angeles to meet with producer Dave Cobb and lay down some tracks. They were now known as the Secret Sisters, and a whirlwind of activity followed: An album of primarily cover songs produced by Cobb and T Bone. Their first tour, with Levon Helm, who Laura called "the father of all things wonderful," their second tour, with Willie Nelson, followed by stints with Paul Simon, K. D. Lang, Amos Lee, the Punch Brothers, and Ray LaMontagne, with others to follow. Trips to New York for performances on David Letterman, to L.A. for Jay Leno, and to England for Jools Holland's *Hootenanny*. A spot in T Bone's Speaking Clock Revue and a

PBS special with T Bone, Jakob Dylan, and Elvis Costello. Collaborations with Jack White, the Chieftains, Dave Stewart, and others ensued. On tour, legendary singer-songwriter Paul Simon met with and played music for the sisters, reminiscing fondly about his time in Muscle Shoals, Alabama, and the history of the region's music. Laura remembers Simon having his assistant pull up songs on a laptop for the three to listen through. He even burned them a CD of Les Paul and Mary Ford, saying, "Take this and listen to it and never stop listening to it." Years later, Laura has a hard time processing all that's happened to them:

> When I tell these stories back—they happened recently, five years ago was not a long time ago—but at the same time . . . I almost feel like I'm telling a story about somebody I don't even know. . . . Did that really happen? . . . I'm standing in my pajamas [it's 3:30 p.m. Eastern Standard Time] in my house shoes on my back porch, I haven't washed my hair in three days, I don't have a tour coming up, and I'm telling you that Paul Simon made me a mix tape. . . . It doesn't check out.[3]

Covering the PBS show, the *Los Angeles Times* took note of the relationship between the sisters' sound and their story, asking, "could it really be that in this age of pop music, often built on calculation and manipulation, that there's still a place for bona-fide innocence?" The answer, perhaps unsurprisingly, brought in the man who had over the past decade become the cultural gatekeeper for such appeal: "There is, at least in the parallel musical universe that producer T Bone Burnett is creating."[4]

Along with traditional songs "Do You Love an Apple," which they had performed together during the tryout in Nashville, and "All About You," their eponymous first album featured cover songs: George Jones, Bill Monroe, Buck Owens, Hank Williams, and others. In a year when Billboard number one singles were saturated with pop music by Kesha, the Black Eyed Peas, Rihanna, Usher, Eminem, Katy Perry, Pink, and other similar artists, the Secret Sisters' album found an audience. For one reviewer, the album "hit the *O Brother* Americana vein" with a "facsimile gem that reimagined and re-created the feel of 1940s traditional country and honky tonk."[5] Another extended the group's influences further: "Their honeysuckle-sweet, flawless family harmonies recall sibling units such as the Everly Brothers or the Andrews Sisters."[6]

Unbeknownst to them, however, in the midst of such a reception there would be challenges. With the purposeful branding harkening back to the midcentury rural South, with the production sessions featuring vintage instruments and recording techniques, with the album chock full of venerable country music classics reinterpreted by the effortless sisterly harmonies, would come debates regarding Southern identity, sincerity, and artistic integrity. Placing them within Burnett's influential circle and marking them with his brand further complicated such already slippery terrain. Their next five years would prove to be a test case for how contemporary Southern artists can attempt to create, record, and perform music with traditional Southern Americana characteristics in a popular context *without* sacrificing their integrity or giving way to the very caricatures they grew up rebelling against. One of the central tenets of their growth would be negotiating their twenty-first-century north-Alabama Southern identity for a contemporary audience without parodying the past in which their music is rooted or glossing over the modern Southern world in which their identity has been constructed.

Just as with Burnett's soundtracks, the role of place is essential for understanding the Secret Sisters. Although they are often referred to—and have often referred to themselves—as being from nearby Florence, the two grew up in the diminutive north Alabama town of Green Hill, also birthplace to former Drive-By Trucker and current solo artist Jason Isbell, which is a thirty-minute drive from its more famous musical neighbor, Muscle Shoals.[7] Green Hill "doesn't have any traffic lights or a Walmart" according to Laura, explaining size in characteristic Walmart-or-no-Walmart Southern fashion. The two sisters were raised in a musical family. Laura describes how they grew up singing in the house with their dad playing musical accompaniment, or outside on the porch and poolside in the summers: "Every Sunday night after church we would usually go in to Florence and eat dinner, and on the way to the restaurant and the way home, the four of us would sing church songs. My dad would sing bass, mom tenor, Lydia and I switching up between soprano and alto."[8]

Their dad still plays in a traditional bluegrass band, Iron Horse, which along with bluegrass staples and originals crafts bluegrass tributes to heavy metal acts like Metallica and Ozzy Osbourne. Though the sisters grew up aware and respectful of Muscle Shoals Sound Studio, its famed house band the Swampers, and the who's-who list of music legends who passed through its doors, famously including the Rolling Stones, the Staple Singers, Paul Simon, Rod Stewart, and Bob Dylan, the duo were more influenced by the music they heard or sang in their home and church. In an NPR interview, the duo recalled the sounds of George Jones, Merle Haggard, and Doc Watson as the soundtrack of pre-church Sunday mornings. Laura remembers learning to sing harmony to her dad's cassette of the Four Seasons.[9] Their grandfather's gospel quartet was called the Happy Valley Boys, and the name stuck with the family, who affectionately refer to their grandparents' home, where Laura and her husband now live, as Happy Valley.[10]

Equally influential in the duo's musical education was their home church congregation: the North Carolina Church of Christ, where Laura still worships, named in honor of the congregation's founding members who settled in Green Hill after leaving the Tar Heel State. Musically, the Churches of Christ have been traditionally distinct for their exclusively a cappella song services. Using just their voices and customarily, particularly in rural churches, without praise teams or choir accompaniment, many congregants grow up learning how to read shape notes out of hymnals, or understanding intuitively how to blend their voices and sing the bass, alto, soprano, or tenor parts. "A lot of the people couldn't tell you what note they're singing, or what key they're in, or what the key signature is, but they can tell you exactly how that melody goes. A lot of it is tradition . . . singing these songs every Sunday over and over again. You just get it," explains Laura.[11] In an interview with NPR's World Cafe, the sisters spoke of the communal and spiritual connections that come from the a cappella singing: "It's pretty magical. I cry a lot in church," Laura admits laughingly. The two also commented on the movement of several congregations in their church tradition toward more contemporary services that include instrumental accompaniment and an emphasis on modern praise and worship songs—perhaps an insinuation regarding the potential loss of the art of harmonizing.[12] During the interview, the sisters were asked on the spot if they would perform a song they grew up singing in church. After a few seconds of brainstorming and Laura setting the tone with a soft hum, the two settled on the eighteenth-century hymn "Rock of Ages":

> Rock of Ages, cleft for me,
> Let me hide myself in thee;
> Let the water and the blood,
> From the wounded side which flowed,
> Be of sin the double cure,
> Save from wrath and make me pure.[13]

It is as pure a musical expression as one can find. The harmonies are effortless. Unhurried by the interview and unrattled by the off-the-cuff request, their slow-paced poise and purposefulness does the song's two-hundred-fifty-year-old poetry justice. The self-effacing sincerity invites the uninitiated to the church pew, to a ride-along seat with the sisters on their car trips back and forth from church. That the song is moving is without question. That the two mean what they are singing, evident. Listeners are let in on how sounds communicate who people are, where they're from, and what they value. When I sat down with the duo before the Fayetteville Roots Music Festival in Fayetteville, Arkansas, in August 2014, the sisters explored how their music connects to shared memories and their past, unsurprisingly interweaving song and stories.

Laura: It's like a soundtrack . . . that reminds you of certain people and stories.

Lydia: It makes me think of our grandmother. We would sit on her lap, and she'd bounce us up and down, and she'd go [*singing*], "Bye oh baby bunting, daddy's gone a-hunting, to get a coon skin to wrap his baby up in."

Laura: And you still remember it. And our granddaddy, our musical granddaddy, had this song . . . [*singing*] "Once I had a kitty, a pretty little kitty cat. Dressed him up with boots on and a great big cowboy hat. Took him out a strollin' on a cold December day. Along came farmer Brown's old dog and chased my cat away. Has anybody seen my kitty, has anybody seen my cat?"

Laura and Lydia: [*laughter*] About a cat!

Laura: Just silly. But, you know, you can still hear it, and you can feel it. . . . And when you're proud of it, and when you love people that have had that kind of impact on you, you just can't help screaming to everybody, you know, in a weird way. . . .

We actually have a family reunion every year, the Parker family reunion. And literally every time some old lady pulls out a stack of song books and starts handing 'em out to people. You're going to sing. You're going to sing if you know what's good for you. At Lydia's wedding in September, they're having Mark's granddaddy lead a song out of the church songbook. . . . It's so sweet and sentimental, and there is so much more than just the song behind it.[14]

As the harmonies in the NPR interview trail off from "Rock of Ages," we hear as Dave Cobb and T Bone may have heard the sisters for the first time, their minds possibly conjuring images of Alan Lomax and the nineteenth- and twentieth-century anthropologists' and musicologists' push to discover the genuine sounds of rural Southerners, or of Ralph Peer and other music executives as they tried to market the music, musicians, and the region's appeal. The sisters' Grand Ole Opry artist profile page features prominently a Burnett quote, speaking to his impression and endorsement: "I have been making music for over forty years and The Secret Sisters album is as close to pure as it gets."[15] Of course, their outsider status and small-town appeal wasn't completely lost on the sisters. As Laura said, "Truth be told, from everything I've heard, that was a very big appealing piece of the story for T Bone because he loved that we were just these girls who had never played a show, never had a demo, a website, or a fan base. . . . We hadn't gone through the Nashville sawmill. We hadn't gone through the L.A. world, and New York world."[16]

Is this what Peer felt recording artists in Bristol, Tennessee, when he first heard the Carter Family and Jimmie Rodgers? Listening to Laura and Lydia sing without rehearsal, we are let in on the producers' dilemma: how to translate such sound through wires, compression, computers, and tape and accompany it with instrumentation? Through the producers' viewpoint we also confront what will become an issue of tension within the debate over the enigma of authenticity: is the music enough, or will the sisters be forced by labels, managers, and audiences to perform their Southern heritage in the way of dress and styling as well?

With "Rock of Ages," we are left unsurprised that the first time they sang in public together was at the audition where they were discovered. It is appropriate that, put on the spot and unprepared, they chose the traditional song "Do You Love an Apple," which would later appear on their first record. Their spiritual connection to music joins them to the region's musical past as well. In the fall of 2010, as the sisters were set to put out their first album, mere months after that Nashville talent audition, T Bone gathered an eclectic consortium of artists at the Beacon Theater in New York for the Speaking Clock Revue. The house band included Elvis Costello, Gregg Allman, Neko Case, the Punch Brothers, Yim Yames, Karen Elson, John Mellencamp, Ralph Stanley, Jeff Bridges, Elton John, and Leon Russell. Laura recalled an interaction with Ralph Stanley that mirrors Burnett's own experience with the bluegrass legend.

We all were kind of practicing on this day. We were doing sound checks and everything. And Ralph Stanley got up there, just him and his little-bitty suit and his guitar player. And the guitar player would play this really pretty lick . . .

and Ralph Stanley sang "Lift Him Up That's All." Everybody in that room, it was us, Jeff Bridges and the Punch Brothers, and Elton John. . . . These amazing people. And we all stood there so reverently because when he sang that song, in that simple, honest way, it was just like this is what *it* is. This is where *real* is. I was so inspired that night, I went back to my hotel room and wrote "River Jordan," after that moment, of meeting and being around Ralph Stanley. . . . I just remember thinking how poignant and how touching songs that are based in spirituality are. And I don't care what you believe. I don't care if you don't think there's a single thing up above us. There's something so precious about seeing someone call out to their creator. The one that they believe in. Even if it's not the one you believe in. There's something so fragile and intimate about that. And that's what we saw with Ralph Stanley.

Born through Stanley's influence, "River Jordan" is by Roger's own admission rowdier than Stanley's song. In the song, the duo calls the listener to repentance, raising voices through song, prayer, and baptism, appealing to Christ's baptism by John the Baptist. The song is an imperative, an urging bordering on prophetic cautioning, and their voices match the tone.

> Go to the river Jordan, said the prophet to the king.
> Wash in that murky water seven times and you'll be clean.
> Yeah, that deep rollin' river's gonna make you new and whole,
> And the faith acquired of you will save your soul.
> Let's go down to the river, raise our voices in prayer,
> And get ourselves a snow white robe to wear.
> Take away all the stains, remove each and every one,
> In the name of the Father and the Son.

Gone are the supple, soft tone on songs like "Do You Love an Apple," "Tennessee Me," and their hit from *The Hunger Games*'s soundtrack, "Tomorrow Will Be Kinder." In "River Jordan" they crescendo and decrescendo forcefully, like a revival preacher whipping a tent full of God-fearers into a frenzy. At times the duo move to call and response, as if the two are standing on both sides of the convert, whispering hauntingly in separate ears: "bury me" in one ear, "bury me" in the other, "River Jordan, River Jordan."

With the promise of mercy and forgiveness, by song's ending the sisters have given a theological treatise on baptism, forgiveness, and the tensions between the pressures of this world and the promises of the next, implying an eschatology of God's restoration and redemption of creation: "I'm a weary broken soul living in a house of clay / and that river's gonna wash my sins away." The sisters' inclusion of unapologetically religious messaging walks a somewhat ironically transgressive tightrope with contemporary audiences and multinational record labels. That the sisters were not merely performing religious sensibilities as a relic of another time is evident in the tensions between artistic intent, sincerity, and their handlers' expectations.

> **Laura:** Early on . . . when we were kind of being shaped, we would sing this old Hank Williams song called "House of Gold," and I would kind of mention something beforehand about being faithful believers, and not really even about, "go Christianity," but more just about our belief that there is something better than what we have here. And I remember one time we had a label person on the phone with us, and he was like, "You know, I know this is who you are and everything, and I'm not trying to tell you what to do, but you should maybe tone it down with the Jesus talk because people in New York and L.A. don't like to hear that sort of thing." And I didn't listen to him. [*laughter*] . . . But no, we're not ashamed of it, and we put gospel songs in our shows because if you want the Secret Sisters and you want them to be true to who they are, that's what we come with. That's what we come with. That's the name that we wear. And if you don't like it, don't come to the show because we are Christians, and we're proud of it, and it affects who we are and the music that we make and how we treat people and how we represent ourselves in the world, and it's such a huge part of our identity.

> **Lydia:** And we're in the process even right now of trying to put together a gospel record. But not cheesy contemporary Christian . . . [but rather] bluegrass gospel.

> **Laura:** Spirituality is such a deep part of the South, and I don't think you can separate the two, no matter how hard you try. . . . People in the South are spiritual people, and they need it, and they love it, and they're proud of it. But, I just think it's important to preserve it. We love gospel music. Some of our favorite songs are up in an old church hymnal that smells funny and musty.

Worth noting is how spirituality in a contemporary Southern context often comes with markers of conservative politics and social views. Yet, interestingly, the sisters' religious belief never translates into political platitudes. Also, as shown earlier with Burnett's own spirituality throughout the years, their connection to T Bone and the artists with whom they tour, perform, and associate helps position their spirituality outside of conservatism's rigid ideological fundamentalism and the Republican Party platform. Yet, as Laura's conflict with her L.A. handlers shows, they are more than just cultural Christians. Instead, they are, as they have always been, regular church attendees. The inability to place them within the stereotypically conservative political religious movement, alongside their pious adherence to and promotion of their faith, complicates the social constructs of Southern identity typically associated with the South's religious. Such complications help forge new ground for a contemporary identity that could be both rooted in religious tradition and simultaneously holding cultural views that could be considered as having both culturally and politically conservative *and* progressive characteristics. This reads against other false dichotomies long plaguing perceptions of Southerners, such as the yeoman and the hillbilly. The sisters avoid overt political statements, yet their social positions can be relatively placed by judging the community in which they participate and, as we will look at later, some of their artistic decisions.

The Secret Sisters' religious belief, mixed with their midcentury sound, with comparisons to the Everly Brothers and the Carter Family, place them at the intersection of history, heritage, and twenty-first-century Southern identity, something of which the two are keenly aware. Identity is a slippery psychological and emotional concept. Mostly, identities are forged with little self-awareness. But when the two were placed in the limelight, from concert halls in the Northeast and abroad to national and international television appearances, their identity construction became more purposeful. Having never lived and barely travelled outside the South, the sisters began coming to terms with what it means to be a Southerner. Their songs purposefully place them in the South, singing about filicide and forbidden love in Iuka, Mississippi, in the song "Iuka," which they performed on *The Tonight Show with Jimmy Fallon*, and turning Tennessee into a verb in the vulnerable love song "Tennessee Me," for example.

The sisters follow the philosophy of such cultural critics as reigning agrarian philosopher emeritus Wendell Berry, who finds "the regional motive . . . false when the myths and abstractions of a place are valued apart from the place itself." He takes to task those who romanticize the South, what he calls "the cult of 'the South,'" commenting on how "morally, it functions as a distraction from the particular realities and needs of particular places." Berry argues that "without a complex knowledge of one's place, and without the faithfulness to one's place on which such knowledge depends, it is inevitable that the place will be used carelessly, and eventually destroyed." Berry, like Burnett's community and the Secret Sisters specifically, believes that without the care and under-standing of particular places, "the culture of a country will be superficial and decorative."[17]

Berry's philosophy regarding community activism, particularly linked to agrarian principles, mirrors Burnett's, and by extension the Secret Sisters' own attitude, a sonic agrarianism advocating purposeful music, relationships, and community in light of the pressures of twenty-first-century culture. Through his soundtracks, Burnett helps draw attention to the music's historical back-ground which in turn helps illuminate how the music's context has evolved, including raising the question as to whether the relationship between social context and musical genre is still as potent. The music purposefully confronts a consumer industry with a decidedly different ethic.

Consumerism, creativity, history, identity, and philosophy collide in the South's most potent culturally and historically contested symbols. And once again, music serves as a vessel by which to explore such complexities. Alongside Karen Elson, the sisters contributed the simultaneously revered and castigated Civil War song "Dixie" for the *Divided & United: The Songs of the Civil War* album, which featured revered performers of old—Vince Gill, Ricky Skaggs, Norman Blake, Dolly Parton, Taj Mahal, Ralph Stanley, and Loretta Lynn—along with contemporary artists like Old Crow Medicine Show, Shovels & Rope, Chris Stapleton, Pokey LaFarge, and the Carolina Chocolate Drops. In a contemporary context in which many liberal-leaning Southerners are distancing themselves from the hero and battle worship of the Lost Cause and its public symbols, such albums could be conflicted in interpretation. The album, however, doesn't feel like an Old South apologetic but rather an attempt to capture the sounds and history of one of the South's darkest times. The artists mentioned stand as testimony to that effect. It reads more like an opportunity to address the complexities of historical and cultural reality with the necessity of progressing from its wrongheadedness. Musician Joe Henry argues that the album reminds us that "this music is still a living thing. They're not artifacts. They may sometimes serve as artifacts, but they are not contained by that idea."[18]

Worth noting is the exclusion of contemporary pop country artists, who, whether rightly or wrongly, carry connotations of conservativism that could arguably confuse what appears to be the album's intent. Instead, the album's inclusion of primarily country legends, Americana, and contemporary neo-folk artists informs the audience intuitively that this is an album about music's history and not propaganda. The sisters' rendition of "Dixie" follows this pathos. Its delicate and mournful tone sounds less like mourning a time lost than that the time happened at all. Laura argues that the song's sadness has been done a "disservice" when sped up and made "peppy [and] uptempo."[19] In opposition to nostalgic celebration, Bryan Sutton, one of the album's producers and musicians, wanted to come up with a way of turning the song into a "cautionary tale."[20] Worth noting is Burnett's own contribution, a mournful song about a runaway indentured servant who after fleeing Ohio for New Orleans is conscripted to fight in the war. After a firefight, the young man connects with his dying brother on the battlefield, watches him take his last breath, and buries him. The personal account from a young man forced to fight for the Confederacy in what would become one of the most devastating battles in American history helps declare the album's purpose and the various artists' intent, complicating trite Civil War apologetics, giving voice to narratives focusing on the perspectives of vulnerable populations, and presenting the historical music born out of the tragedy. Other songs like Old Crow Medicine Show's "Hurray Hurray" help unpack the contested narratives within. Lead singer Ketch Secor maintains that the song is a celebration of liberation from the slaves' perspectives, a call to arms for the Yankees, and a "death cry" for the rebels.[21]

The Civil War album example speaks to one of the complexities regarding contemporary Southern identity which many young people face, and in particular those with a large platform and wide-ranging audience. Like many Southerners, the sisters are keen on embracing their regional identity but are simultaneously somewhat defensive and protective.

Laura: I feel like we are Southern without being the tacky Southern, annoying. We try not to be that weird kind of Southern that gets a bad rap. . . . Backwards, ignorant, kind of unintelligent, uneducated . . . hateful.

Lydia: We get a bad rap.

Laura: Just kind of slow, and I mean maybe that is true in some cases, but I feel like it is just different. People don't realize how special the South is. The stories, the folklore, the history. . . . It's modeled with really amazing things and really horrible things, but it's still our story, and I just love the people that come out of the South. I love the artistry that comes out of the South, not just musically. I think the South has put out the best music in the history of the world. . . . I would argue it to anybody that the South is the most important geographic location that will ever be. I don't think it will ever be replicated in any other way. We don't shy away from that. In fact, we like to let that be what people know us as. It's funny, in certain instances, especially when we travel overseas, people love it. They think it's so charming that we're Southern, and have a drawl, and say "bless your heart." They think that's really special in a weird way. I don't know why.

Lydia: Everybody in the South is a product of that Southern music heritage that just made it so rich. You think of black slaves working during the Civil War times, working the songs in the fields that created this blues culture that kind of created so many other branches, and I would like to think that what we do is a product of that, indirectly.

Laura: A long way down the line, I think that it's all related. The music that the South is known for has a common ancestor, and I think that a lot of it is credited to slave culture. Gospel music, I think it has a lot of roots in that. And then there's also elements of Southern music that come from Irish roots: there's a whole lot of that in there. If you pay attention to it, you can hear it. But yeah, the South is really special, and I'm really proud to be from here.[22]

Beyond music, the Rogers sisters draw inspiration from other Southern cultural channels. Laura admits that "Iuka" conjures the character Bob Ewell from *To Kill a Mockingbird*. In doing so, they channel the abused Mayella's desire for more. After having her life set for her at nineteen, complicated by Bob's unwillingness to change, Mayella's search for power in the form of an attempted affair with a black man shows she is willing to cost a man his life to exert her agency. "Iuka" summons that desperation with the violence of Cash's "Delia's Gone" and a Faulknerian rage right out of Yoknapatawpha. Here, they highlight the complexities behind the exalted ideal of Southern community and family: a potential for stifling choice and originality, leaving little room for rebellion from the community's norms. Decidedly grounding them in their Alabama upbringing, Laura also counts as an influence Alabama author Rick Bragg, most known for his trilogy *All Over But the Shoutin'*, *Ava's Man*, and *The Prince of Frogtown*, which recount his family's rural Alabama life.

Yet, their musical ardor comes less from any one artistic influence but instead an entire mise-en-scène. Their sonic ecology is born out of family life, history, and connection to a place.

Laura: I think, too, there is something about the landscape of the South, the actual geographical landscape . . . that affects us as musicians. There is a tie to it that we feel. When we're away from the South for too long, we start needing it again. We actually had one of our managers a couple of years ago say, "I'm starting to realize that Southern people"—because he wasn't a Southerner—"that all the Southern artists I work with don't need to be out of the South for too long." Because there is almost like this connection back there that you need to go back and revisit.

Lydia: We were having a really hard time a few years ago being away from home for so long. We would be away for four or five weeks at a time, and it just weighs on you. After the three-week mark, we just felt so drawn back to it.

Laura: And it wasn't enough to have our family members come on the road with us, or meet us in a certain city. That wasn't enough. It was like, no, I want to be in Alabama, with my familiar landscape, and my place and my people around me. That's something that's unique to the South, in a very big way, is that people are so connected to their family, their roots, their history, their story, and there is a pride in each individual.

At the same time, in order to understand who they were in relation to their roots, history, and story, to be able to appreciate the unique value of their culture while also affording a critical eye, the sisters had to get out of the South, out of what Lydia called their bubble.

Lydia: I think we are really lucky to have left when we did. I was twenty years old, Laura was twenty-two, and we had lived in Florence, Alabama, our whole lives. At least for me, I was so tired of it, and I wanted something more out of life, and then all this music stuff happened, and we got out of our bubble, and we realized how special our bubble was.

Travelling to L.A., New York, and overseas afforded the duo perspective, and it put them into a unique role. For the first time in their lives they were a part of the Southern diaspora. They were outside of their familiar environment, where audiences would instinctively understand them and shared similar contexts. Instead, they were now not only being asked to perform this traditional Americana sound, but audiences and record label execs expected them to look and sound the part as well—leaving the two, less than a year removed from their first public performance, with nuanced decisions to make regarding Southern identity. They were left to negotiate what kind of Southerner they wanted to be publicly; in what community did they belong?

Laura: When we first got started in all of this, they kind of labeled us as country music artists. And we are that, and a lot of people were trying to pitch us to open for these pop-country singers, but we didn't want to do that. We chose a different route. . . . The music that we love doesn't really utilize those sorts of caricatures.

The music that influences us the most is not the stuff talking about sittin' in the back of a pickup with your girl who doesn't have a name and drinkin' out of a moonshine jar. I don't love that kind of music at all. . . . It can be cheesy, and a little bit taking advantage of something that's almost sacred. And I get really annoyed whenever I hear artists who are not from the South faking a Southern accent in the way they sing. That grinds my ears.

H. C.: So is it fair to say that you are kind of trying to reclaim a certain Southern image from that crowd?

Lydia: I think we're part of that movement for sure.

Laura: More than reclaiming it, we're just showing how ridiculous it is, how silly it can be, and how absolutely inaccurate it can be.

Lydia: That you don't have to play it up, you just be who are, and it will come out in your music, regardless.

Laura: Too, this is interesting, because I remember the first time we went overseas to do any touring, but the general consensus from people in that part of the world is that they really do have this idea that we all just sit around on our front porches playing music and drinking sweet tea. And while that may be true in a lot of instances, we love doing that, but you have to kind of find ways to teach them about Southern culture without disappointing them. You don't want to . . . burst their bubble, but you also don't want to portray something that isn't real. So for us, it's just a matter of being who we are, and we've really had to learn, you just show up and be true to who you are, and you sleep easy at night knowing that you were genuine in whatever way. And then, if they enjoy that and think that it's charming, and they are won over, then that's fantastic. And if they think that it's a different idea than what they're looking for, well, then, they're just not right for you.

Yet, in the beginning, as novices, the two relied on the advice of their label regarding branding and styling. The first album featured the sisters in polka-dotted dresses, bright red lipstick, and their hair in victory rolls, not-so-subtly connecting their sound to the look and feel of the 1940s. As Lydia remembers it, the two walked off a photo shoot set once and some label people, either from New York or L.A., said, "We love this! You have to embody this." She laughed dismissively, recounting the story: "We get all our clothes from Target!" But the message was clear, and it worked, both for good and ill. In many reviews of the first two albums, the duo's appearance was as much a matter of critique as the albums; often the two were interconnected. NPR's Meredith Ochs writes, "Porcelain complected, red-lipsticked, blue-eyed and raven-haired, the Secret Sisters' look seems cultivated to match the duo's sound." Ochs further connects the duo's sound and aesthetic by evoking the period-piece television drama *Mad Men*, the 1950s pin-up model Bettie Page, and the harmony-singing duo the Everly Brothers.[23] Quoting Laura—"Sometimes, when I'm out walking with my dress on and my hair all curled, I feel bad getting my cell phone out. . . . People will think I'm such a phony"—the *Guardian*'s Alexis Petridis took to task the carefully crafted image of "historical recreation rock," claiming that the duo's label markets them as "an anthropological find." Petridis argues that the marketing strategy is no "less contrived than Lady Gaga emerging from a giant plastic egg with a lobster on her head."

For the critic, the stylings bely artistic decisions on their debut album, too, in which "august Nashville session musicians and carefully selected cover versions . . . speak of a world of chaste romance, where hearts skip a beat when you walk down the street and men are chastised for honky-tonkin'." Particularly problematic were such songs as the traditional British folk tune "Do You Love an Apple," which as sung by the Secret Sisters, Petridis notes, "removes the verses suggestive of domestic abuse and takes the song's dark, doleful power along with them."

Implied within what Petridis doesn't say is that the sisters have undeniable talent, and their context and story warrant telling. Perhaps inferred within the critique is that their small-town Southern upbringing provided them by proximity and ancestry a connection to the authentic roots of the music's heritage. With that in mind, Petridis echoes what would, two years later, be the duo's mantra and what many music lovers who champion substance over image would find worthy: "It works best when everyone stops worrying about conjuring a chocolate-box version of the past and allows the duo's raw talent to shine through."[24]

A disagreement in the comment section to the review is particularly revealing, speaking to the slippery contradictions over authenticity and kitsch and foregrounding the internal struggle Laura and Lydia soon found within themselves.

Username: Benulek 18 Feb 2011: . . . this reeks of try-too-hard *in*authenticity.

Username: lauralfp 20 Feb 2011: I presume we'll only be able to buy it on 78 format, then? 10" shellac? Antediluvian twaddle.

Username: neorich 22 Feb 2011: Why is it that these album "reviews," take up so much time telling us very little about the quality, or content of the songs, or performances? This is completely, like so many of these "reviews," totally up its own backside.

These gals, retro, or not are the real deal, they sing together with exquisite vocal harmonies which are a joy to listen to as anyone who heard them performing without any whistles and bells, or backing tracks on BBC Breakfast will have heard.

What we first, many of us witnessed on Jools on New Year's Eve was no accident, they put "artists," such as Cheryl Cole and the like into perspective.

Given time to grow, I'm sure they'll move into other areas and produce some interesting work, or at least be assured of a damn good and honest living doing what they do very well.

I, for one, will buy the album, not least because they're talented, but also because it's great to see artists being taken seriously because of what they can do, rather [sic] whether they feel they have to look like they belong on a cat-walk in order to be a success![25]

After the first album, Laura and Lydia engaged issues of value, motivation, integrity and sincerity in recording, performing, and writing music. And they began inching toward taking control over their own narrative.

Laura: What people don't realize is that if you don't have a really clear identity of what you're going after when you enter the music world, you will be shaped. You will be molded, you will be cast a certain way. They will try to tell your stories. They'll spin you. And when you're just finding your way, unless you're very strong-willed about it, it is so easy to trust them because, at least in our case, we were like, they have to know better than we do. We've never done this before. We've never styled ourselves.[26]

Navigating how best to translate the sounds and life they lived in Florence, Alabama, and their Southern heritage without giving way to a theater-like performance was a challenge. Hyperaware of the thin line between authenticity and insincerity, they began to debate how best to be sincere, true to their context, themselves, and their music, without giving in to a facsimile of the very stereotypes they had grown to reject about the South and Southerners. What had been intended as what Laura calls a "tribute" had "started crossing over into, this is a little bit like we're on a movie set. A little bit shtick." The Secret Sisters were on the tightrope other conscientious artists have found themselves walking when attempting to look backward and forward at the same time, trying to preserve something without giving way to either hackneyed karaoke or stagnation but rather offering a reinterpretation and re-presentation of heritage. Carrying the T Bone brand could also be a double-edged sword, as the debates surrounding *O Brother, Where Art Thou?* confirm. Undoubtedly, the sisters benefitted from Burnett's encyclopedic knowledge, his decades of recording and producing experience, his wide network of friends, and his musical taste. However, while benefitting from the post–*O Brother* roots music resurgence gave them their break, it also left them attempting to deftly navigate the folk-fatigue terrain bands like Mumford & Sons both felt and left in their wake.

Lydia: I think we're fortunate to be doing what we're doing right now because of a movement that T Bone started with *O Brother, Where Art Thou?*, this resurgence of really old music, and people loved it.

Mentioning bands like Colorado-based the Lumineers, the Icelandic band Of Monsters and Men, alongside Mumford, Lydia felt that while "we're kind of on that train, I hope we're not just on that train. I hope we're moving past that too."

Laura: The Lumineers had this huge success with this kind of chanting "Ho, Hey" song. Good song, but I feel like because that was so successful now everybody is, like, "I'll pull out a banjo, kick on a kick drum like this, play this way, say 'Hey.'" I think it's really easy to stand from a place of a creative mind and look at those kinds of bands and kind of turn your nose up at it, and I was that way admittedly for a little while about Mumford & Sons, but I think my main reason I was that way was because everybody loved them! And every time I turned on the radio I heard something. Every time I opened up a magazine it was something. And I was just, like, "Oh, my word, this is ridiculous." Then we were a part of the *Inside Llewyn Davis* performance that T Bone put together, and Marcus Mumford was there, and he stood and sang a Bob Dylan song, just him and a guitar, brought me to my knees. It was so good. This person knows good stuff, he's got a real sincerity about him, and I gained a lot of respect for what they do.

Within the creation and performance of music for a popular audience, with musicians, producers, stylists, executives, a host of distribution outlets from YouTube and Spotify to intimate concerts and CDs, the conflicts among context, identity, purpose, authenticity, artistic intent, and the construction of meaning and message swirl around. Benjamin Filene's fears of a superficial reaction to the music's context resonate. Are the Rogers sisters unwitting participants in an industry attempt to brand the past for an audience interested in nostalgia over cultural subversion, wringing out any trace of transgressive potential with each stereotypical hat-tip to a bygone, supposed golden era? Is it possible to translate the Secret Sisters's youthful family sing-alongs and church pew harmonies outside the confines of Florence? Can Burnett recreate through his soundtracks and through his inner circle of artistic productions his Fort Worth early years for popular audiences without sacrificing what made both contexts unique?

In *Wake Up Dead Man*, folklorist Bruce Jackson collected and analyzed African American prison work songs born out of the psychological, physical, emotional, and spiritual hell making up prison life for African Americans in the Deep South. Jackson comments on the transformation of songs taken out of one context and recreated in another. He contends that the songs' art and beauty can only be fully grasped by being there: "Sung outside such a context . . . there is an academic flavor—a sense of *performance* or a sense of doing a song-*with*-a-context, which is quite different from being in a context and singing a song."[27] Jackson's folklorist sensibilities set the dilemma in stone for artists like the Secret Sisters and Burnett. It is impossible to translate the nuanced complexities of family, place, theology, and cultural identity onto rolls of recording tape and into digital files to be compressed, housed, and sent off into the world with less control over interpretation. It's easier in live performance, but as they move further outside their north Alabama town, at what point do they, unintentionally or not, give in to that "sense of performance" Jackson so eloquently noted? Are they performing their Florence Southern heritage for audiences eager for a show, with expectations that they dress and talk a certain way and, apparently, abstain from using cell phones and other modern devices in manners more likely for the Amish than contemporary Southerners? Perhaps, though, the critics set up a false dichotomy of either unblemished authenticity or farce, when in fact popular music consumption of a region so rich with history, myth, and characters can never be read so easily.

The arguments themselves are nothing new, as the recording boom of the 1920s and 1930s saw "authentic" rural musicians willingly transferring their sounds and look out of the coal mines and cotton fields to a popular audience, often in metropolitan areas. One need look no further than convicted murderer Huddie "Lead Belly" Ledbetter leaving the infamous Angola prison farm in Louisiana to be whisked around New York City by John Lomax, often dressing the part of down-home black man come to the big city for his urbanite audience. For one hundred years, Southern musicians have purposefully crafted identities by using the tools of branding and music, birthing tall tales and legends surrounding bargains with the devil and railroad ramblings, such as with myth-men like Robert Johnson and Jimmie Rodgers. Furthermore, as country music's popularity soared in the midcentury, shows like the Grand Ole Opry, Ozark Jubilee, and later Hee Haw became outlets for new and established artists to perform amidst skits that purposefully played on Southern stereotypes. For the Secret Sisters, despite charges of lapsing into an image-over-substance sentimentalized nostalgia through branding, there yet exists transgressive potential to cut against the grain, as the sisters' second album and the consequences of attempting to take back control of their art and narrative indicate.

With the second album, the sisters shed the protection of cover songs, venturing instead into songwriting. The result is darker in tone, investigative in approach. Gone are the victory rolls and polka dot dresses, replaced now with all black. With the growth in songwriting, they explore gender roles, love, and place more openly. Refusing to give themselves over to kitsch marketing and the unblemished utopian presentation of the first album, however, would come with consequences. The follow-up to their eponymous debut album signaled more than just shifts in fashion.

Lydia: We quickly learned that if we were to stay with that image we would forever be known as these traditional, sweet country girls, and we didn't want to be boxed in like that. We wanted to surprise people and have something different every time we released music.

Laura: And too, in a way . . . our progression in our dress and our attire represented a deeper progression in us growing up and figuring out how we're going to do this and what we want to sound like and establishing a level of confidence that we didn't have when we started, so the clothing progression became a kind of shallow indicator of us also progressing as musicians and writers and in our mentality too.[28]

This "deeper progression" purposefully extends to gender expectations as well. Growing up in a culture steeped in the connotations of what it means to be a "Southern lady" (read genteel, pure, white, moneyed, and submissive) or its opposite, the "redneck woman" popularized by Gretchen Wilson, the two here resist those poles to explore the complexities within what it means in contemporary terms to be a Southern woman:

> **Laura:** I think that it's a fine balance, a pretty delicate line, and we've not had a hard time navigating it, really, because I feel like for the most part we're very true as artists to who we are as individuals when we're not being "The Secret Sisters." And so there is a certain level of be a lady, be delicate when you need to be, be feminine when you need to be, but don't be afraid to go and be strong and don't be afraid to be assertive, and it's okay to be confident, and it's okay to want to look pretty, and it's okay to not want to look pretty, and it's just okay to be whatever you feel like being that day. And you know, we still get the thing, our mom says, "Don't sit like that," or "Don't say those things because you're a girl." That's just the nature of Southern mothers. They want their girls to be socially inoffensive. But I don't think of myself as a redneck. I think of myself as a Southern woman. But to me the redneck thing is, I feel like there are rednecks everywhere, if you really want to get serious about it. You can find a redneck anywhere you look. It's more about a mindset and a mentality and approach to things.

Behind the direction of T Bone, *Put Your Needle Down* saw the Secret Sisters moving from the comfort of cover songs, with the exception of the P. J. Harvey track "The Pocket Knife," and into writing their own songs and collaborating with writers like Brandi Carlile. Purposefully attempting to carve out their own sound, to take control of their own narrative, and to avoid the kitsch folk narratives dominating the airwaves, the music had to evolve as well.

With T Bone's "psychosphere" production philosophy and the sisters' harmonies and thematic exploration, the album received due attention. *Rolling Stone* noted how the "haunting harmonies combine with the spooky nuances of T Bone Burnett's country baroque production for an album fit for a horror film," citing the combination of "swampy atmospherics . . . ethereal vocals and cherubic charm."[29] Noting how their first album could have trapped them "into a dusty back-alley country corner stylistically," *AllMusic*'s Steve Leggett complimented their second album on how Burnett and company, with a "mesh of folky honky tonk, garage rock, and girl group ballads," place the Secret Sisters's sound in company with "Daniel Lanois-like swampy noodling," comparing their album with "Emmylou Harris' Lanois-produced *Wrecking Ball* as sung by the Everly Brothers' little sisters while fronting the Cowboy Junkies."[30] An NPR review commented on how the two "have mastered the art of looking backward and forward at the same time."[31]

In *Put Your Needle Down*, the Secret Sisters travel familiar Southern thematic roads with religious homilies like "River Jordan" and violent Southern gothic tracks like "Iuka" sharing the same sonic and cultural space with universal psychological and mythological issues surrounding religion and violence, love and lust, family, community, and rugged individualism, all inherent within the contradictions of country music and the South writ large. They take on race in their video for "Rattle My Bones," filmed in an Alabama prison with hat-tip to Johnny Cash intended, which features scenes of a white warden's daughter and a black inmate dancing in contemporary fashion, at the encouragement of the music and the other inmates. The scenes are not overtly sexual, but rather connote a sweet innocence, an idealistic longing between the sexes and races. At video's end, utopian longing is shattered by reality as the two are forcefully separated by prison guards. Above all, the album unpacks the back-and-forth disjointedness and psychological and emotional complexities of sexuality, love, and identity. Throughout the album, they explore the contradictions between stifling fear of marriage and the anxiety of loneliness, between individualism and relationship.

The album's tempo and Burnett's ability to adapt several genres within the same space work well with such thematic contradictions. Upbeat rock and roll numbers like "Rattle My Bones" combine with the tempered, twangy, country straightforwardness of "I Cannot Find a Way" in exploring the tug and pull of desire and vulnerability. In the duo's cover of English singer-songwriter P. J. Harvey's "The Pocket Knife," Burnett pairs swamp rock and punk dissonance with the psychological discord of young women's fearful expectations of marriage and settling down. The fifties-inspired pop playfulness on "Good Luck, Good Night, Goodbye," asserting their standards and declarations in getting rid of an unappreciative love interest, contrasts with "Bad Habit," a sultry, slow anthem of resignation, of not being able to give up on the wrong kind of man, evoking lowly lit bars where down-on-their-luck folks drown their sorrows.

The backhanded and assertive straightforwardness of the rapid-fire rhetorical questions in "If I Don't" conjure Cash's "Walk the Line" themes of loyalty, agency, and lover's games:

> Who's gonna love you if I don't,
> Who's gonna give you what you want,
> Who in the world will put up with your little schemes?
> You better get yourself in check
> If you've got any self-respect.

Themes of desperation and lamentation in spurned love continue with the minimalist piano, tambourine, and guitar-backed soliloquy in "Let There Be Lonely," which harmonizes well with the whimsy and dramatic declarations of a life lived in solitude in "Lonely Island." "Black and Blue" jars listeners' attention again with fifties-styled hand-claps-and-finger-snaps rock and roll. The sisters also add to Bob Dylan's unfinished lyrics for "Dirty Lie," turning it into jazz-blues beatnik playfulness.

Lyrically, "Iuka" relies on tropes of Southern identity more than any other track on the album. In "Iuka," everything is percussion: the piano, drums, voices, and guitars, the constant thumping supporting the threat of violence. The pounding is complicated by delicate tambourine play and whining horns, foreshadowing the implicit sexuality in forbidden love. It's sex and hostility, battle lines drawn in red-clay Mississippi earth. It's the struggle to break free from the suffocation of family and place. In this way, "Iuka" can also be read as an artistic death of sorts. With the second album, the sisters lay to rest the branding aesthetics and cover-song nostalgia of the first album, and, rather than getting caught in a type of Southern Stockholm Syndrome by which Southerners take cues from popular culture's expectations of Southern-born performers and in turn create and perpetuate the very images they hope to rebel against, the duo attempt to assert their own voice and sound. As the song says, "two headstones for two lovers who finally got away." As violence, love, lust, longing, resolve, and religion share narrative space, the album reads like a Flannery O'Connor or Bobbie Ann Mason novel backed by Burnett's jaunts back and forth between swampy, sultry, rock, jazz, country, and pop, all with those harmonies that can be both delicate and then forceful.

The distance between their first two albums is best summarized by a PopMatters review: "*Put Your Needle Down* doesn't sound like it's something the godmothers of country would have made. It doesn't sound like it could have fit into another era. It stands on its own."[32]

Perhaps the best way to place the Secret Sisters' cultural intent is by travelling with them in the community of artists in which they reside and the venues in which they perform. In support of their second album, they toured and recorded with a host of Southern bands and pop-folk artists operating under a similar cultural ethos, including M. Ward, Dylan LeBlanc, Striking Matches, Iron and Wine, Jamestown Revival, and Old Crow Medicine Show. They have crisscrossed the South, East Coast, Midwest, Texas, and the Pacific Northwest performing in venues and festivals such as Bluegrass Underground at Cumberland Caverns, the Carolina in the Fall Music and Food Festival, Southern Ground Music and Food Festival, AmericanaFest, Panoply Arts Festival, 30A Songwriters Festival, the Outlaw Roadshow, Bunbury Music Festival, Brandywine Folk Festival, Wakarusa Festival, and the Grand Ole Opry, among others.

With the backing of Burnett, the two were afforded the opportunity for a wider audience as well. Their performance of "Iuka" on *The Tonight Show with Jimmy Fallon* best exemplifies the cultural negotiations that take place when Southern musicians perform for a popular audience outside the South. In conjunction with the release of their second album, the duo secured a partnership with the homestyle Southern cooking chain restaurant Cracker Barrel, selling an exclusive deluxe album in stores. Founded in Lebanon, Tennessee, in 1969, Cracker Barrel now exports its Southern-inspired sentimentality—oversized rocking chairs, old-timey candy, and general-store appeal, where families can play checkers in front of a fire while waiting for cornbread and chicken-fried steak—across America, with restaurants dotting highway exits in forty-two states. While introducing the band before their *Tonight Show* performance, host Jimmy Fallon, wry grins and condescension intact, declared his contrived love for the Southern-staple restaurant chain to announcer and comedic counterpoint Steve Higgins. As if to assure his audience that the Secret Sisters were more than his comedic pretensions may have suggested, Fallon assured them that cultural gatekeeper T Bone Burnett had given his stamp of approval. Meaning, these two aren't cracker-barrel yokels.

Cracker Barrel may be the perfect symbol to flesh out the narrative transactions Southerners wrestle with, both within themselves *and* with their non-Southern counterparts. Southerners acknowledge the restaurant's facsimiles of the dinner tables and small-town country stores that still exist along forgotten highways outside the reaches of tourist traps and the bright lights of Charlotte, Atlanta, Nashville, and Charleston. Southerners leave the Cracker Barrel satisfied at the re-creation, but knowing it's a far cry from the family spreads or mom-and-pop meat-and-threes they have enjoyed. It is an identity negotiation of sorts, a restaurant-chain reminder of displays of family and community many Southerners might say they long for, some still have, and others only want to remember in a haze of nostalgia. Simply put, Cracker Barrel is to grandma's table and her small-town general store what pop country's blue-collar bluster is to Loretta Lynn's Kentucky mining community upbringing. And that's how outsiders see it, too. It's a performance of a kind of Southern identity that, like the African American prison-chant songs in Jackson's book, doesn't translate easily outside original context.

Therein rests the Secret Sisters performance on the *Tonight Show*: allusions to Southern stereotyping from a New York City comedian, T Bone Burnett, a song about forbidden love, family, and violence in a deep South Mississippi town, and two sisters from Florence, Alabama, best known for the harmonies they perfected in their small country church and their parent's home. Those symbols bouncing around for popular consumption signify the difficulty when Southern bands with similar contexts attempt to popularize their sound and ethic while staying just outside the confines of stereotyping the very thing they value and love. Sometimes the either-or dichotomy holds firm, pairing purposeful stereotyping like a Jeff Foxworthy "You Might Be a Redneck If" routine against an "authentic" cultural expression like a gathering of folk musicians around a courthouse square. When cultural expressions are presented for popular consumption, the conclusions are typically more complex than such dichotomies suggest. Communities, performances, and associations all help, but so does motivation, which can often best be judged over time. Responding to a question about where they hope to position their careers, the sisters were adamant that, though folk-inspired trends come and go, they were in this for the long haul.

Laura: For us, it's a slow trajectory. . . .

Lydia: We don't want to be following any trend.

Laura: I think it can be challenging. . . . We could've done another, a second album of cover songs, of really great old country standards. And that would have been fine, and it would've still been who we are, but I think that for our own sake we needed to know that we could write from our inspiration. And that we could somehow grab the important parts of the music that inspires us but also tell our own story with it. . . .

Lydia: And that will inevitably progress on its own.

Laura: It will grow as it needs to.[33]

While a noble ethic, their philosophy comes at a price. Kitsch sells, as indicated by the success of the pop country music coming out of Nashville and entertainment such as the Blue Collar Comedy Tour and the television show *Duck Dynasty*. After their summer 2014 tour, Republic Records decided to end their relationship. Laura explains that they anticipated this next phase of their careers and, happy to have made two albums they were proud of and having had the opportunity to work with T Bone and a host of their music heroes, they felt no hard feelings. "We're an indie band now," Laura laughs. In the midst of the transition, however, the two had a "nasty" falling out with their manager, culminating in a year's worth of lawyers, suits and countersuits, and ultimately bankruptcy, all while trying to promote their latest record. Left without a manager and unable to hire a replacement due to the legal wrangling, the sisters had to plan a tour and manage it, hitting the road with Laura driving six or seven hours a day and Lydia planning, marketing, and arranging the logistics and details from the passenger seat.

In contrast to their first headlining tour, which included a full backup band, the duo were to rely on stripped-down shows, just the two of them and a guitar. Though they felt insecure without a band, questioning whether they had just been a fad, a string of sold-out intimate venues in Mobile, New Orleans, Dallas, Austin, and Little Rock were reinvigorating, reminding them of the centrality of music and messaging.[34] The New Orleans show at Gasa Gasa was emblematic of the tour's success. Gasa Gasa is the kind of Uptown New Orleans quaint venue that is as likely to host a music show as it is an art exhibition or film screening. The sold-out crowd may have numbered only a hundred people, but they were spirited and engaged all night as the duo led them through songs from *Put Your Needle Down* and covers of Pete Seeger and the Everly Brothers among others. The sisters saved the best for last, as they ventured away from their mics and stage lights and into the crowd. With the audience snapping the beat, the two sang "Tonight You Belong to Me" in a circle surrounded by their new friends.

The sisters are purposeful in making sure their shows reflect the character-istics of music and culture they most value, giving a glimpse into who they are and where they're from.

> **Laura:** I guess in a way, I really like to make the short time we're on stage a kind of encompassing snapshot of just who we are and the experiences we have and the kind of life that we live, and the way that we were raised, and the humans we ended up becoming.[35]

The Gasa Gasa show was a stark contrast to the first time I saw them. The 2014 Fayetteville Roots Music Festival's lineup was in keeping with the sisters' typical associations, with Jay Farrar of Son Volt and Uncle Tupelo fame, New Orleans–based Americana rock outfit Hurray for the Riff Raff, and outlaw country queen bee Lucinda Williams all on the bill. The audience, however, was decidedly old, middle-aged, and white. Cushy chairs and an air-conditioned pavilion, where locally grown food was whipped up for concertgoers to purchase, stood in stark contrast to the Gasa Gasa show. Yet, the two polarities are representative of the sisters' typical audience. The first record had encouraged a cultural brokering between the white-haired crowd and their grandchildren. Their song on the *Hunger Games* soundtrack helped introduce them to a much younger audience as well. Such intergenerational appeal was purposefully crafted.

> **Laura:** From the beginning, we've always said that we want to make the kind of music that a grandmother can come to the show with her grandson who's in his twenties, and they both love it in equal amounts. And we have little kids who can sing every word of our record, and we have ninety-, ninety-five-year-old women who know it . . . . There's a guy we know who came to one of our shows, and as it turns out he found out about us because his grandmother asked for our CD for Christmas, and he bought it for her, just thinking, "Well, I'll get her what she wants." And he looked at it and was, like, "Who are these girls? What is this?" And he listened to it and ended up loving it. And his grandmother, who's like, eighty-five, introduced him to a new band. . . . I love that contradiction, flipping traditional roles on their heads, a little bit.[36]

The sisters' touring setup was decidedly different, too, from the Fayetteville show's tour bus and backing band to the NOLA show's DIY grit. The decision to choose artistic integrity over kitsch appeal came at a high price, testing their motivation and resolve. The years in between the two albums presented disappointment, financial struggle, and discouragement, leaving them to organize, plan, and execute a tour on their own. In a summer 2015 Instagram post, Laura summarized what was at stake, simultaneously offering a glimpse of what it's like behind the scenes.

> **@laurarogers:** We found ourselves faced with a month long run of shows, with very few people to help us organize it. Going in, it was black and white for me: if the tour went smoothly, I would hang in there and keep singing until it comes time to quit . . . If it went poorly, I would hang it up and get a stable 8–5 job with benefits. But here we are, 20 shows in 29 days all done, and done successfully. Without a record label, without management, without a tour manager, without a band, without any financial help and paying for everything up front, we made it. I am deeply proud of what @llslagle88 and I could accomplish in the simplest of ways ... With 2 voices, 1 guitar, and a bunch of people who somehow want to come hear us sing. So after it's all done, it seems the road has chosen us to fight another day, another tour, and onward we will go, choosing the hard road of quality music. So long as you guys keep showing up to hear us, we will sing for you. Thank you for restoring my faith in myself and the music I love so dearly to create. Homeward, we go![37]

As the post suggests, "choosing the hard road of quality music" over an easier way that compromised the integrity of their art for clichéd branding that plays on a preserved-in-amber Southern heritage comes at a high price. Weekend runs to shows in places like Mobile, the two might earn three or four hundred dollars a night. Festival gigs could pay anywhere from five to seven thousand. It is unpredictable. At one point, Laura put ads on Facebook looking for people who needed help with babysitting, housekeeping, or "organizing their kitchen cabinets": "I can clean a house today and make fifty bucks and that will cover my water bill and groceries." During these times, community became essential to their well-being, as support from family and the music community helped sustain them. Laura noted how often people like Brandi Carlile would call or send emails of support, while also helping them shop for managers and flying the sisters out to open a series of shows for her in Seattle. The famous Muscle Shoals music community has supported them as well. Former Civil Wars front man John Paul White, with his Single Lock Records, is another supporter, asking the sisters to back him on tour and his new album. Laura confides that they make more backing John Paul than they did headlining their own shows. With support from the community, coming in the form of both encouragement and gigs during thin financial days, the Secret Sisters appear for the time being to be back on their feet.

> **Laura:** We feel a little more free than we ever have. Not that freedom is comforting, actually freedom is terrifying. . . . Now that we don't have a record label or a domineering manager telling us what to wear and that our outfits look ridiculous . . . at the end of the day now it's all about what we want to do. . . . Maybe I don't want to wear a dress when I perform, or play this kind of song, or tell this story. . . . I feel a lot more peace about my music career . . . than I have in a long time.[38]

The strength of the contemporary music scene in which they participate is not lost on Burnett, either. Citing bands like the Avett Brothers, he maintains that the "traditional American music scene is probably the healthiest music scene in the country right now. It's still strangely underground and alternative or marginalized . . . but it's extraordinarily healthy with . . . a lot of people devoting their lives to it."[39]

For Laura and Lydia, Burnett's role in introducing them to the community, putting the weight of his name and ethos behind them, remains a defining moment of their young careers. Noting the "camaraderie and partnership," the "communal effort to do something good" that exemplifies Burnett's "inner circle," Laura comments on the circle's and Burnett's ethos:

> **Laura:** It's just this group of artists that he counts on, and anytime he does a project or one of his revues that he's so famous for, these are the people that are staples in it. I think that we are not like the Punch Brothers, and we are not like the Carolina Chocolate Drops, and we are not like Gillian Welch. There are a lot of differences in the artists he has in his inner circle, but it's all for the same purpose and the same goal, and I think it goes back to that whole preservationist mindset of "we're going to get it covered." Between all those people that T Bone kind of puts together in the same circumstance, we've got all the good stuff covered. And I think he knows that. And he doesn't ever call anybody to do something that isn't true to who they are. And so, instead, he finds the people that do it right, and brings them into the world. And so there's this family kind of thing. . . . Our T Bone connection provided us with our relationship with Chris Thile, which provided us with our entire summer of touring opening for Nickel Creek. So, T Bone being the common factor in everything, we're all able to help each other out because

we're not, none of us, individually as successful as T Bone, but he uses his power to put us all together, and we all benefit from knowing each other.[40]

After *O Brother*, T Bone used the next decade to help produce a number of artists re-presenting art made in the spirit of traditional American music: Ralph Stanley, Ollabelle, Cassandra Wilson, B. B. King, Willie Nelson, Robert Randolph and the Family Band, Ryan Bingham, Gregg Allman, Steve Earle, the Chieftains, the Punch Brothers, Rhiannon Giddens. Burnett's reputation allowed him, at a time when a Led Zeppelin reunion tour would have sold out stadiums around the world, to bring Robert Plant and bluegrass queen Alison Krauss together for a stripped-down album with delicate, tightly woven harmonies and rockabilly, Appalachian folk, rock, bluegrass, and blues tones. Burnett's community reads like one of his albums, combining the revered and the recent by intermingling genres and re-interpreting sounds and contexts. Any one album has swamp rock, bluegrass, rockabilly, country, and blues riffs blended such that it's hard to note the point at which one ceases to be something and instead becomes something else. Taken together, they are the representative soundtrack for traditional American music reinterpreted for contemporary audiences, which is as good a commentary on the significance of Southern music, past and present, in American popular culture as one can find.[41]

Karl Marx said, "The philosophers have only interpreted the world, in various ways; the point is to change it." Burnett eschews this implied dichotomy between philosopher's gaze and activist's rally. For him, ethic feeds action. As he did with staple folk performers like Emmylou Harris and Alison Krauss and rockers like Jack White, Burnett continued to work with artists like the Secret Sisters and the Carolina Chocolate Drops' Rhiannon Giddens to reinterpret traditional songs and covers, while interspersing originals to create a sonic continuity between the past and the present.

Using the tools of popular culture, Burnett remains interested in the philosophical and cultural implications of re-presenting and reinterpreting roots music. This regenerative and philosophical quality holds true in Burnett's work, particularly in his studio philosophy, with the Secret Sisters, and in their attempt to be to some degree cultural preservationists of their heritage.

Laura: We are trying to preserve the tradition of real voices that are not robots that are tuned beyond belief, that are not produced to the point that they aren't human anymore. We're trying to preserve styles of songs that maybe are not popular anymore or at least not being made in large amounts, that kind of music that we just love. We love it so much, and it's so deeply rooted in who we are.

Lydia: And I also think the kind of harmony we do is pretty unique, too, because it harkens back to that Church of Christ roots. And not many people have that. I think that we're in a way paying tribute to that time so we don't forget how to harmonize with each other, and how to read music.[42]

Laura purposefully connects Burnett's studio philosophy, how the idea of preservation "trickl[ing] down from him" had an "absolute effect" on them, with their desire to present music that is accessible and as open to the imperfections of a live performance as can be achieved in a studio.

Laura: I've actually talked to producers and engineers who will sit in these very popular artist recordings, and they will tweak every little note. They'll listen to 10 or 12 passes on a couple words and choose the best one. And when they choose the best one and still have to tune it, and it's just like, what are you doing? . . . So, I guess for us, it's just a matter of showing people it's okay if you hit a bum note every now and then, and it's okay if there is a moment of vulnerability in your song or where you get feedback in your guitar, because you're a human, a human playing a piece of wood in front of other humans.

According to the sisters, though he is particular in the studio, and though nothing is done "out of impulse," Burnett ultimately presided over their sessions like a "master curator."

Laura: We would come in and usually just have a rough acoustic demo of us and the song, and he would play it for all the musicians, and some of them would already have parts . . . or they might have the songs charted out already or whatever. And he would kind of guide it along. But as far as being very heavy-handed and everything, he really wasn't. He was really more like the master curator of things. And it was more about him bringing certain people into the same space and turning on the recording switch.

The image of Burnett as the curator of Americana's soul speaks to the T Bone brand of authenticity, for which many of his admirers are hunting, at work in his artistic productions. The idea that an album made for popular consumption cannot be as authentic as an unscripted folk concert creates an unnecessary false dichotomy. Burnett's "psychosphere" creations—*True Detective*'s Louisiana, *Crazy Heart*'s West Texas, *Cold Mountain*'s Appalachia, *O Brother*'s

Delta, *Walk the Line*'s exploration of Cash's mind—and all the other artists and albums don't pretend to be what they aren't. They aren't competing with the fruits of folklore, with church singings and courthouse picking sessions, juke joints and country line dances. It is not an attempt at identifying and defining an enigmatic concept like authenticity. It is a re-creation of music, and contexts, that deserve re-presentation in popular contexts.

> **Laura:** It's almost like a Rolodex in his brain of these artists . . . from late 1800s, early 1900s. People that nobody knew about. And he knows so much about them. How they were recorded, and how they impacted society. Who discovered them, and the songs they wrote, and who they stole songs from. He's just so smart. Not only does he know how to capture sonically, but he knows so much about the history and the importance and the cultural relevance of it.

It's a guidebook to what Burnett and his friends feel are important about music, a focus on community and context that takes its cues from cultural honesty over kitsch. Laura and Lydia have tried to carry that ethic into their art, following some advice Burnett gave them early on in their career.

> **Laura:** "The goal is not the accolades and the praise and the affirmation that you receive. Money and success will come. It will come as it's supposed to. The trick is to just always make it good. Make it something you are proud of, that you're proud to listen to, and that you know you put your heart into. All the other stuff is just kind of secondary." Financial stability is fantastic, and it's important, and being able to tour and travel comfortably, all of that is really needed, but I can't imagine wanting to do this if I didn't feel good about the music we were making. If it felt like it was contrived or insincere in any way, I don't think that any amount of money or comfort or material success would fulfill that need in us. And it's different for different people.

Seminal sociologist Simon Frith, exploring the relationship between identity and music, argues that "in examining the aesthetics of popular music we need to reverse the usual academic argument: the question is not how a piece of music, a text, 'reflects' popular values, but how—in performance—it produces them."[43] In a contemporary music climate dominated by pop idols like Miley Cyrus, Katy Perry, and Beyoncé and hip-hop megastars like Jay-Z, Kanye West, and Drake, with shows like *American Idol* and *The Voice* dominating television, and where people listen to music on a host of portable electronic devices, most notably via digital streaming services like Spotify and iTunes that offer consumers virtually any genre of music at the click of a button, it's worth noting why the Secret Sisters' sound and identity, and, by implication, Burnett's circle, have struck a chord.

> **Lydia:** I think people miss that time. The radio, especially, is so saturated with that pop sound, just completely auto-tuning every note. I think people miss an older time. . . .

> **Laura:** You have to wonder at times. I think people are just hungry for something simple, that life is so complicated. We live with screens in front of our faces all the time. And we connect with people, but we *don't* connect with people. And we're losing our sense of who we are, and culture is shifting so much. And that's just the natural way of things, but I feel like people are still trying to hold on to something of the past. The good parts of the past.[44]

It's no surprise, then, that noted rock critic and author Greil Marcus, when asked by Henry Rollins what artists currently excited him, listed two Burnett productions: Rhiannon Giddens and the New Basement Tapes.[45]

Looking toward the now decades-long careers of venerable musicians like Dave Rawlings and Gillian Welch as inspiration, the Secret Sisters entered 2016 filled with the hope of a new album. Laura was focused on a more stripped-down product, with fewer instruments and "no impressive solos." Instead, they were looking to create music that more closely resembled their 2015 shows, that reminded them of who they are artistically and as people: two sisters, one guitar, and crowds of supporters.[46] Their new album saw the duo coming full circle as well. At her Nashville audition for Interscope back in 2010, Laura sang the Brandi Carlile song "Same Old You." For this third album, aptly titled *You Don't Own Me Anymore*, the duo recorded tracks at Bear Creek Studio outside Seattle, produced by Carlile and backed by Tim and Phil Hanseroth.

> **@laurarogers:** If you had told me, in the midst of our dark chapter, that the world would right itself, that I would be able to buy more acreage, that we would get a new, wonderful manager, that our finances would slowly improve, and that we'd be given the opportunity to have our third album produced by one of our heroes, I wouldn't have thought it possible to go from such distress to such elation. . . . We are ecstatic and amazed and humbled and grateful, and though it isn't popular to say, we are both sure that our faith is what held us together when we very certainly would've fallen apart.[47]

Furthermore, the new album tested the bonds of community and fan involvement, as the sisters set up a "pledge music" campaign to fund the album through donations. In a Facebook post announcing her involvement, Carlile placed this decision in a historic and theoretical framework.

"Boys they can't take my refrigerator now!!"

Who said it? No no—it wasn't a bandit on the run from the law fearing the dreaded appliance repossession . . . it was Patsy Cline not long before she left us in 1963, why is it important? Because Patsy Cline had a slew of number one hits under her belt while she frequently pondered the real possibility of repossession of her prized possession . . . her refrigerator.

This is a problem because at the time the music business (and most businesses) had created for itself and [sic] environment where what women created became the property of the institution and the men who controlled it.

By default the uncomfortable truth about our beloved industry of art and honesty . . . is that we are what we create, making women themselves actually the property.

What a rough road for our heroes! Glad to know it's in the past? I think deep down we know that quietly, it still happens. We are seeing blatant misogyny constantly making music headlines and I am not happy with it.

The bumps and bruises that The Secret Sisters have earned on the road are entirely their own. Their life and their music are their story to tell. Young women in their 20s, they belong to no one regardless of their gender. At some point they said we aren't owned . . . and they grew up.

You and I "their fans" might not have been able to save them from the pain and humiliation of lawsuits and bankruptcy (a small price to pay for their freedom)[.] But by contributing to this pledge campaign and the making of this album we're standing up and saying—Boys you can't take their refrigerator now!

Let's make this record friends
Thank you
Xobc
amplifywomen[48]

The Sisters' fans heeded Carlile's clarion call, and the results speak to the ethic at the heart of the community's spirit. The Secret Sisters were able to raise enough money through the pledges of fans and friends to make the album, releasing it with New West Records. They were able to put together headlining tours along with continuing to play festivals and opening for friends like Carlile as well. Their hard work and uncompromising values were honored by a 2017 Grammy nod for Best Folk Album, alongside Laura Marling, Offa Rex, Cat Stevens, and winner Aimee Mann. That the sisters produced an album on their own terms with the help of a close friend, one that was funded by friends and fans who wanted their music to be made and released to the world, speaks to the values inherent within the community. That the album was recognized by popular music's supposed gatekeepers implies an audience of fans, critics, and writers alike who are attracted to a set of intrinsic principles—sincerity, integrity, and honesty—within such artistic productions.

A youthful photo of the sisters' late paternal grandmother, Marcie Lou Rogers, graces the album's cover. Unsurprisingly, before officially releasing the album, the two performed the songs for family and close friends on Laura's Happy Valley property. In attendance were Marcie Lou and their maternal grandmother Mable Evelyn Parker, whose husband had built the very house where Laura now lives and where the sisters' mother was raised. Lydia's husband Mark Slagle and his 1504 production company cohorts produced a short documentary for *The Bitter Southerner* covering the making of the album. The scene featuring the family-only concert offers visual confirmation of Laura's fears when they were going through bankruptcy, laying bare the prominence of place and the values negotiated in trying to carve out a career in music: "I would rather walk away from music for the rest of my life than lose Happy Valley."[49]

Wealth measured in adding to their family's land in Happy Valley, community, music, and faith all serve as symbols for the Secret Sisters' sense of themselves in relationship to their Southern context and their music. Yet, they also upset the implications of such complex symbols. Their close friendship with Brandi Carlile, a Washington State–reared musician identifying as both lesbian and Christian, their willingness to explore gender and race relations in their songs and videos, and their obstinate refusal to play the stereotypical roles preferred by their record executives and handlers all seem to conflict with their Southern, conservative upbringing. Yet their story is a not-uncommon tale of contemporary Southern identity construction that is more kaleidoscope than monochromatic. The Secret Sisters are indicative of a South on the move, representations of a new Southern renaissance that defies simple liberal-conservative dichotomies. Instead, the movement has characteristics that could be considered not "either-or" but "both-and" simultaneously: Conservative Christian churchgoers who are not defined by rigid fundamentalism nor full-stop relativism. Southerners who explore gender roles and community expectations more than gun rights. Sisters whose music connotes blue-collar church pews yet who are college educated and equipped to both criticize and revere their small-town upbringing.

The sisters' music, community, and purposeful identity construction reads against the old story assuming that the sum total of contemporary Southern identity consists of slow talking, dropped *g*'s and extended vowels, homages to dead cultural symbols resurrected for self-serving purposes, or vibrant symbols made trite by exploitation and oversimplification. There is a transgressive nature within such identity construction when it purposefully seeks to run against cultural expectations and stereotypes. Enveloped in their identity are complex negotiations regarding place, history, the present, the future, and the weight of all the coded symbols that carry Southern connotations both musically and culturally. Their purposeful participation in a community of Southerners seeking to reignite a cultural renaissance, born out of a shared interest in cultural preservation, re-presentation, and creation, is undeniable. Like their pristine harmonies, the community appears to abide by a simple code. Yet, upon second listening, the nuances and complexities, the richness hidden in the harmonies is evident. When that fullness combines with tradition and consistency, a recipe for sustainability and cultural creation ensues. As we pivot outside Burnett's immediate circle, it becomes ever clearer that his ethic has a wide reach, extending to other artists-and-producer pairings and into other facets of culture at large.

CHAPTER 5

THE T BONE INFLUENCE AND
A MUSIC COMMUNITY'S ETHIC

Featuring Bonnie Montgomery,
Jason Weinheimer, and Joe Henry

> Are the hats, the boots, the pickup trucks, and the honky-
> tonking poses all that's left of a disintegrating culture? Back
> in Arkansas, a way of life produced a certain kind of music.
> Does a certain kind of music now produce a way of life?
>
> **— JOHNNY CASH**

"Are you a redneck at heart?" asks the website for W. T. Bubba's ("Soon to be World Famous") Country Tavern. If so, the site promises that you will feel right at home in the bar and grill where you can drink beer and eat a smoked bologna sandwich: it is "all about being Southern and being country. . . . Our décor says it all!" Sitting in the heart of Little Rock's River Market, right off President Clinton Avenue and within eyesight of the River Market Amphitheater and the Arkansas River, W. T. Bubba's minimalist exterior, a simple round sign above an understated canopy, does not match the ostentatious display of self-congratulatory and cheerfully hyperbolized "redneck" design of the interior.

The inside looks as if Disney World had created a redneck theme park. Several "exhibits" of purposefully stereotypical rural poor-white culture are on display throughout the bar. This includes a pickup truck bed "garden," a trailer inside which patrons can eat and drink, complete with artificial grass and plastic lawn ornamentation, and a garage-framed stage for performers. The walls feature rural-white cultural ephemera: NASCAR, guns, eagles, a poster of Johnny Cash "flipping the bird." The space also has barroom staples like pool tables, neon beer signs, a dance floor, and an old jukebox. As we entered, a friend whispered, "All this place needs is a divorce lawyer and a rehab clinic and there will be nothing left to exploit."

This night, W. T. Bubba's was the site of an after-party for the Little Rock Film Festival's Horror Picture Show. The after-show was to feature the country music musings of local artists Bonnie Montgomery and Nathan Howdeshell. Since 2011, Montgomery and Howdeshell have recorded *Live at the Cake Shop* in New York City, along with two EP's, *Cruel* (2012) and *Joy* (2013), and a self-titled full-length album (2015), all of the latter of which were recorded at Fellowship Hall Sound in Little Rock under Howdeshell's Fast Weapons record label.

Though she now spends all her energy writing, playing, and promoting country music, Montgomery's transition into the genre comes from an unlikely place. Receiving a bachelor's degree in music from Ouachita Baptist University in Arkadelphia, Arkansas, and a master's in ethnomusicology from the University of Missouri–Kansas City's Conservatory of Music and Dance, Montgomery is a classically trained pianist who once pursued a career as an opera singer. This training led her to coauthor and score a self-described "folk opera" titled *Billy Blythe*, telling the story of President Bill Clinton's early childhood. The opera premiered in New York City and was well received, garnering positive media attention from the *New Yorker*, *U.S. News*, the *Daily News*, the *Christian Science Monitor*, the *Economist*, and MSNBC, among others.

Though committed to classical music, Montgomery admits that the pull of singer-songwriter Americana music had long been percolating in the background.[1] She grew up singing in church, part of a musical family that still owns the music store on the courthouse square in Searcy, Arkansas, where she spent many days of her youth. Like most teenagers, she went through different phases of musical interest, so her lifelong love of classical music was always in the context of flirtations with the nineties grunge scene, the Beatles, and country music. She tinkered around with writing songs as an undergraduate and even played a few solo gigs during her year-long postgrad stint teaching English in China. It was her graduate school experience, however, that was a decisive turning point. At UMKC she was drawn to the Marr Sound Archives, where she listened attentively to countless hours of old Americana classics. Immersing herself in the sounds and history of these songs, she started better understanding the rich and complex history surrounding American roots music. She began to see it in the same light she saw classical music: as infused with historical context. When she commenced seriously writing songs, they naturally veered toward a roots-country genre, inspired by what she says had always been the "scenery" of her life.

After a brief stint in Nashville, where she became more serious about writing music and began tinkering with self-recording, she landed back in Little Rock more committed to the idea of becoming a professional musician. Though she admits a wide range of influences, including country darling Dolly Parton and paterfamilias Hank Williams, from the beginning her primary muse has always been "the Man in Black," Johnny Cash. She was drawn to Cash's early sound—the Tennessee Three setup with Marshall Grant on upright bass and the great "boom-chicka-boom" guitar sounds of Luther Perkins: "I thought, if I could get a band, that would be it." The "raw, rudimentary sound" Cash's Tennessee Three produced was "the best in American music." "I knew when I started writing songs that I wanted the Johnny Cash setup, and I knew it seven years before I started really playing," she confided.

Though Howdeshell and Montgomery knew each other through school in Searcy, Arkansas—a county seat 50 miles north of Little Rock—their musical pasts involved travelling distinctly different roads. Howdeshell was an instrumental presence in Searcy's small but vibrant punk scene. After high school he moved to Olympia, Washington, and Portland, Oregon. After forming the genre-bending (dance-rock, soul, electronic, postpunk) band Gossip with fellow Arkansan Beth Ditto, who grew up in neighboring Judsonia, the group went on to achieve widespread acclaim in Europe with their 2006 album *Standing in the Way of Control*. Since their breakout success, the band has recorded an album with legendary producer Rick Rubin at famed Shangri-La Studios in Malibu, toured Europe and Asia extensively, played the exclusive 2009 Paris Fashion Week Fendi party, and became certified European rock stars with their single "Heavy Cross" hitting triple gold. The band continues to enjoy acclaim and commercial success, yet in between Gossip albums and touring, Howdeshell moved back to his childhood sixty-acre farm in Center Hill, Arkansas, started a record label, Fast Weapons, and began recording, producing, and managing a variety of artists and playing on and sometimes touring in support of Montgomery's albums. Howdeshell's senior quote in his high school annual speaks to his philosophy and the duo's contrast: "If you want to be in a band, and you love music, nothing should stop you. Talent is not an issue."

Montgomery cheerfully admits that Howdeshell's playing has "changed everything. . . . He has taught me about collaboration, and though the parts he creates are minimalistic, his tones are so intuitive, precise, and perfect. He exceeds everything I thought I could have in a guitar player." Howdeshell's punk music background, a fast and noisy blend of early Nirvana, Olympia, Washington–based band Bikini Kill, and Sonic Youth, serves as an interesting counter to Montgomery's classically trained precision. Together the two balance each other out in the search for a stripped-down roots-country sound that is at once minimalistic, raw, genre-blending, and experimental, while technically sound. With its countercultural and anti-consumerist focus, Montgomery's outlaw country has more in common with punk music's ethos than one might initially presume.[2] In the spirit of Burnett's soundtracks and community of artists, including the Secret Sisters, Montgomery is ultimately in search of participating in a resistant country music community, rooted in tradition and Southern identity, achieved through performance, songwriting, musical styling, branding, and community participation.

Montgomery places her music within the folk-rock, roots, Americana, outlaw country spectrum, implying the historical tradition while purposefully tipping her hat to her branding and musical ethos. Yet, putting her music in its broad historical context, complete with multiple genres, is problematic. Bill Malone's look at the diversity of the South helps illustrate how difficult even regional definitions could be. He argues that the South's culture and music have been "remarkable blendings of ethnic, racial, traditional, and modern traits. Kentucky coal miners, North Carolina textile workers, and East Texas oil drillers worked and lived in dramatically different settings."[3] Malone's statement suggests the class consciousness that permeates definitions of roots music—and implies many different races and ethnicities, such as African American Delta cotton pickers and Mexican migrant workers, who undoubtedly influenced folk music traditions and further complicated any hopes of a homogeneous genre-grouping.

Music seen through the lens of regional identity persists throughout genres owing lineage to the roots tradition. For example, Malone sheds light on how a particular genre of music can be born out of a specific demographic, in this case traditional country music and the Southern working class. A similar observation could be made regarding the blues, gospel, and various forms of rock music. Thus, the blending of sentimentality, cultural identity, musical performance, and lyrical messaging further obfuscates an attempt at cohesively defining roots music. Perhaps rock journalist Richie Unterberger, speaking particularly about the folk-rock movement of the 1960s, says it best: folk "was a crazy-quilt of connective threads between musicians, styles, generations, politics, the record industry, and the mass media."[4]

Burnett protégé Joe Henry, a polymathic artist, producer, author, and cultural critic, believes there are inherent problems regarding obsessions with musical categorization.

> It just doesn't serve us very well, if we're so anxious to put you somewhere and attach a handle to you for easy carrying. I understand the need for shorthand sometimes, but I think as a rule that putting music into tidy categories—you know, I pick this up and I want that flavor, and I pick this up and I want that—is very limiting to the way music actually works on us. . . . And to speak about things in only very particular categorical terms limits the way that we perceive them, and I'm not comfortable with it. I mean Duke Ellington called himself a folk musician, so did Charles Mingus, and so did Joe Strummer.[5]

For Montgomery, then, the value of genre is more linked to its history, style, and ethic than a fully defined label. Furthermore, through group identity and regional identification, Montgomery participates in a resistant tradition and community of artists opposed to the isolation and passive consumption of music, particularly music carrying loaded symbols of Southern identity which oversimplify more than complicate.

Montgomery's sound consists of a cocktail of Tennessee Three and Hank Williams–inspired instrumentation mixed with whipped-dog honky-tonk howling and stripped-down, sweet-sounding, and precisely delivered alto vocals. When combined with her songwriting penchant for telling stories concerning love, loss, homesickness, lament, escape, and carousing, she clearly participates simultaneously in multiple incarnations of country music's past. The thematic concerns of her songs complement the "nostalgia, fantasy, romance, and pure escapism" in traditional country, which feeds into "warring impulses" such as "piety and hedonism, home and rambling, companionship and individualism, and nostalgia and modernity" that are engrained deeply in the consciousness of performers and lovers of country.[6]

Montgomery feels that fans are hungry for a more roots-oriented raw approach because it has become a forgotten sound. She also feels that its sincerity resonates as a response to a materialistic, consumer-driven economy and serves as a counter to Nashville pop country. This is an ethos she consciously promotes in her recorded songs, and perhaps even more when she performs live. Performance has always been a key component of the roots music experience, and as such, Montgomery plays in a variety of venues on a consistent basis. She is a regular in the central Arkansas and Austin, Texas, music scenes, playing gigs in Little Rock at places like the local dive favorite White Water Tavern, or opening for the NPR show "Tales from the South" and playing at the *Oxford American*–affiliated restaurant South on Main—where she performed in a Ray Price tribute concert. In Austin, she regularly performs at a variety of venues including the White Horse and the Clive Bar, along with playing the famed sxsw music festival. Montgomery solely supports herself by playing music: a week doesn't go by where she isn't playing a gig in central Arkansas or Austin, and she makes annual trips to California and New York. She has played alongside the likes of Wayne "The Train" Hancock, Hayes Carll, Dale Watson, and the legendary Billy Joe Shaver. Outside of the South, Montgomery has toured the Pacific Northwest and the East Coast, including cities like Portland, Oregon, and Brooklyn, New York. She and Howdeshell even opened for Gossip on a European tour, allowing Montgomery to play for audiences in France, Belgium, Italy, and Germany.

Montgomery notes the variety of audiences she has encountered in her travels. Her usual crowd consists of a hybrid between classic outlaw country seekers, those George Jones and Johnny Cash fans looking for that vintage country sound, young indie music fans interested in a sound that resides notably outside the conventions of mainstream pop, and those in her contemporary outlaw country-rock scene. She also finds it interesting when fans in markets like Portland and Brooklyn approach her Southern-infused country, so far outside of the audience's urban context. Montgomery claims fans in these metropolitan cities have certainly been open to the music and the ethos, but were definitely not used to the sound. However, overall, fans have appreciated the uniqueness and authenticity.[7]

Like the Secret Sisters, Montgomery is alert to the tendency to play the Southern card in those contexts, aware that the audience has expectations regarding how she dresses and her personality. This foregrounds not only issues of branding and consumerism, but the history of roots music in these contexts. In Europe, where Montgomery played in front of as many as fourteen thousand people, she observed how open and polite most European fans were, particularly noting how many of them seemed to romanticize the South. Here, Montgomery was participating in a long-standing trans-Atlantic exchange between Europe and the American South. Stories of the Beatles and the Rolling Stones scouring American record stores in search of their favorite blues and rockabilly artists gives modern credibility to Montgomery's experience abroad. Malone comments on the image of the South perpetuated by the music and the musicians.[8] Though Southern culture and music were notably diverse, travelling through many states and incorporating multiple genres, Southerners "nevertheless shared a rural context and social history that linked them in various ways."[9] Furthermore, he notes the "century-long obsession with the South in . . . popular culture," arguing that "when the fascination with Dixie was combined with the themes of nostalgia, home, and domesticity, the resulting potent mélange of images proved irresistible."[10] Perhaps this is what Montgomery had in mind when she said that regardless of her performing context, her Southern identity permeates everything she does.

Montgomery's participation in this marginal scene foregrounds the complex negotiations between fans, artists, labels, and the music market at large. In her study on the history of commercialism—understood as a "complex social construction—in country music, Diane Pecknold sees commercialism as in a constant state of evolution.[11] Pecknold uses commercial frameworks to study how there are "cultural meanings attached to the system that produces the music."[12] Offering the Country Music Hall of Fame and Museum as symbolic of that system, she argues that its "self-consciously elaborate edifice . . . remind[s] us that commercialism has been no less powerful a cultural discourse than authenticity, and that it has equally profoundly shaped the social narratives country music offers."[13]

Pecknold argues that modern country has been tainted by commercialism "as both an indictment of bad taste and a marker of social identity."[14] In her study of commercialism in country music, she notes the widespread expression of similar concerns, including *New York Times* arts reporter Neil Strauss "lamenting," in her words, that the "economy [of popular music] controls and distorts audience tastes," that it "makes for aesthetically bad music," and that "the legends and traditions of country were being tossed aside for hunks in hats singing love songs to suburban housewives in the interest of peddling personal care products," thus pulling the music away from the heritage on which it was founded.[15] However, she also suggests that such critics would have to understand that perhaps both the producers and the audience are aware of the commercial space modern country claims. So, whereas Montgomery's music attempts to fight against the tendency of popular imagination to castigate country music as lowbrow, giving cultural efficacy and weight to the roots-country ethos for a contemporary audience, Top 40 country is arguably as purposeful in its presenting, in Aaron Fox's phrase, "poetic self-regard as a commodity."[16]

The search for the authentic and traditional is undoubtedly grafted into the branding and commercialism that remain an essential aspect of country music. Indeed, Montgomery maintains that branding and image are at least "fifty percent of the equation," mentioning aspects of entertainment, personality, and presentation—to create an aesthetic feel—alongside songwriting, sound, and singing.[17] Montgomery carefully crafts a public image while being aware of the fine line between the genuine and the pretentious. Her album covers are a great example of the aesthetic appeal she intentionally creates, which grounds her both in the past and in place. The *Live at the Cake Shop* cover has Montgomery adrift on a river, riding a makeshift raft loaded with a trunk, a guitar, a fiddle and a dulcimer and an old ribbon mic—a Huck Finn damsel in gingham-clad distress. The *Cruel* EP has a close-up of Montgomery complete with vintage-style photo tinting, evoking midcentury Patsy Cline. The *Joy* single features a dramatic black-and-white shot of Montgomery and Howdeshell on his family's farm, each all in black save for Howdeshell's white kerchief, he with a cowboy hat and classic white Gretsch Falcon in hand. Her 2014 self-titled album gives us a portrait of Montgomery in the middle of a black background with yellow vines and neon-pink flowers lining the borders. With red roses directly behind her in the portrait itself, her dark hair, pale skin, and red lips—all set against the black—convey beauty, darkness, and neon electricity. The cover photo on 2018's *Forever* forecasts her life on the road, with Montgomery, her back to the camera and face shown in profile, standing in the foreground as a West Texas highway and landscape extends before her. Collectively, all of these images invoke a brooding sensuality in a Southern context, helping establish an aesthetic and commercial design frame for her songwriter narratives and vintage rockabilly, outlaw country-rock sound.

Her sound and songwriting themes leave Montgomery outside, looking in at the contemporary Top 40 Nashville scene: "I don't like the instrumentation, aesthetic, branding, [or] image [of Top 40 country]. It's just not my thing."[18] She is clearly in search of a more traditional country sound, reinterpreted for modern audiences. However, like "folk" and "roots," the term "tradition" is layered with history, symbolism, and negotiations of identity. Folklorist Henry Glassie maintains that "tradition is the creation of the future out of the past. A continuous process situated in the nothingness of the present, . . . tradition is stopped, parceled, and codified by thinkers who fix upon this aspect or that, in accord with their needs."[19] Montgomery, then, arouses tradition through recording, presentation, and performance, while both recreating the past for the present and allowing consumers a participatory role in creating tradition as well.

Anthropologist and folklorist Dell Hymes places tradition in a similarly evolving context, believing that "the traditional begins with the personal" and that "intact tradition is not so much a matter of preservation, as it is a matter of re-creation, by successive persons and generations, and in individual performances."[20] For Hymes and Glassie, understanding tradition—and, implicitly, the notion of the authentic—depends on particular circumstances, creativity, and performance. Benjamin Filene agrees, arguing that "tradition always depended on its adaptability."[21] With this in mind, Montgomery's creative activities are a production of and a participation in tradition rooted in her Southern identity.

It is within the seeming incongruence of Top 40 versus historical country that the debate over authenticity often flares. Bill Malone argues that much of the divide concerning modern country, which he claims now sounds like "refurbished 1980s-style rock," rests in modern musicians and promoters disassociating from the music's historically Southern, blue-collar audience. Malone contends that, though modern country still gives a hat tip to the South and working-class people, it "may have become merely symbolic for a generation of entertainers who grew up in suburbia."[22] He points to Johnny Cash, who raised the same issue: "Are the hats, the boots, the pickup trucks, and the honky-tonking poses all that's left of a disintegrating culture? Back in Arkansas, a way of life produced a certain kind of music. Does a certain kind of music now produce a way of life?"[23]

Combining Malone and Cash's criticism with the definitions of tradition from Glassie and Hymes raises interesting questions. If contemporary country audiences have seemingly moved away from the themes, sound, and blue-collar leanings of historic country, could it be argued that Top 40 country is actually simply mirroring the shift of what it means to *be* blue collar, particularly in the American South? As the working-class Southerner has moved further right on the political spectrum and as what constitutes the working middle class has grown and become more slippery to define, popular contemporary country music has responded in kind to its audience, more closely resembling those consumers it now represents. Yet, the symbol of the blue-collar Southerner still often keeps its cultural, simplified, and stereotypical panache. That's why both popular artists and those making music in the margins can claim inspiration from country's past, particularly the working-class musicians of old.[24] As the definitions concerning tradition suggest, though she comes from a classically trained background and grew up in a suburban middle-class household, a generation removed from rural Arkansas farmers, does Montgomery's purposeful participation in a roots-country sound and narrative recreate the slippery notion of the traditional?[25] By doing so, does she make a transgressive statement about Southern identity in opposition to the values of pop contemporary country dominating Nashville? Perhaps the answer to both questions is yes. Glassie states, "When humans commit to willful acts of creation intended to express cultural or social connection, they are participating authentically in traditional culture."[26] Both Top 40 and those on the outside can lay claim to versions of the "authentic" and to be part of the evolution of tradition, though markedly different: one as a purposeful reinvention with a unique hat-tip to the past, the other as notably removed, yet with intentional evocation of archetypes and cultural symbols, such as the display in W. T. Bubba's.

Burnett's and Montgomery's community, as an antithesis to stale, consumption-centered and hackneyed nostalgia, relies on active, regenerative preservation. "Nostalgia is the death of what we're talking about," Joe Henry declares. The producer eloquently describes the relationship between the past and the present.

> I always go back to Faulkner: "The past isn't dead, it's not even past." If I picked up my grandmother today, which I just now have, she is now alive and active in my day, and she'll remain a part of this day for me after this conversation. Because I have conjured her into my present moment, that's real. I think music is like a séance. You call spirits into the room, and they change things. I'm not being flippant when I say that. I believe very purely in enlivening the past into the present, not leaving the present to visit the past.[27]

For this active community, "enlivening the past into the present" involves exploring several avenues by which to present music, including popular-culture tools like film soundtracks and television scores, to an audience that might not otherwise get it. Some so-called folk purists turn their noses up at the attempt to blend popular culture and roots-based music, as indicated by Burnett and the broad community. Henry reacts strongly against this tendency.

Anything that puts music into the air—vinyl, CD, computer hard drive—whatever it takes to get it up and out, I'm not prejudiced about any of it, though I certainly have preferences sonically, among other things. It's easy for people to slip into the mindset that "old-time folk music" is a relic. It's not a sustainable, living, and engageable thing, and I do everything I can to remind everyone, myself primarily, first and foremost, that this is a fire that has to be tended. It's not a dusty book on a shelf. Even as I say that, literature works the same way. If you crack it open and engage it today, it is brought forward and into a real-time present moment. . . .

There's a lot of power and authority to the folk tradition, and people can forget it has to be taken up, it has to be nurtured and cared for. It has to move like blood in your veins. It's not music, it's an idea. . . . But T Bone has always, and more expansively now than ever I think, just worked out of genre assumptions and limitations. [He] refuses to be marginalized by anybody else's expectations, or anybody else's sense of what's possible and what might be relevant. . . . "Purists" of any discipline, whether it's music or culinary or anything else, work really hard at building fences, and people look really hard to hop over them or dismantle them.

I don't think T Bone thinks in terms of popular music versus any other kind of music. I think that T Bone thinks [in terms of] authentic music, serviceable music, and how we hold it up. I think he's always—I know because we talk about this all the time—just looking for new opportunities to make music that we haven't made before, and [looking for] new ways for music to be heard. So if a film or a television show offers that platform, fantastic. The delivery system of pure recorded legal music is bankrupt. . . . It's not music or the interest in music that is broken. . . .

T Bone is looking for another way through. . . . I promise you he doesn't spend any time worrying about what's supposed to be popular music and what is marginal and what is "roots" music. It's just music standing up in front of me like a living thing; it's deep. That's real music to him, and it's everything to me. . . . [By] serviceable . . . I'm talking about music that actually has function in our lives. It doesn't live like a relic behind glass. Or it is not important and someone has to explain why it's supposed to be. I'm talking about music that is invariably and sometimes undefinably . . . demonstrating. You don't need anybody [to tell you] why it's supposed to matter to you, you just know that it does when you hear it. That's what I mean by serviceable music.[28]

Country-rock artist Chris Stapleton and pop star Taylor Swift epitomize two different approaches to the debate over when regeneration of sounds and symbols is "serviceable" and sincere and when it gives over to cliché designed for passive consumption, at the least, or to cash in on stereotypes, at worst. Most representative of the divide are two award-show performances by the different artists. With closed eyes, Stapleton's voice carries intonations of soul, country, and Southern rock music: Wilson Pickett, Ronnie Van Zant, and the Allman Brothers all mixed together. It's biracial and gritty; it's Saturday night, not Sunday morning. It's what the sounds of Hank Williams and Jimmie Rodgers were always supposed to evolve into. It's what Elvis might have sounded like if he hadn't abandoned his genre-blending youth to become Las Vegas "Elvis." It has the tones of Memphis, Nashville, Muscle Shoals, and the Mississippi Delta: the church, the juke joint, and the honky-tonk, all collected in a pair of vocal chords. With eyes open, his long hair, beard, and cowboy hat are unmistakably outlaw and country-rock. An accomplished songwriter—having written songs for artists such as Adele, Luke Bryan, Kenny Chesney, and George Strait, among others, and as lead man for the bluegrass band SteelDrivers—Stapleton's 2015 solo album *Traveller* elbowed its way into Nashville's Top 40 contemporary-country-saturated music world. It was not an easy sell, however. The album was not eagerly received by country radio, which has traditionally been the gatekeeper for country artists looking to break out. As of November 2015, right before the Country Music Awards where Stapleton would win New Artist of the Year, Male Vocalist of the Year, and Album of the Year, *Traveller* had 5,000 spins on country radio, as compared to 753,000 spins for Kenny Chesney's *Big Revival*, 680,000 for Jason Aldean's *Old Boots, New Dirt*, and 418,000 spins for Little Big Town's *Pain Killer*.[29] The lack of country radio airtime undoubtedly came from Stapleton's sound residing outside of clear categorization: "I don't know that my voice ever makes sense anywhere, necessarily. . . . I would sing bluegrass music and I don't fit in there; I would sing rock music and I'm probably a little too hillbilly for that. And country, I'm too much rock 'n' roll for there sometimes," he explains. Instead, early on he was left "piecing together [a] loose coalition of forward-looking tastemakers, anti-mainstream dissenters and old-style purists—a group with limited reach."[30]

Stapleton's breakout moment, and the spark that put the Nashville music community on notice that they could no longer ignore a thriving music scene in the margins, came at the 2015 Country Music Awards, where the singer shared the stage for a duet of his single "Tennessee Whiskey" with a seemingly unlikely partner, Memphis-born mega pop star and movie actor Justin Timberlake. Interestingly, country star Brad Paisley, an artist who has throwback appeal yet is embraced by the Nashville country machine, introduced the two with a purposeful declaration of the moment's symbolism, noting that with this performance "the Nashville Sound meets the soul of Memphis . . . the home of the blues." That Stapleton's sound and ethos could hardly be categorized as marked by the "Nashville Sound" is evident from the rest of the night's winners, most of whom were decidedly within the frame of contemporary pop, Top 40 country, including Luke Bryan, Miranda Lambert, Little Big Town, Florida Georgia Line, and Keith Urban, among others. Stapleton is the clear outlier. Earnestly, Stapleton and Timberlake trade verses and harmonize through the song, backed most prominently by horns and Stapleton's electric guitar. They follow that song with a thematically complementary version of Timberlake's "Drink You Away." The CMA crowd filled with Nashville country elites rises to its feet. The cameras catch country stars with cell phones taking videos of the performance. Keith Urban's mouth is open, flashing a smile showing top and bottom rows of whitened teeth.

Timberlake is himself, and that is the key to the moment. There are no country pretensions in his delivery or styling. He reminds us here that, removed from his boy-band beginnings and the Britney Spears years, the Hollywood films, the SNL performances, and the "History of Rap" bits he does with Jimmy Fallon, his art has been moving its way back to Memphis, carrying intonations of Stax soul, hip-hop beats, and R&B rhythm. His falsetto runs and soulful inflections placed alongside Stapleton's gruff Southern soul-rock vocals and electric guitar cause viewers to revisit him again. Detached from his celebrity and pop culture history, the performance begs a revisiting of Timberlake's *20/20 Experience* album as a direct descendent of the sex appeal of Memphis music's past. Perhaps for the first time in his career, he seemed like he may belong—or could be, if he chose to accept the inheritance—at the table with heirs apparent to the sounds of Memphis's past. Timberlake is keen to hammer the point home as well, shouting, "Nashville, how y'all doing tonight? Can I put a little Memphis up in here!" Timberlake's performance with Stapleton reads and sounds like what it is and by implication takes a stance on what it isn't. It's a model of the South in transition and a challenge to Nashville's status quo. That Stapleton is the grandson of Kentucky coal miners, that he spent time studying at Vanderbilt, and that he went through Nashville without compromising his integrity all speak to the demographics and ethos by which he and those in the community produce music: educated Southerners interested in participating in their heritage without compromising its integrity by giving in to stereotypes. That two Southern white boys are singing biracial music conjures images of the cultural and musical exchanges happening in the South for a few hundred years. Combined, these two characteristics denote a contrasted shift from the conservative pop ethos and identity of most of the music coming out of Nashville.

It wasn't just the CMA audience that took note of the moment. Music Row leader Joe Galante, who was at the helm of RCA Nashville and led the launch of Sony Music Nashville, referencing the uptick in Stapleton's success after the performance, stated, "That just goes to show you, if we all do that on a regular basis and we can get that kind of artistry, there's a solution to the music business, and it started with Chris Stapleton that night."[31] The music world at large has taken notice as well, as *Traveller* eventually topped the overall Billboard sales charts, won a Grammy for Country Album of the Year, and also received a Grammy nod for Album of the Year alongside pop star Taylor Swift, Muscle Shoals soul-rock band Alabama Shakes, hip-hop star Kendrick Lamar, and pop singer The Weeknd.

Stapleton did not fall out of nowhere and he does not exist in a vacuum. Having paid his dues writing songs and playing bluegrass, he illustrates the willingness to pursue music outside the limelight and in the margins, something many under the broad umbrella of country and Americana have done for decades. Further, Stapleton is just one of many operating within the contemporary community of musicians. A GQ story titled "Meet Three Country Badasses Who Are Shaking Up the Nashville Establishment" features Stapleton alongside former Drive-By Trucker Jason Isbell and Kentucky native Sturgill Simpson, all produced by T Bone community-mate Dave Cobb. In the piece, writer Will Welch offers the threesome up as an example of a community of artists who are the antidote to a contemporary country scene that he feels is the "musical equivalent of Walmart—monolithic, cheap, and eroding the soul of small-town America."[32] Implicit within the rebuke is the purposefully transgressive potential of their community, which includes many lesser-known artists like Montgomery toiling away at bars throughout the South and West.

In contrast to Stapleton's rise to acclaim, nothing could be more prototypically contemporary Nashville country than Taylor Swift's dazzling rise from country darling to synthetic pop-princess mega-stardom. Swift found early success as a teenage singer-songwriter in Nashville, with her songs typically speaking to the issues involved in teenage relationships. Yet, some argue that Swift's relationship to country was "always one of convenience." In a cover story for *Time*, Jack Dickey argues that "the Pennsylvania-reared Swift—no more authentically country than a coastal Cracker Barrel—found in Nashville a chance to make it on the strength of her songs."[33] It was unsurprising that with her album *1989*, which beat out Stapleton's *Traveller* for Album of the Year at the 2016 Grammys, Swift traded any semblance of country music for Beyoncé and Katy Perry–like pop. It was a natural progression, and one which the Nashville country music scene seems to promote.

Yet, before the shift, Swift was purposeful in playing up a rural, down-home, girl-next-door Southern image. This was on display most notably in the 2012 Grammy performance of "Mean," a song about the causes and effects of bullying, directed at the bully from the victim's perspective. Seeing the bully's future, Swift paints the picture of a has-been alone in a bar talking to himself about football, still fixating on the singer. Swift is merciless in exacting her revenge while calling out her tormentor's cruel character. It's an emotional track, powerful because of its sincerity and universal thematic appropriateness. There are undoubtedly thousands of people young and old who identified with the song's protagonist. The song is further evidence of Swift's gift for emotional honesty and transparency and her ability to move from inward to outward, using a specific circumstance to speak to the whole.

For the Grammy performance, however, Swift chose to dress up a song about exerting her willpower and identity in the face of a bully's persecution with Beverly Hillbillies–like, cornpone-porn Southern connotations. Strumming a couple of chords on the banjo and surrounded by what is supposed to mirror a dilapidated wooden shack, Swift is out front dressed in what looks like a poor farmer's daughter's housedress, complete with torn edges, exposed slip, and disheveled, braided hair. The camera pans outward to show her backup singers and bandmates dressed similarly, playing by the dim light of faux oil lamps, the men looking like they're about to head out to till a field instead of play pop music in Hollywood. Knocked-out windows, wooden blocks, detached shingles, an "udder" dairy basin, a sign reading "Mary Ruth's Dry Goods," and other rural ephemera litter the stage like a shabby-chic strip-mall emporium booth. The set even includes brief awkward synchronized dance moves. The music has country tones: mandolin picking, a banjo, fiddle, and stand-up bass mixed with other acoustic instruments. The pop bluegrass number garnered a standing ovation, by which she was charmingly surprised and obviously humbled, *despite* its tacky, stereotypical, and unnecessary routine meant to evoke a rural, small-town, informal gathering of musicians. The song was clearly personal, resonating particularly well at its conclusion. Smiling and staring straight into the camera with her Nordic blue eyes, arms extended over her head leading the crowd in congratulatory hand clapping, she sings directly into the camera, taking her victory lap in front of millions of people while confronting her former tormentor simultaneously.

Swift should not have relied on such ostentatious country pretensions, and her choice to do so on arguably popular music's biggest stage was unnecessary for her career. That rural Southern life and its virtues and vices are not her culture was evident. Swift's strength lies in purposeful pop songwriting designed for a specific audience, not in dressing up to pretend she carries the mantle of roots music. That she was the darling of Nashville is telling, as so many Top 40 musicians follow a similar pattern to Swift's Grammy performance by playing pop songs with country tones set to overplayed Southern tropes, appropriating cultural symbols for consumption at the expense of "serviceable," regenerative creation. The sincerity of the song's context, of which she is an appropriate spokesperson, is confused by the insincerity of the styling. And the latter is the great divide separating Stapleton's and Timberlake's CMA performance from Swift's. The former abandon slick stage production and stereotypical tropes in favor of being themselves, a decidedly different pairing stylistically, and letting the music speak for itself. Ironically, without any props, their CMA performance was a much clearer re-presentation of a musical and cultural ethos.

As shown, the complexities involved in thematic concerns, sound, branding, and commercialism intermingle with complicated notions of tradition in an artist's and listener's understanding of identity. Though multifaceted, this formula is nothing new. Music insiders and musicians alike have long been keen on crafting various public identities. This has undoubtedly contributed to the branding of certain genres, performers, and cultural groups. Filene's cultural study shows "how Americans have remembered their country's musical past, how these memories have been transmitted, and how these conceptions have both reflected and shaped Americans' cultural outlook."[34] Filene unpacks what the roots-music movement looked like behind the scenes as music industry insiders helped shape what audiences would recognize as authentic folk music. He contends that, by doing so, these different groups "'romanced' the folk, in the sense both of wooing them as intimates and of sentimentalizing them as Other."[35] Perhaps here is where Burnett's and Montgomery's music, community, and aesthetic feel reside. By purposefully connecting with an idealized version of country music's past, Montgomery can distance herself from the commercially successful Top 40 country scene, thus enabling her, for a particular music demographic, access to the "traditional authentic." As Filene argues, "to highlight a person's marginality in relation to the mainstream helped authenticate him or her as an exemplar of American grit and character."[36] As Malone, Pecknold, Cohen, and many other scholars show, country musicians from Jimmie Rodgers and Hank Williams to more contemporary, yet equally mythological, musicians like Johnny Cash and Willie Nelson have always crafted particular identities to reach specific audiences.

Montgomery and Howdeshell's relationship to the South and their contemporary Southern identity has been an evolution, particularly for Howdeshell. As a high schooler in small-town Arkansas, Howdeshell's punk leanings and aesthetics were notably outside the norm. In a markedly religious small town even by Southern standards (the local cable provider did not offer MTV until circa 2000 due to the religious culture's influence), Howdeshell's penchant for making music characterized by being fast and noisy and for wearing duct tape, safety pins, and once a dog collar to school stood out even more. The dog collar was apparently noteworthy enough to make the high school newspaper. Scouring local supermarkets for magazines through which he could write in for subscriptions to zines and gain access to mixtapes and new worlds, he began a subversive education that would later define Gossip's overtly feminist and queer messaging.[37] Howdeshell's escape from Arkansas to Olympia and Portland seemed inevitable; his return fifteen years later to live on his family's farm and produce roots-country music seemed unlikely. One of Gossip's first EP's, *Arkansas Heat* (2002), speaks unflinchingly of how he viewed his Southern hometown: a place stuck in time, where the power structures and the humidity are equally suppressing. Through Howdeshell's lyrics and Ditto's punk growl, they promise to never come back.

Yet, twelve years after he penned that scathing rebuke, Howdeshell returned to Arkansas, having achieved worldwide critical acclaim. His partnership with Montgomery and other Fast Weapons–produced artists, including eclectic rockabilly musician, author, and filmmaker Tav Falco (Falco grew up in rural Arkansas before moving to Memphis in the 1970s; his band Panther Burns is named after a Mississippi plantation), is indicative of a characteristic of Southern identity within this community: a reclamation of certain aspects of Southern culture and heritage and a reaction against other aspects. For example, Howdeshell is currently in the process of running his family's farm and has plans for incorporating crop production with the livestock they currently have. Furthermore, his work with Montgomery indicates a purposeful attempt to marry his punk past with roots music with decidedly Southern connotations. Howdeshell's label's catalogue is testimony, too, to the South in transition, defying overly simplistic categorization by its inclusion of dissonant sounds and global reach. A Fast Weapons compilation disc amounts to an artistic statement in which genres bounce off one another, with artists such as Melbourne, Australia, new wave band New War, postpunk and new wave Portland-based bands Soft Kill and Litanic Mask, Sonic Youth frontman and punk icon Thurston Moore, funk-soul outfit Magic Mouth, and Vancouver-based punk band Nü Sensae, alongside Montgomery's outlaw country crooning and Falco's rockabilly. Howdeshell's eclecticism, punk-country aesthetics, and rural agrarian principles confound simple dichotomous declarations of Southern identity.

Contrary to Howdeshell, who as countercultural teenager confronted his small town's expectations, Montgomery, like many Southerners being embedded in her context, didn't think much about Southern identity growing up. She recalls working for a summer after her freshman year in college in Yosemite National Park and remembers masking her Southern accent, afraid her peers would mock her as "Baptist, ignorant, barefoot and pregnant, and all that." From there, her opera training and stint in graduate school in Kansas City saw her distancing herself from being recognizably Southern. She admits, however, that she was most likely rebelling against her family and her conservative Southern upbringing as well. She later decided to embrace her Southern identity, especially the pride in the Southern musical heritage in which she had grown up, singing in church and with family, speaking of the global dominance of music inspired by Southern contexts and particularly the legacy of Memphis. She has also confronted the slippery notion of dealing with the racially coded symbols of the South's past, and of how heritage can be an enigmatic and problematic ideal which must be clearly communicated, that it can be used for good or ill, for oversimplification or for a more complex revisiting of the past. In the song "Keep Quiet," which she wrote during her stint teaching English in China, Montgomery relies on the hook from the controversial Confederate tune "Dixie," even using the word a few times in the song. Montgomery has never recorded the song, and, after having offended audience members leave shows, she shelved it from her performances as well. The violence of the summer of 2015 and the reignited debate over the Confederate flag left Montgomery reflective on why she wanted to include that tune in a song she wrote a decade ago. Recalling her grandfather singing the song on their drives in his truck to the farm as a little girl, she never knew it was an anthem for the Confederacy and later for Jim Crow atrocities. To her, the inclusion of the tune was communicating "how much I miss home and my grandfather, and *my* South, which has nothing to do with some hateful murderous thing. I was hoping my version would be a rewrite." Her "rewrite" impulse speaks to her desire to confront the despicable aspects of the South's past without whitewashing the history or its consequences, while simultaneously gleaning from history worthy virtues and characteristics that swell the present with purpose and meaning.[38]

Unsurprisingly, this ethic comes with political connotations as well. In her interview, Montgomery cited Beth Arnold's 2015 *Huffington Post* article "The De-evolution of Arkansas," which laments the turning of Arkansas from Democratic Southern outlier to a state, much like the rest of the current South, that "had been swallowed in red and had subscribed to the prevailing values of ignorance, hate, and intolerance—as well as that nasty elephant in the room: racism."[39] Like Arnold, Montgomery embraces her yellow-dog Democrat upbringing, remembering a time of "commonsense," "moderate" politics that she feels was "community-driven." Montgomery's contemporary Southern identity is therefore represented in her politics, self-identification, and family- and heritage-centered ethos. These lenses combine with her penchant for writing songs about independent women who sometimes break convention, even the law, by doing things such as smoking weed to cope with hardships, to confuse attempts to place her Southern identity within any one easily definable set of characteristics.[40]

Howdeshell's and Montgomery's seemingly disparate musical paths make sense in light of their shared cultural identity, history, and ethos. Within that context, it's interesting to imagine how audiences must have felt when the two opened for Gossip across Europe, Los Angeles, and New York City. When Beth Ditto joined Montgomery on stage, as she often did, for duet country song covers like Kitty Wells's "It Wasn't God Who Made Honky Tonk Angels," the non-Southern crowds, there for the countercultural, genre-bending, notorious Gossip performances, were treated to a cross-cultural exchange and an introduction to the contemporary outlaw country scene. Ditto's participation is further evidence of an eclectic Southern diaspora defying conventional cultural expectations. Though she hasn't lived in the South for over a decade, Ditto still maintains a distinctly Southern accent, as one journalist noted her habit of dropping g's and adding an r to rural ("rur-ral").[41] She has frequently talked openly about her poor upbringing in small-town Judsonia, Arkansas, and about eating "trees full" of squirrels, meeting then-governor Bill Clinton at a fish fry, and watching her grandma speak in tongues.[42]

Since leaving Arkansas, Ditto, via the Olympia and Portland riot grrrl punk scenes, has become a European icon as an outspoken advocate on body image, gender, and queer issues leading a paparazzi-filled London life—palling around with supermodel Kate Moss, founding a clothing line, and writing an advice column, "What Would Beth Do?" for the *Guardian*. She is known for her bold fashion style and her lack of inhibitions both on stage, where her voice flawlessly travels from gospel and soul to punk rage, and in the press: at just north of five feet tall and over two hundred pounds, she has been known to perform in her underwear, posed nude on magazine covers, and altered her hairstyles and colors and eye make-up designs with rapid frequency. Hearing her harmonize with Montgomery, backed only by Howdeshell playing an electric guitar and Montgomery setting the acoustic rhythm, works so well it's startling.[43] Ditto reminds her audience that the song's context is hers—and her and Howdeshell's relationship to Montgomery, particularly in having Montgomery open for them, stands as a statement regarding how much the two seemingly opposing styles of music have in common characteristically. It's no shock that in a BBC *Breakfast* interview Ditto, explaining that she's a morning person, says that she likes to get up and "listen to Loretta Lynn and mop the floor."[44] The performance solidifies that Montgomery's own outlaw ethos has more in common with an outspoken lesbian, feminist, European fashion icon and disco-punk rock star than it does contemporary Nashville country.

The progressions of their Southern identity echo the realities of many Southerners, both those who have stayed and those who have left. Raised in North Carolina and Georgia, Joe Henry moved to the Midwest before his tenth birthday. He admits to spending "a lot of years trying to expunge my Southern heritage from my DNA because as a boy growing up in the '60s I was not proud of the connotation of the South." Leaving the South at a young age, Henry was placed in a position early on to analyze both what the South meant to him and how it was perceived by outsiders, while coming to terms with the virtues and horrors of the South of his youth.

> Once I got to the Midwest, I knew what the idea of the South conjured, not only to everybody else but to me. I've realized, over time, with maturity beyond the shame of my young years in the South and some things that I witnessed and knew to be true about that landscape, . . . that Thelonious Monk was from North Carolina . . . and John Coltrane, and John Cage at Black Mountain College. There was a lot more to that heritage that I was responsible to.[45]

For Henry, the key to wrestling with the past was that "if you want to have history, you have to have all of it. You can't have just a piece of it."[46]

Outside of branding, songwriting themes, and community, Montgomery admits that achieving the particular sound she is chasing can be a unique challenge both in the studio and on stage. The right instruments are one key part of the puzzle according to producer and engineer Jason Weinheimer.[47] Montgomery's *Joy* EP and eponymous album were recorded, engineered, and produced at Weinheimer's Fellowship Hall Sound in Little Rock. In Fellowship Hall, vintage Les Paul and Gibson guitars and Jerry Jones basses line the walls and are standing up, mingling with a Wurlitzer piano, analog tape machine, and other vintage equipment throughout, foregrounding the producer's recording philosophy. Weinheimer was raised in Tulsa until age fourteen, when his family moved to Shreveport, Louisiana. He recalls at age fifteen driving around Shreveport buying up records. It was 1987, hair metal was everywhere, and people were replacing their old records with CDs. In his formative years, he recalls seeing a Peter Case record, with the eclectic roots-rock musician on the cover "wearing a funny hat, vintage jacket, and vintage guitar," all of which were decidedly different than the teased-bangs-and-spandex style dominating late-eighties music culture. Asked what the Case record sounded like, the guy manning the counter said, "Oh, it sounds like your typical T Bone Burnett production." "I didn't know that was a thing," Weinheimer admits. From then on, he started buying anything Burnett was attached to, particularly enthralled by *The Criminal under My Own Hat* and the recordings of Burnett's then-wife Sam Phillips: "Those records were major touchstones for me, [particularly] the way they approached production, hanging things around songs." After graduating from college in northwest Arkansas and earning an MA in English from the University of Tulsa, and before he became a full-time engineer and producer, Weinheimer played in several bands, including the Boondogs, who recorded at famed Ardent Studios in Memphis under renowned producer and musician Jim Dickinson.

For his own production space, Weinheimer followed Burnett's lead. He even connects his teenage experience with the Peter Case record in a Shreveport record store to the popular-culture reaction to Burnett's *O Brother* soundtrack. It was an aesthetic and sound that were in stark contrast to everything else that was dominating the airwaves at the time. For his production ethos, Weinheimer was purposefully after a certain sound, and keying in on particular components for achieving the roots-based and raw sound artists like Montgomery seek. Weinheimer purposefully crafted a studio space for bands to record live. He contends that the spontaneity a live performance affords figures into a more genuine sound: "Part of what makes roots, authentic music distinct is the sound of people in a room playing music together." Therefore, like Montgomery's live shows, her recording sessions are an avenue for performing in the studio. Weinheimer learned early on that the particular sound he was after had much to do with the microphones and how he chose to place them around the studio. The ribbon mic is based on some of the oldest mic technology and notoriously produces a certain vintage sound, and Weinheimer points to the success of Burnett's recordings of the past ten years as evidence.

Following the lead of Burnett, Weinheimer mics the entire room, allowing him to take sounds from different mic placements for various instruments. For instance, he can take a guitar part from a drum mic, a process called bleeding, and, with the movable recording "clouds" hanging from the ceiling in the studio, manipulate his space, literally bouncing sounds off the clouds and the walls and bleeding them into the track in whichever way makes the most sense for the song. This technique produces music in which instruments do not sound separate from one another; it mirrors the live performance, both instrumentally and vocally. Weinheimer insists this not only allows musicians to react and play off each other in the moment, but it creates a notably different sound from recording a drum machine and laying the bass, guitar, and vocal parts over it separately.

Weinheimer has a similarly purposeful modus operandi when capturing live performances. He first records the songs onto a 1982 analog recorder, based on technology pioneered in the 1960s. It allows for sixteen tracks of audio onto a two-inch tape machine that records magnetically, before later transferring to digital. The multitrack recording allows him to turn instruments up and down as he wishes and helps produce a more pure sound. This plays directly into his use of processing: anything an engineer does to manipulate the sound. This includes compression, which involves taking the quiet parts and turning them up, and the louder parts and turning them down, leveling the audio so there are not peaks and troughs. Weinheimer's style of compression varies from more modern radio engineering, which turns everything up until the sound hits the metaphorical brick wall, called limiting. He claims this is why most songs on the radio sound so loud, separate, and overly compressed. The live performance, purposeful mic placement, and sound manipulation feed into his system of analog and minimalist processing techniques to create the unique vintage tone singers like Montgomery are pursuing, highlighting the importance of an engineer's recording philosophy in creating an older sound.

Weinheimer's motivation mirrors Burnett's *O Brother* production philosophy and setup, which relied on recording techniques Decca Records used in the 1930s: By "placing ribbon mics in a triangle . . . [we] captured all the ambience bouncing around the room. We didn't use any artificial ambience, we used hardly anything artificial at all. . . . Most of it was recorded with the band standing in a semicircle around that one microphone." The sound Burnett wanted to create was as if "you were right there in the room with the people. . . . You can feel the musicians around you, you hear the room . . . the resonance . . . the reflections. It's not this cold sine wave coming at you."[48]

Burnett's recording mantra is more than marketing kitsch or nostalgia-making. His production ethos reads as a resistant statement to the contemporary culture where music is often consumed and produced. He argues that "recorded music is to the United States as wine is to France. It's part of our national identity. We conquered the world with it, really."[49] Within that cultural power, the producer contends, rest the quality and art of production and a rallying cry to treat recorded music with the respect and attention that its cultural tradition deserves. Evoking the age-old debates surrounding the unintended consequences of technological advancements, Burnett argues that "digital sound has dehumanized us. . . . When I first went into a recording studio, I heard music a whole new way, and I've been trying to figure out what that was ever since. I fell in love with sound. . . . How you can twist it and shape it."[50]

Unsurprisingly, as Joe Henry's "professional godfather," Burnett influenced the way the producer-artist perceived the art of production:

I worked with him for the first time when we first produced [Henry's] *Shuffletown* in 1990. . . . T Bone invited me to be his apprentice as a producer. I never thought anything about doing such a thing. I sort of blanched, probably, and said, you know the saying, "Those who can, do, those who can't produce." In fact, he challenged me immediately, and should have, that production was part of his artistry and didn't supersede what he did for himself. . . . What T Bone has always done and continues to do is to blur those lines for everybody. And I don't mean just a line between artist and producer, I mean the line between music and any other action of love in your life—what you devote yourself to, how you present it.[51]

For Henry, there is no distinction between how he records, the artistic creation in a particular moment and space, and how the past informs the present:

I'll do anything to make music feel alive when it comes out of speakers. But sonically, I find the bleed between instruments and microphones to be a terribly romantic thing. I find people playing music together in real time observe a certain pulse and occupy atmosphere in the same way, create this weather in a very particular way together that doesn't happen any other way. I don't get people [to play] live together because I'm a purist, I get people in a room together because that's the most immediate way to create music that feels immediate and moves like we do. . . . I still go back, and I go back like a religious zealot, to Louis Armstrong's Hot Five and Hot Seven recordings all the time. Those were people standing around facing a microphone in a room. It was a camera . . . [and T Bone] invites people into a room and takes a picture. That's what that microphone did. The only way to achieve that was to play music together.[52]

Henry's Grammy Award–winning body of production work mirrors Burnett's in many other ways as well. For example, Henry's work on the album *The Wexford Carols* combined the soprano vocals of Irish folk singer Caitríona O'Leary with guests such as Rosanne Cash and Rhiannon Giddens. With these pairings, Henry combines traditional Irish folk with the roots sounds of Americana, gospel, and blues to highlight the now century-long trans-Atlantic folk music exchange between the American South and Ireland. Similarly, Henry has worked with other artists who produce music directly settled into the contemporary roots scene, such as British folk musician Billy Bragg, country artists Ramblin' Jack Elliott and Rodney Crowell, folk musician Loudon Wainwright III, Americana queen Emmylou Harris, genre-bending New Orleans musician Allen Toussaint, contemporary folk band Carolina Chocolate Drops (whose *Genuine Negro Jig* won the 2010 Grammy for Best Traditional Folk Album), and R&B and soul artist Solomon Burke, among others. Henry has taken this recording philosophy further in some of his own art as well, particularly on *Reverie* (2011). Regarding that album, Henry opened up about the philosophy of the recording process, granting insight into how he perceives music functions, particularly how the past relates to the present, and how sounds are created.

> I just had a conscious thought when I was writing that batch of songs. The songs don't appear in a vacuum. I'm sitting in my room trying to write, my children walk through, the FedEx man comes, or I have to leave to drive the carpool, or whatever it is, there is a lot of literal and figurative noise happening all around me.
>
> The idea that now that I have the song, that for it to get articulated I have to disappear into a black void of silence, is absurd. When I had that thought it wasn't a gag. I'd just finished that batch of songs. I wanted to hear musicians playing from a very few and very primary and primitive instrumentation. The idea being that, if we're taking very old instruments, upright bass in this case, drums, which is the oldest musical instrument, a piano, and acoustic guitar and say, "We can do anything we want, but we're doing it from these positions"—the idea being that if something needs to be more exotic, we'll reach for a more exotic instrument.
>
> We have to play that way. If we want it to be bigger, we don't add more instruments, we just play bigger. And I was very much inspired by Duke Ellington's trio record called *Money Jungle*, his album with Charles Mingus and Max Roach. They hit a room, they're playing very aggressively. You can hear everybody's instrument; you can hear everybody's microphones; you can hear it hit the walls. As a real drama, that engaged me, and I wanted to linger with that.

But I didn't want to stop there. I thought, if I want to hear this music compress-ing against the wall, I want to know what's on the other side of that wall, so we left the windows open and pointed the microphones at them so that the ambient noise of life happening around us was part of the fabric for the music. It wasn't just an idea. I realized that the instant I turned the microphones off, for instance, when mixing, the whole thing was diminished. And it was part of what made it feel three-dimensional.[53]

Like Henry, Weinheimer, as a protégé of Jim Dickinson, keenly understands how achieving a particular sound plays a key role in issues regarding music and public memory, reminiscence, and emotional connection, what he calls the "subconscious response" to music. He explains how some of his technology is based on the recording equipment used by John and Alan Lomax on their trips for the Smithsonian around the South attempting to capture music at its roots, recording in prisons, fields, and homes, among other places. Now, engineers like Weinheimer, in the midst of great technological advancement, are inten-tionally trying to achieve a sound that approximates those earlier recordings.

Dickinson felt similarly, once trying to convince Weinheimer that the suc-cess of U2's uber-popular and defining album *Joshua Tree* was based somewhat on how the producer had mic'd the drums. The producer applied the same microphone technology that had been used to record Ringo Starr two decades prior. So, for Dickinson, the success of *Joshua Tree* was in part due to the lis-tener's subconscious connection to the early Beatles. Weinheimer was clear on what he thought about this theory: "Jim could be full of shit at times." Yet, he admits that there is something to the subconscious response to sounds, crafted purposefully in recording studios, that feed into complicated notions of mem-ory, identity, and heritage for fans. This has borne fruit in Burnett's critically acclaimed and commercially successful productions.

Similar to Dickinson, Weinheimer talks about the "distinctly Southern idiom" of the way drums and bass interact with one another in recorded music, what he calls "the groove" or "the pocket." Citing the 1930s and '40s recording boom, particularly in roots blues and country and their progression into rock and roll, he notes the "unspoken rules about the way the bass player fits in with the drums," which were set in place by Sam Phillips, field recordings, and the records put out by furniture companies that needed a musical product to give away when they sold Victrolas. Citing the great Chess blues recordings and artists like Jimmy Reed as examples, Weinheimer unpacks how putting the drum back of the beat creates a completely different feeling than if it's on top and in sync with the metronome. He feels that even though a passive consumer is not consciously picking up on the producer's purposeful non-metronomic placement of drum beats, they are subconsciously connecting the rhythm to artists, genres, and places. "For me, it's not quite as big as the Jungian collective unconscious," he admits, "but that's the way I think about it." "From a production standpoint, there's a thread from those records. The records I love all have this thread that ties them together that all comes back to Southern music, whether it is rock and roll, rockabilly, country, [or] whatever." Citing artists like blues musician Jimmy Reed, roots artist J. J. Cale, and Bob Dylan's mid-sixties output, including *Highway 61 Revisited*, *Bringing It All Back Home*, and *Nashville Skyline*, which leads to Dylan and the Band, Weinheimer also eagerly extends the principle to seemingly disparate albums like Atlanta hip-hop group Outkast's *Speakerboxxx/The Love Below* and country artist Charlie Rich's *Behind Closed Doors*, claiming both as part of that Southern thread.[54]

Yet, for Weinheimer, those connections evoke private memories as much as or more than public associations. He remembers, like Montgomery, the Secret Sisters, and Joe Henry, not appreciating the richness of his Southern heritage until it was in his "rearview mirror." He had spent his formative musical years surrounded by Shreveport's fertile musical heritage, where the radio and television show *Louisiana Hayride* had helped ignite the careers of Elvis and Hank Williams. Looking back years removed, he realized how fortunate he was to "cut his teeth musically" in such a place, noting that "through osmosis I was taking it in and not even realizing it." Yet, critically analyzing one's Southern identity and heritage reveals complexities beyond a romanticized place and past. Weinheimer's great-uncle owned and operated the majority of jukeboxes in Tulsa from the 1940s through the 1970s. He also had a record store on Route 66—11th Street in Tulsa—where he sold all the old 45s from his jukeboxes. Surrounded by the richness and eclecticism of the music, Weinheimer had a similar experience to Burnett's in the Fort Worth record store of Stephen Bruton's father. Yet the familial connection was contradictory. While the music supported the interconnection between the races in the South, particularly how each culture often fed off the other artistically, a connection infused with a dynamism that changed the breadth, depth, and reach of popular music forever, Weinheimer remembers the political fights dealing with racism he had with his uncle, conflicts that had him leaving in tears of frustration. He recalls the segregated infrastructure of north and south Tulsa, which in effect created two altogether separate cities.[55] The concentric circles of memories involving racism overlapping with all that the music had to offer created the complicated heritage informing the producer's present identity. As such, Benjamin Filene's thoughts on public memory can equally translate to private heritage as well: "Public memory is formed by a recursive process, one that involves revisiting and reevaluating the culture of the past in the light of the present."[56]

Back at W. T. Bubba's, as Montgomery, Howdeshell, and her stand-up bassist Jimmy sound-check, the conflicts between consumerism, branding, country ethos, Southern identity, place, sound, and tradition come to the forefront. Considering Montgomery's Hank Williams, Johnny Cash, and Dolly Parton leanings—a stripped-down yet energized potpourri of honky-tonk, rockabilly, and country soul harkening back to the outlaw country sincerity of decades past—she's set to perform in a venue that seemingly stands in stark contrast to her values. The sparse crowd consists of people trickling in from the Horror Picture Show, a few dressed as bloodied cheerleaders, bar regulars who seem more intent on watching basketball on big screens and drinking Budweiser on tap than listening to music, some older folks who sit up front and are tuned in with the music all night, and one diehard cowboy boots and hat-wearing country aficionado—who I later learn is an outlaw country DJ. By and large, the crowd is polite but unenthusiastic; dancing and yelling out are replaced by courteous clapping at the end of each song. This is in stark contrast to her shows I have previously attended, where country hipsters and middle-aged outlaw country fans danced, hollered, and joyfully participated in the night's performance. At W. T. Bubba's, the crowd unfortunately matches the décor.

This does not, however, prevent Montgomery and company from putting on a spirited performance as she graciously and enthusiastically encourages the crowd throughout. Her songs hit many of the established themes of outlaw country—family, nostalgia, love, loss, and escapism—and her pacing and tempo are designed to keep listeners involved. "Joy" is a fast-paced boom-chicka-boom song that jumps around in time, beginning in 1924 and ending in 1963. In it she sings of mountain life, death, church, family, blue-collar work, and farming, culminating with the bold and escapist hopefulness in the chorus: "Well they say I've got the gall, and I'm gonna have it all / I was born up in the sky, and I'm never gonna die."

She marries such bravado with the slow melancholy of "Daddy's," which opens with her smoking dope on the way to visit her dying father, concluding that she'll "think about that tomorrow, in the light of another day." Here, Montgomery's voice is tender yet strong, displaying a commanding precision, undoubtedly from her years of classical training, yet infused with a subtle hint of country twang. The soft and supple tone works in contrast to the story's narrative of grappling with facing the death of her father.

"But I Won't," "Cruel," and "Lost at Sea" deal with relationships. "Cruel" relies on a slow-paced Hank Sr.–imbued guitar line. Yet the lyrics speak of a hyperbolized evil in a broken relationship: "Sometimes I feel like you are so cruel. . . . / Like Judas Iscariot and Catherine the Great, / Ivan the Terrible and Henry the Eighth / Then there's you." "Lost at Sea" uses the metaphor of the turbulence of the ocean's winds and unpredictable waters to speak to the uncertainties and consequences in love. "But I Won't" is an aggressive assertion of power as she shouts out, backed by rock and roll country rhythm:

I could talk a little louder, but I won't
I could load the pistol, but I won't
I could burn the house down, but I won't
I could publicly ruin you, but I won't

Montgomery is willing to play with points of view and gender roles, displaying opportunities for power and vulnerability among lovers. Yet, her feminism doesn't read like Amy Schumer-esque ribaldry. She's unafraid to be sexual, both vulnerable and aggressive, and in her songs she can be both tough and sweet, tender and hard-edged. Like the Secret Sisters, she has no interest in the false dichotomy between lily-white Southern belle and "redneck woman." Her lyric gender identity doesn't rest neatly into easily definable categories. Participating in the outlaw country community, Montgomery admits that though people often tell her, complimentarily, that she's a "badass bitch," she admits to not feeling tough: "I feel pretty demure," she confesses. Citing an industry where she works primarily with men, Montgomery wishes she had more of an aggressive personality. "I actually just had a tough week where promoters treated me with disrespect, and I was really coy about it. After the fact, I was really mad." Being raised in what she calls a conservative, traditional Arkansas community, Montgomery admits that though her mother was a working woman herself, she didn't raise her to be a feminist. "She raised me to be straight submissive, actually," she declares. Interestingly, either due to being "really progressive" or as a product of the "Depression-Era survivalist mentality," it was her grandmother, Francis, who taught Montgomery to "think for [herself] and to never rely on a man for money."[57]

The complexities of her negotiations of identity manifest themselves throughout her music. "Zydeco" offers pure escapism from the difficulties of death and romance, boldly claiming that she cares neither for family nor responsibility and "only want[s] to dance that zydeco with you." She anchored the W. T. Bubba's set with a hat-tip to Cash, performing his "Cotton Fields"—harkening back to the old mythologized cotton fields of yore. The song evokes memories of Montgomery's childhood ventures with her grandpa Ivan to his farm in Garner, Arkansas, and to Montgomery it reads like one of the diary entries he made from 1948 until his death in 2001. Not surprisingly, she is a student of his written thoughts, poring over the diary and using it as an inspiration for her songs, even admitting that "Joy" has several quotes lifted directly from her grandfather's writings.

Collectively, both her latest self-titled album and those preceding are not apocryphal. They do not read like a novel playing on Southern tropes for nostalgic marketing. Her life certainly bears out the album's complexities. In high school, Montgomery watched helplessly as a schoolmate and close friend drowned in a river. In college, she survived a commercial airline crash that killed over a dozen passengers. Not many years later, she experienced the heartbreak and loss of a failed marriage. As such, her sincere explorations of the human condition and her personal connections to place and time doubtless leave an impression that her music passes Henry's "serviceable" test. Her songs marry indignation and peacefulness, confusion and clarity, anguish and relief, passion and resignation, joy and sorrow. Her terrain is uncompromisingly Southern, as she grapples with the past's relationship to the present and future and as she debates whether she should leave or go, conform or carve her own way. "Black County" best explores the latter theme. In it she lays bare the inner strife between restlessness and rambling.

> Should've stayed in Black County and married my John
> Would've been better off never leaving the farm
> But the wide world was calling, so I said that I'd go
> So I left old Black County just to search for my soul

Leaving for California and overseas, the singer laments that "when you come from Black County, you can't find your peace." Montgomery's conclusions are never bastardized into simple morals. They read as the complexities inherent when relationships between time, place, and the human collide. Furthermore, the album's sounds mirror the thematic diversity. "Black County" is a slow-moving, purposeful country song with a distorted, hard-rock guitar riff trembling through the tempo, the sonic dissonance mirroring the protagonist's inner turmoil. "Nashville" and "But I Won't" feature the Sam Phillips pioneering "slap-back" echo sounds on guitar and vocals that harken back to Sun Records rockabilly and Luther Perkins's boom-chick-a rhythm, conjuring early Cash songs like "There You Go." As songs like "Nashville" lean on traditional country slide guitar, "Take Me or Leave Me" marries hollow electric dissonance and strings with fast-paced country acoustics, while "Lost at Sea" features a jazzy blues piano. Within the sounds and narratives of the album, we hear her bounce around among the contradictions of her life, laying bare once-forbidden or discouraged thoughts and shameful actions, matching sounds with the narratives.

Montgomery admits that she loves to tell stories in her songs. Her emotional honesty, accessibility, and harmonic precision, alongside her penchant for avoiding theatrics and vocal embellishments, support her narratives. Her combination of opera precision and outlaw country, along with her unflinchingly honest and compelling lyrics exploring human actions and the psyche, fit well with descriptions regarding others in the community. The *New York Times*'s Jon Caramanica calls Chris Stapleton's voice "a scraped-up but muscular Southern rock howl that's the stuff of the Allman Brothers or Lynyrd Skynyrd," and comments on how "his songwriting favors interior depth over frivolity. There's no breeze in his music."[58] Sturgill Simpson's songwriting lives up to his album title's promise of *Metamodern Sounds in Country Music*: "I want all that dirt and grime and life-sauce. . . . A lot of my favorite old soul records have it, but you don't hear it on country records anymore."[59]

Montgomery's pursuit of a resistant country sound exists in the narratives of her songs, her outlaw-indie country sound, her aesthetic appeal, her performances, and the recording booth. She has a dream of recreating the early Cash-era excitement in country music, envisioning restoring the "HWY 67" touring spirit. It's not surprising that Montgomery venerates Cash both as musical and cultural role model. In her book *Johnny Cash and the Paradox of American Identity*, Leigh Edwards, exploring the cultural effects of Cash's contradictory public personas, argues that "Cash embodied the tensions in the American character without resolving them."[60] She unpacks the many cultural forms in which Cash's public persona evolved. He was the "drugged rock star," "devout Christian," and "the Man in Black," creating space for the musician to be "a progressive voice for the disenfranchised, but also the Southern patriarch performing at Nixon's White House. He was the outlaw hillbilly thug, and he was the establishment."[61]

It's no surprise, then, that both Bonnie's community and the contemporary Nashville scene would gladly claim the Cash ethos. As such, while harkening back to the do-it-yourself spirit of early Sun Records–era rockabilly Cash, Montgomery realizes the difficulties in navigating the material consumer culture in which her music is created and disseminated. In the pursuit of genuineness, her intent, purpose, and motivation serve as the best metric for the authentic.

Similarly, Joe Henry's production of *Look Again to the Wind: Johnny Cash's Bitter Tears Revisited* sought to revisit a part of Cash's motivations and ethos that can get overlooked in the contradictory popular-culture myth Edwards hones in on. Reprising Cash's *Bitter Tears: Ballads of the American Indian* album, which focused on the harsh and unfair treatment of Native Americans, Henry's album refocused the contemporary consumer's attention on the resistant, progressive impulse of much so-called Americana, country, roots, and folk music.

Well, fundamentally it was my understanding that it was a project that Johnny Cash had been extremely passionate about, and through my close friendship with his daughter Rosanne, I learned that he was through much of his life disappointed at the way it was received, or I should say the way it was not allowed to be received because Columbia had done everything they could to keep from having to release the record.

He had just come off an immense success with Ring of Fire for them, and they thought he was going to continue his road to superstardom, and instead he said, "Now that I have some capital and a platform, I'm going to do what I want, and what I want to do is make concept records that are socially important and engaging and challenging." And so he set out to make the Bitter Tears record, and journalists wouldn't write about it; the label didn't want to release it; it was never really heard, certainly not the way he intended.

Because of my tremendous debt to him, when I was invited to be involved, I learned from Rosanne that he had always felt a great disappointment that it hadn't been heard. I felt that it was a sort of duty, if I had the opportunity to help bring it back into the light and to offer it the chance to be heard and for the work to be engaged as a real-time conversation, not as an archival piece.[62]

Henry put together a who's who of contemporary and legendary Americana artists for the project, including Gillian Welch and Dave Rawlings, Emmylou Harris, the Milk Carton Kids, Rhiannon Giddens, Bill Miller, Steve Earle, and Nancy Blake, alongside Kris Kristofferson and Norman Blake. However, as producer and curator, Henry was particular about how these artists fit into not only the spirit of the re-creation but the intent of Cash's original context.

> I wanted it to play like an album, and like a true collaboration, not just a bunch of disparate artists to have a track and send it to me. I didn't want it to play like a compilation. I wanted it to play like an album that was created to be that, and to be heard as a statement. So I started thinking about artists that I thought artistically and creatively [would] reside spiritually in relationship to music and folk tradition. It's like casting a movie, not only who might be great as individual artists, but who might make a whole . . . that plays as a very deliberate and cohesive statement.[63]

Henry thought it would be "morally wrong" not to invite Norman Blake, "the last musician alive who actually played on Johnny Cash's original version of *Bitter Tears*," and felt similarly in regard to Kris Kristofferson. "I thought it was important to have somebody of stature that could represent the gravitas and the importance of Johnny Cash, and somebody who also had a very real and personal connection to Cash, and Kris certainly did."[64]

While her music has yet to take on such overtly political tones, Montgomery's proclivity to make music on the margins of contemporary country, her fidelity to a sound and an outlaw-country code of DIY road life and stripped-down shows and narrative songwriting positions her firmly outside of contemporary popular country. As with the Secret Sisters, Montgomery is left making little money and relies on a rigorous touring schedule. The plight of many such artists in trying to eke out a living playing "serviceable" music raises interesting questions regarding the sustainability of roots-oriented music in a contemporary music climate where Spotify, YouTube, Tidal, Pandora, and other streaming sources provide artists an opportunity to find new fans while simultaneously making it more difficult for them to get paid for their art. "The entire infrastructure that supported the world of music for a century has been dismantled, and in its place we've got these little things, these little handheld devices," complains Burnett. The producer is adamant that smaller artists are getting squeezed out by the current system. He argues that instead of "democ-ratiz[ing] everything . . . [and] creat[ing] a level field," the web generated a vacuum. He maintains that "this is the problem of ubiquitous data . . . that the power's been consolidated in very, very few companies, and the middle class of musicians really has just been wiped out. I mean, the Internet has been an honest-to-God con."[65]

Despite the hardships, Montgomery plugs along with seemingly boundless amounts of touring energy, fueled perhaps by aspiring to something larger than just creating good music: "In my quest, I am eventually trying to say something larger than just a cute country girl in boots. I want to bring people together with a spiritual element. Cash's body of work inspires me to see a spiritual dimension in life. I want to write songs about redemption and forgive-ness; I want to raise the quality of people's lives."[66] Echoing the Secret Sisters and authors like Eudora Welty, Montgomery's "spiritual dimension" seems to encompass not only an ecclesiology but the ethereal spirit of a region, through its landscape, people, history, folklore, and sounds. Montgomery aspires to be a regional regular, leaving her unique imprint on this genre and promoting its sound, quality, and thematic concerns for another generation of music lovers.

Montgomery's and the Secret Sisters' touring regimen and stripped-down shows evoke Burnett's past as well, and arguably the beginning of the T Bone sound he's best known for now. In 1984, Burnett hit the road touring solo with only a 1938 Gibson J-45, and was then, as he is now, philosophical about what such performances signify: "Playing with just one guitar lets you get into all the subtleties. A stop with one guitar becomes gigantic. It's a real jolt of play-ing to be allowed to play very quietly and draw people in."[67] When touring with Elvis Costello in the spring of 1984, Burnett played bare, stripped-down, folk-like performances. After playing their own sets, the two would encore as the Coward Brothers to play roots country, folk, and blues music.[68] According to Bradley Hanson, when T Bone produced Costello's *King of America*, a roots-infused album using players from Elvis Presley's backing band along with some who had played with Dizzy Gillespie and Duke Ellington, and later produced Willie Dixon's *Hidden Charms* (1987) using pioneering blues musicians, he "foreshadowed many of [his] later endeavors into older American styles as well as his developing skill for merging renowned roots practitioners with contemporary stars."[69] His touring and production ethic began to ferment in his own albums as well, particularly the self-titled *T Bone Burnett*, in which Burnett further "demonstrated [a] growing interest in uncomplicated, intimate, older studio practices."[70] It's no wonder, then, fast-forwarding thirty years, that when Burnett was asked to reflect on how the *O Brother* cultural moment had catapulted roots music into arguably mainstream status, even reviving the career of the legend Burnett had been introduced to in his Fort Worth youth, that T Bone would talk of the touring ethic of his roots forbearers: "Ralph Stanley would drive from Washington, DC, to St. Louis, Louisiana, to play for two hundred people in a church basement." Burnett claims that Stanley and other "pioneers" like Howling Wolf and Muddy Waters "drove those roads and played those joints and those churches for years to build up this thing that we have now."[71]

Contemporary American music resides in a culture without originals. Unlike other works of art, like paintings or sculptures, there are no original CDs, only copies of copies. Particularly with a technology of shared compressed audio files and streaming services, American musical products exist within a culture of mass production. Perhaps that's why Burnett, the Secret Sisters, Montgomery, Henry, Weinheimer, and others in their community put such value in their performances and production. Perhaps that's why their purposeful re-presentation of music with rich historical ties to America's cultural past resonates strongly with contemporary audiences. Perhaps their pursuits lie within a framework of the search for something original within a culture of copies. Perhaps their live-performance ethos, their throwback appeal and sound, and their thematic concerns are a testament to re-creating music that the mainstream market has forgotten. This subconscious response is in line with theorist Walter Benjamin's idea of "aura"—the almost mystical feeling of standing in front of an original, a feeling that is lost in mechanical reproduction.[72] Perhaps that's what sociologist Simon Frith means when he argues that "Music is more like clothes than any other art form—not just in the sense of the significance of fashion, but also in the sense that the music we 'wear' is as much shaped by our own desires, our own purposes, our own bodies, as by the intentions or bodies or desires of the people who first made it."[73]

In this vein, Burnett's community, including the thread running to smaller artist-producer combinations like Montgomery and Weinheimer, resists being categorized as novelty. Rather, the collective aspires to re-create and simultaneously produce cultural values for contemporary audiences, linking musicians and music lovers to the past to guide the present and give hope for the future. In this way, Montgomery and Burnett's community can best navigate the contemporary cultural milieu, wherein music with historical, roots leanings can be "serviceable" in the future without being, as Richard Peterson puts it, "'absorbed' into popular music, 'elevated' into art, or 'ossified' as a folk music."[74] In Montgomery's music, we see Bad Blake navigating the demons of the past and the function of country music in the present. Winning the 2016 Ameripolitan Music Awards "Outlaw Female of the Year" and the 2018 Arkansas Country Music Awards "Female Vocalist of the Year" further solidifies that her peers feel the same.[75] In Weinheimer and Henry, we see how the art of production conjures the spirit of the past for usefulness in the present. We see how recording spaces like Muscle Shoals Sound Studio, Sun, Stax, and Ardent stand with Fellowship Hall Sound as a tangible and philosophical heritage for the South's cultural imprint. In all four artists, we see a Southern cultural community defying simple categorization, evoking the traditions of the past for active engagement and negotiations of identity in the present. In the last chapter, this ethic and spirit extends from playing and producing music into the various cultures in the South explored through documentary filmmaking, journalism, preservation, and popular culture discourses at large, solidifying the argument that Burnett's cultural ethic is at the heart of a broad-sweeping Southern cultural renaissance.

CHAPTER 6

T BONE AND THE NARRATIVES OF
THE SOUTHERN RENAISSANCE

Featuring Dust-to-Digital, 1504, and the Southern Foodways
Alliance, with a Comparison of *The Bitter Southerner*,
the *Oxford American*, and *Garden and Gun*

> Tell about the South. What's it like there. What do they do there.
> Why do they live there. Why do they live at all.
>
> — **CANADIAN SHREVE MCCANNON,** Harvard roommate
> of Mississippian Quentin Compson,
> in William Faulkner's *Absalom, Absalom!*

The September 8, 2015, debut of *The Late Show with Stephen Colbert* was a
decidedly Southern affair. Particularly noticeable was the special musical performance. Led by Colbert's new band director, Jon Batiste, the then twenty-
eight-year-old New Orleans multi-instrumentalist musician, Colbert put
together an eclectic performance with contemporary Southern musicians
mingling with legends. The centerpiece featured Mavis Staples and Buddy
Guy. Raised in the renowned gospel, soul, and R&B group the Staple Singers
with her family, Staples grew up in Chicago, a part of the great migration of
black workers who left Mississippi and other parts of the South for opportunities in the North. Similarly, Guy, the Louisiana-reared Chicago bluesman
who played with Muddy Waters at Chess Records, further represented the
Southern diaspora. Playing alongside these two legends were Batiste, a Julliard-
trained, Louisiana-raised eclectic musician in the New Orleans jazz tradition
known for playing piano and melodica, Brittany Howard (Athens, Alabama)
lead singer of the rock group the Alabama Shakes, pop musician Ben Folds
(Winston-Salem, North Carolina), Paul Janeway (Birmingham, Alabama)
lead singer of six-piece soul-rock band St. Paul and the Broken Bones, and
the blues-rock band Tedeschi Trucks (Jacksonville, Florida), alongside the

two non-Southern artists, California soul singer Aloe Blacc and New Mexico-based indie artist Zach Condon of the band Beirut. That the supergroup sang the Sly Stone song "Everyday People" was appropriate, as Stone, who was born into a religious home in Denton, Texas, performing gospel music with his siblings before moving to the San Francisco Bay area, himself represents well the eclecticism that comes from Southern roots music.[1] On display during the energized performance that had the studio audience on their feet and clapping were the Southern-inspired traditions of R&B, electric blues, jazz, soul, and rock and roll, and the music and artists represented an overlapping and inter-locking assemblage of the South's sounds, past, present, and future. As such, the live performance read like a T Bone Burnett soundtrack production. That Kentucky-born actor George Clooney, along with former Florida governor and then presidential hopeful Jeb Bush, were guests both solidified the night as a decidedly Southern affair while simultaneously, albeit perhaps coinciden-tally, connecting the performance with Burnett's *O Brother* soundtrack fame.

Throughout this book, I have tried to show how cultural moments like this are layered with meaning. There are narratives chock-full of Southern conno-tations being told within these seemingly innocuous displays. Like Burnett, Colbert and Batiste remind their New York crowd and global audience of the interracial and genre-bending vibrancy of Southern music. It's a hint that much of what we know of popular culture was created out of Southern contexts. Yet it's also important as a transgressive read on what it means to be a Southerner, particularly the influence of the diaspora, and in that vein Colbert is on display, indicative of the Southern character that transcends eas-ily definable and stereotypical categories. Charleston-raised, Colbert had at one time been so embarrassed of the South's reputation for ignorance and anti-intellectualism that he masked his South Carolinian accent, trying to mimic nightly news anchors instead.[2] Yet, in his opening night performance, join-ing with the expression of Southern cultural exchange happening in front of millions of television viewers, Colbert seems characteristic of the current Southern cultural renaissance.

Having with great success parodied a neoconservative pundit in his for-mer gig on Comedy Central, Colbert appears to be the television personal-ity reimagining of Mark Twain. The former Southerner residing in New York works against the stereotypical Southern gentleman and elite "Yankee" media intellectual mold by being a Northwestern University–educated, politically liberal practicing Catholic, raised in antebellum stronghold Charleston, South Carolina. Colbert still maintains active community ties, for example joining the march across the Arthur Ravenel Jr. Bridge in Charleston to honor the victims of the shooting at the city's historic Emanuel African Methodist Episcopal Church in June of 2015. He's an intellectual satirist/activist who uses his whip-smart intelligence as a weapon against politicians, secular humanists, and the religious right, among others. Furthermore, his and Batiste's selection of musical artists speaks to the cultural renaissance's mantra: a multiracial, cross-cultural exchange between the past, present, and future.

This book has looked at T Bone Burnett's participation in a movement, most notably through his soundtrack and artistic productions, and at artists and producers who are either directly inspired by or are infused with a similar ethic. Like the Southern Renascence of the 1920s and 1930s, this movement seeks to address the complexities of Southern identity through cultural history, with particular focus on race, class, and gender, exploring that identity by creating art that best uncovers the Southern cultures standing resistant to the oversimplified, often stereotypical, perceived homogeneity of contemporary Southern identity. Like the Renascence, which Richard H. King argues was much more than a literary movement, representing "an outpouring of history, sociology, political analysis, autobiography, and innovative forms of journalism," this movement extends well beyond the boundaries of music, encompassing the study of how literature, food, fashion, film, preservationists, and community builders are leading a contemporary Southern cultural renaissance.[3] This concluding chapter aims at building on Burnett's contributions by extending his ethic into other artistic mediums with similar aims. Here, we'll look at outlets that blend scholarship and popular culture, while highlighting Southern stories past and present and addressing the complicated notions of tradition and heritage.

Running the record company Dust-to-Digital from their nondescript basement in Atlanta, husband-and-wife team Lance and April Ledbetter represent the terrain between Colbert-like popular culture moments, Burnett's hybrid folk-pop collaborations, and traditional scholarship, with similar aims. Dust-to-Digital's catalogue includes episodic jaunts through the South's musical past: West Virginia folk musician from the 1920s *Blind Alfred Reed: Appalachian Visionary*; *Joe Bussard Presents: The Year of Jubilo: 78 RPM Recordings of Songs from the Civil War*; 1960s old-time Appalachian music performer *Ola Belle Reed and Southern Mountain Music on the Mason-Dixon Line*; *J. B. Smith: No More Good Time in the World for Me* from Bruce Jackson's recordings from Ramsey State Prison Farm in Rosharon, Texas; old-timey roots music in *Arkansas at 78 RPM: Corn Dodgers and Hoss Hair Pullers*; informal spiritual and gospel songs recorded from 1965 to 1973 in *Sorrow Come Pass Me Around: A Survey of Rural Religious Black Music*; *Voices of Mississippi: Artists and Musicians Documented by William Ferris*, presenting the lion's share of the famed folklorist's work; and *Rev. Johnny L. "Hurricane" Jones: Jesus Christ from A to Z*, a vinyl LP of live congregational singing, among others. Not simply musical compilations, most albums come with hardcover books featuring pictures and introductory notes or essays by leading folklorists, cementing a direct connection to the music's historic contexts. Though their catalogue also includes global music, such as *Don't Think I've Forgotten: Cambodia's Lost Rock and Roll*, the label's ethos seems firmly grounded in Southern tradition. In doing so, the Ledbetters occupy unique ground in the musical market by connecting popular music consumption, scholarship, multimedia artistry, and preservation. Their first production, *Goodbye, Babylon* (2003), best announces Dust-to-Digital's philosophy and motivation.

As a Georgia State University student, in 1997 the then twenty-year-old Ledbetter heard Harry Smith's *Anthology of American Folk Music*. In it, like Dylan, Burnett, and the whole of the 1960s folk revival, Ledbetter discovered the American roots music heritage. The gospel section on the anthology was nothing like the Wesleyan hymns of his youth; they were, instead, as one *New Yorker* writer put it, "ecstatic, apocalyptic."[4] Ledbetter was hooked. Soon after, Ledbetter landed a local radio show and began playing songs from the *Anthology*, eventually venturing beyond to blues and country reissues: "The one thing I had a hard time finding was early gospel," he told the *New Yorker* in a profile piece. "I kept thinking, who's got these records? Who's got them? They have to come from somewhere." Surfing the internet, Ledbetter came across a story about a rabid record collector of prewar folk and gospel music named Joe Bussard: "Bussard's got shit that God don't have," another collector claimed.[5] Ledbetter called Bussard with a list of gospel records he was hoping to find, and soon the two had a relationship where Lance would send a list with a check and shortly thereafter receive cassette tapes, Bussard charging him fifty cents per song. After purchasing over a hundred tapes and upwards of five thousand songs, Ledbetter began to visualize what would become Dust-to-Digital. As

Burkhard Bilger writes, "What was needed, he realized, wasn't another record collector. What was needed was a go-between, an anthologizer—someone to collect from the collectors. What was needed was another Harry Smith."[6] The husband-and-wife team worked on *Goodbye, Babylon* from 1999 to 2003, concentrating "very much on the presentation, the song selection, the aesthetics. What we were doing was building a foundation of aesthetics and structures and frameworks that would carry the label to current day and, hopefully, for many years on."[7] His intent was twofold, to answer one question—"what were the greatest gospel recordings in the early twentieth century?"—while simultaneously "highlight[ing] as many subgenres of gospel music as we could."[8] The anthology included a sprawling six CDs and a two-hundred-page book, with contributions from dozens of scholars, that were housed in a cedar box with a sliding lid packed with raw cotton from a relative's Alabama farm. He and April spent untold hours transcribing and meticulously working on the songs and packaging. "I wanted everything to be old, old-looking, like something you might see in a general store in 1929."[9] The public and critical reception was electric.

> The whole *Goodbye, Babylon* experience was crazy because we put them all together by hand, and I really did not think they would sell. We had no distribution and all these things. . . . The press went crazy for it, and we were just putting them together left and right. . . . It went from October 2003 until we ended up going to the Grammys in Los Angeles in 2005. And we've gone through that whole experience which is like a year and a half. . . . What happened?[10]

A few months after returning from the Grammys, Ledbetter received an email from an NPR Weekend Edition producer informing him that he would want to tune in to their interview with Neil Young that day. A few minutes into listening, he heard Young start talking about *Goodbye, Babylon* and how Bob Dylan had gifted it to him as a Christmas present: "What that meant to me is that my wife and I were hand assembling these, and it went from our hands to Dylan's hands to Neil's hands. . . . I mean, I almost fainted."[11]

Ledbetter points to the usual suspects for inspiration: Alan Lomax, Art Rosenbaum, George Mitchell, and Bill Ferris, but he acknowledges revered music collector and amateur scholar Harry Smith as his "top inspiration." Ledbetter acknowledges Smith's ability to "mix the scholarly in with the art world," noting how the anthologist was apt to talk about "using alchemical powers to produce those types of compilation."[12] The dictionary defines alchemy as a "seemingly magical process of transformation, creation, or combination." Perhaps that is why Smith's Folkways *Anthology*, with three volumes and eighty-four selections, was identified by Robert Cantwell as the "musical constitution" of the '60s folk revival, reimagining as it did the traditional music of "the poor, the isolated, and the uneducated" into a "curriculum in mystical ethnography, converting a commercial music fashioned in the twenties out of various cultural emplacements and historical displacements into the 'folk' music of the revival." Influencing academics, musicians, and fans alike, the *Anthology* "led into an endless proliferation of new recordings . . . of rediscovered Anthology performers, as well as newly discovered younger musicians . . . who could be encouraged to take advantage of the growing commercial viability of traditional music."[13]

With his productions aiming at "a deeper meaning than just audio and text," Ledbetter is analytical about Dust-to-Digital's audience and the potential for their productions to be regenerative in the mode of Smith and the 1960s.

> I think a lot has changed in the twelve years we've been putting out records. The technology and the way people listen to music has changed tremendously in just a short span of time. I think people are drawn to the type of releases we put out [for various reasons]. One, its accessibility and duration, where you go on to YouTube or Spotify and you have thirty million songs to pick from. . . . Even with *Goodbye, Babylon* back in 2003 . . . a hundred and sixty tracks was considered [to be] so much music. Nowadays, no one would bat an eye at that quantity of music. I think people look to us for curation, but I think there's also this other aspect where people are—maybe you can call them adventurous listeners where they're looking for something they haven't found yet or they're willing to hear something they'd never heard before. . . . Then, you add to that what we try to do with our packages. We try to offer in-depth scholarship but also artful packages. We're trying to blend the art world and the scholarly worlds together to hopefully create a lot of variety in your experience.[14]

This unique approach, marrying popular culture and art with the scholarship of folklore and ethnography, by its nature expands and diversifies Dust-to-Digital's audience, extending from record collectors and musicologists to musicians and general lovers of music and history, while decidedly grounding the music in its Southern context. This reach highlights the potential overlap between preservation and inspiration. Not surprisingly, then, musicians as diverse as Bruce Springsteen and Elvis Costello are fans. Ledbetter, humbled by the attention, was amazed when Canadian indie-rock band Arcade Fire's lead singer Win Butler claimed that their album *Neon Bible* is based on *Goodbye, Babylon*.[15] Addressing why she feels their output resonates with contemporary music lovers, April speculates that "people are looking for ways to have context for their lives." She believes that "getting to see something like these sets, you might imagine that this is what it was like in your family, for your grandparents or great-grandparents."[16]

Ledbetter's own reaction to Smith's collection speaks to the hankering after the past. For him, this was a direct connection to the South. Speaking of connecting Smith's collection to his own life, Ledbetter echoes the experiences of Montgomery, Weinheimer, and Henry.

I can just remember playing the CDs and reading the book, and it just floored me. I cannot believe how powerful it was, and for me, personally, as a Southerner, I've grown up around a lot of music like this. In high school, that was the furthest thing from what I was buying. I was buying indie rock and punk rock and things like that, but when I heard this, what it did was it took me back to the '50s with early rock and rockabilly [and then] back to the '20s, and I hear the music that I'd grown up [hearing].

When I was growing up, we'd go to cattle auctions and land auctions for the town, and there'd be a band there playing string-band music or somebody playing guitar, singing folk traditional songs. You just take it for granted, but, to me, what the *Anthology* did was it put a lot of pieces and places in my mind of where this music came from. When I looked to do *Goodbye, Babylon*, almost all that music is from the South. . . . I think what the *Anthology* did for me was it basically made me pay attention to music that is taken for granted in the South. It's almost like the third eye was open. Once I looked around, I was, like, "Oh my God, there's so much incredible music." It's just—for whatever reason, [that music] had been in my background and then, all of a sudden, it put a lot of that into my foreground. . . . I started talking to a lot of 78 collectors.

In fact, walking into the Anthology of American Folk Music was like walking into this house with all these windows and then, all of a sudden, I found out from all these collectors that the eighty-four tracks on the Anthology are a drop in the bucket to what they recorded back then. In the '20s and '30s, they were making so many recordings in the South. It gave me an appreciation for what has been around me, but then also opened me up to a lot of music from that era that I just had never known about.[17]

Coincidentally, *Goodbye, Babylon*'s release coincided with the popularity and acclaim of Burnett's *O Brother* soundtrack, leaving the two as an easy comparison for many. Not surprisingly, Lance and April were fans, attending the soundtrack's Down from the Mountain tour when it came to Atlanta. Ledbetter, with his characteristically understated demeanor, still seemingly in shock regarding the album's success even twelve years removed, recalls *Entertainment Weekly* comparing the two albums: "If *O Brother, Where Art Thou?* is the coffee table album of the year, then *Goodbye, Babylon* is the coffee table."[18] Ledbetter hones in on the historic significance of Burnett's and Dust-to-Digital's successes in the light of folk revivals of the past.

> *The Anthology of American Folk Music* came out in '52, and then you get all this great folk revival stuff in the early '60s. If you look at the time span of the *Anthology* being reissued on CD for the first time in '97. . . . In 2003, you get *Goodbye, Babylon, O Brother* [in 2000]. . . . It's almost like you could see a second roots revival for the *Anthology*, the digital one versus the LP version.[19]

Perhaps his optimism, historical acuity, humility, and passion inspired the *New Yorker*'s Burkhard Bilger to describe Ledbetter as "a child of the New South, which is to say, an amalgam of anachronisms. He had an easy drawl and an ironic wit, the tastes of an urban aesthete and the manner of a small-town innocent."[20]

With such charisma and over a decade's worth of consistent reproductions under its belt, Dust-to-Digital has cemented itself as a cultural tastemaker. *The Bitter Southerner* endorses the Ledbetters as "perhaps the most important preservers of folk music in the modern world, and they do it all from the basement of their little brick house."[21] The roots music website *No Depression* argues that "the rise of Dust-to-Digital has been perhaps the most important catalyst in exposing younger generations to traditional American folk music since Harry Smith's 'Anthology.'"[22] Indie music site *Pitchfork* places Dust-to-Digital in the world of folklorists in the field and ancient performers, arguing for the debt owed the Ledbetters: "The bulk of the material might have been lost—or, at the very least, tethered to archives, readily accessible only to curious faculty, paper-writing students, and bespectacled researchers."[23]

Beyond critical acclaim, Dust-to-Digital has been nominated for nine Grammys, winning in 2008 for Best Historical Album with *Art of Field*

Recording, Volume I: Fifty Years of Traditional American Music Documented by Art Rosenbaum. The award was symbolic, as Ledbetter's relationship to the folk revivalist and record collector par excellence was instrumental in Dust-to-Digital's early success. The similarities and differences between the two men are crucial to how the label has navigated the worlds of scholarship and popular culture. As Bilger notes, while Rosenbaum "believed that traditional ballads, blues, spirituals, and fiddle tunes are among the glories of American culture," Ledbetter sought to "research, remaster, and repackage it as beautifully as possible—to make the old songs seem new again."[24] The four-CD release featured a sweeping exploration of Rosenbaum's recordings, "everything from ring shouts and murder ballads to a song about twenty frogs going to school. It was full of throaty voices and clanging banjos and the incidental music of daily life—babies crying, bar glasses clinking, cicadas on a summer night."[25] Beyond the Grammys, the duo have both been nominated for and won many awards from organizations like the Jazz Journalists Association, the Society for Ethnomusicology, *Living Blues* magazine, the Florida Historical Society, and the Association for Recorded Sound Collections. They have also ventured into working with contemporary artists, producing Lonnie Holley's 2013 album *Keeping a Record of It*. Furthermore, working with an organization called Music Memory, they continue their dedicated efforts to digitize forgotten sounds while giving a voice to unheard artists and unwitnessed contexts, "by placing equipment in the homes of record collectors who are methodically processing their own holdings. The group will assemble lyrics, liner notes, discographic data and audio in an online collection."[26]

According to Ledbetter, the combination of scholarship, photography, and music creates a platform by which people can engage with their productions through more than just nostalgia, but rather by probing essential questions of identity: "Where do we come from? What were these people like? How long ago was this? Where are we now? How have things changed? This is in your hand, and you're basically having to face your own thoughts."[27] As such, the albums are as much about the present as the past, and that's why Ledbetter is eager to adopt tools of popular culture while also jarring the popular audience's trained inclination for passive consumption—and jarring more traditional scholarly pursuits in equal measure, to make sure that these sounds and histories are not relegated to folk gatherings and archives alone. As he puts it, the music, stories, and contexts "should be available and accessible to whoever wants it, whoever is turned on by it, should be able to access it. . . . I want our releases to have that capability to reach someone and turn on a switch.[28]

With that instructive and regenerative capability in mind, Chuck Reece argues that Dust-to-Digital output like *Parchman Farm: Photographs and Field Recordings: 1947–1959* matters: "You hold it in your hand. You read the stories. You listen. And it puts you *there*, inside Parchman Farm, in 1947. It's a place where every Southerner needs to go, so that we learn never to go back there again."[29] The Ledbetters are navigating the slippery connections between popular consumption and scholarship. William Ferris catches several aspects of their work's importance in regard to contemporary Southern contexts.[30] Ferris believes the Ledbetters "create an environment within the confines of a box" and "make very imaginative uses of art to frame and amplify the music." Calling their compilations works of art in themselves, Ferris argues that Dust-to-Digital, "in tandem with people like T-Bone Burnett . . ., are taking Southern music to places that were unimaginable in an earlier period."[31]

Arguably, the success of Burnett's community—extending to those like Dust-to-Digital also participating in this renaissance, in its various aspects—depends on narratives past and present. Meanwhile, there is evident desire across artistic platforms and audiences for stories set in Southern contexts to be told. Beyond the academic journals, presses, and studies programs across the South, magazines and online journals like *The Bitter Southerner*, *Garden and Gun*, and the *Oxford American* serve as examples of this impulse. Not surprisingly, each of the three outlets grants Southern music a particular place of honor. *Garden and Gun* features an online "Back Porch Sessions" concert series presenting live performances from numerous Southern artists, including Nathaniel Rateliff and the Night Sweats, Sturgill Simpson, Drive-By-Truckers, Jason Isbell, Carolina Chocolate Drops, the Avett Brothers, the Punch Brothers, Holly Williams, and more. Similarly, *The Bitter Southerner* has a host of music videos and essays from contemporary Southern artists. The *Oxford American* takes a more historical approach in its annual music issues, each affording a glance at that state's musical context—past, present, and future—with articles, features, and reviews that unpack the stories of the songs and the vibrant complexities of the sound's historic and present background. Through back stories, interviews, photographs, and narratives, the music issues channel the intent of Burnett's soundtracks. The accompanying CDs blend genres, races, and time periods to make a cultural imprint of the state's evolution. For example, the

2013 two-disc Tennessee compilation features a diverse range of artists, with a cappella ensemble the Fisk Jubilee Singers (founded at Fisk University in the late nineteenth century) and 1950s Sun Records doo-wop group the Prisonaires alongside performers like Emmylou Harris, Elvis Presley, B. B. King, and Al Green.

Though with seemingly similar aims—to tell stories of overlooked and underappreciated aspects of the American South and to highlight cultural tastemakers—*Garden and Gun, Oxford American,* and *The Bitter Southerner* are decidedly different in approach and audience. Award-winning Charleston, South Carolina–based *Garden and Gun* focuses on various aspects of Southern life, with online and magazine articles covering sporting life, food, music, art, literature, home and garden, arts and culture, and travel. The magazine bestows annual Made in the South Awards with categories including style, crafts, home, drink, food, and outdoors. Its website was once home to the "Mercantile & Co." online store, now the "Fieldshop." They also host an annual Made in the South Jubilee, featuring a host of Southern makers and including dinners, trunk shows, book signings, sporting dog events, and more. That their audience leans toward the affluent can be seen through typical advertisers in the pages of their bimonthly magazine. In between stories of Southern places, people, and culture are advertisements for Volvo, Rolex, private jet travel, exclusive real estate, and exotic vacation destinations. These partnerships have in the past made the magazine the target of criticism, most notably from former *Oxford American* editor Marc Smirnoff: "I don't play golf, or make big business deals or tell racist jokes, so the idea of hanging out in a sauna with a bunch of good ole boys at The Club just does not do it for me. (I overheard one wag say, '*Garden and Gun* is a magazine for Republicans produced by Democrats.')" Mr. Smirnoff wasn't finished, calling the magazine "superficial" and questioning its motives in "dumbing down (and commodifying) a subject that I love" and "promot[ing] a vulgar and aggressive materialism." According to Smirnoff, *Garden and Gun* "worship[s] at the veranda of The Old South Plantation Myth."[32] Smirnoff's critique confronts the debate pursued throughout this study, squarely analyzing the points of tension between an exploitative commodification of regional ways—the opposite of Wendell Berry's "local life aware of itself"—and a desire to celebrate the unique aspects of the South's present artistic output in light of such creation's roots in the past.[33] Can culture be appreciated and celebrated without giving in to the fetishized and voyeuristic?

The *Oxford American* began in 1992 in Oxford, Mississippi, and has over the years been published by author John Grisham, At Home, Inc., and, since 2002, the University of Central Arkansas. The quarterly magazine bends more toward the literati, having featured revered Southern authors like Charles Portis, Roy Blount Jr., and Eudora Welty alongside visual artists such as William Eggleston and Carroll Cloar. The typical *Oxford American* issue contains photographs, poems, fiction, and profiles of people, places, and events unique to the South. The typical contributors are professional writers, with some connection past or present to the South, whose CVs feature significant publications that might variously include articles, essay collections and other nonfiction books, novels, and poems. The magazine's "Points South" section, what current editor Eliza Borné calls "a refuge for literary miscellanea,"[34] proposes to offer a space for a variety of artistic and literary mediums in order to give snapshot glimpses of the broad Southern condition. The "Omnivore" section features criticism and commentary, such as film, book, movie, and cultural analysis from a variety of critics, with regulars Chris Offutt and John T. Edge also commenting on food culture. The bulk of the magazine holds long essays, journalism, fiction, and poetry. For example, the spring 2016 issue included, in Borné's words, an author's "meditation on ancestry and her . . . connection to Florida's Fountain of Youth legend; . . . [a] short story about the birth of a child in rural Kentucky; . . . [a] report from the Mississippi Delta, where [the authors] sought the source material for Lewis Nordan's fiction; . . . [a] tale of an unforgettable soccer season for a New Orleans team; and new work by C. D. Wright, the brilliant Arkansas-born poet" who died in January 2012.[35]

The *Oxford American* straddles the line between literary journal and popular magazine. Its mission is to feature "the best in Southern writing while documenting the complexity and vitality of the American South," and in doing so, the magazine has won four ASME National Magazine Awards, among other honors.[36] Ostensibly, the *Oxford American* and *Garden and Gun* have a similar destination, with the goal of celebrating and uncovering cultural aspects of the contemporary American South. Yet, they travel divergent routes. *Garden and Gun* operates more as an introduction to cultural tastemakers, with striking photographic spreads. Their magazine invites readers to appreciate the South as a land of creators. Their aesthetic and narrative approach creates an appealing, albeit safe and borderline utopian representation. On the other hand, the *Oxford American* attempts to convey the situations and psyches of the region's overlooked and underrepresented, and is filled with gritty explorations of race, class, gender, politics, sexuality, religion, and culture writ large.

The narrative differences rest mostly in the tension points of their two purposes. Geared toward a more popular audience, *Garden and Gun*'s president and CEO Rebecca Wesson Darwin offers an explanation of the magazine's name evoking traditionally abstract Southern symbols: "It is a metaphor for the South—its land, the people, their lifestyle, and their heritage."[37] A useful example of the debate surrounding the slippery terrain between "authenticity" and commodification is found in *Garden and Gun*'s April/May 2015 issue highlighting the "50 Perfect Southern Things: Funky Juke Joints, Hidden Gardens, Hot New Restaurants, and Lots more Reasons to Love the South Now." The issue's cover shows Merigold, Mississippi's Po' Monkey's Lounge, a dilapidated, windowless, wood-frame juke joint with hand-painted signs and show bills decorating the front. Settled in between the aforementioned advertisements, the issue begins with an interview with soul and R&B legend Bill Withers. The "Talk of the South" features include food, sport, and art, with short pieces on "Mexican-style lamb barbacoa," three small-batch Southern distilleries in Charleston, Miami, and San Leon, Texas, homegrown ingredients from Chesapeake–region chefs, and a how-to guide to preparing soft-shell crawfish (batter with beer, drizzle with remoulade, and serve with spicy slaw). These stories weave in and out with reviews of music (Richmond native Matthew E. White, the Alabama Shakes, and a special duo album of Elliott Smith covers by Seth Avett and Jessica Lea Mayfield) and literature (Southern photographer Sally Mann's *Hold Still: A Memoir with Photographs*). Lastly, the section includes a look at the revamped Bahamian "Tuna Alley" fishing tournament and a retrospective by PGA golfer Ben Crenshaw about his last Masters Tournament. The "Made in the South" section features a Jackson, Mississippi, insurance executive's custom knife collection, an event designer's revival of a rural Georgia antebellum estate, and Monterey, Kentucky, resident Gray Zeitz's hand press bookbinding shop. The "50 Things" spread operates on a similar trajectory, featuring food (livermush, hot sauce, and farmer's markets, to name a few), landscapes, music (Helena, Arkansas's King Biscuit Time radio show and informal "guitar pulls," in which musicians take turns playing songs), hunting, college football, and Southern staples like the scent of magnolia, etiquette, and storytellers. Craftsmanship abounds as well, as the magazine features a Southern quilter, a wicker furniture maker, a custom saddlemaker, and Preservation Virginia's Tobacco Barn Preservation Project.

The magazine goes on to feature a trip to Memphis hot spots, a few short profile pieces, and a calendar of events for the next two months for each Southern state. The Po' Monkey's piece is an exemplar of what irks critics like Marc Smirnoff. The eight-page spread features models wearing the season's latest fashions in and around the Delta juke joint's grounds. One two-page spread features a stunning red-lipsticked brunette standing in a field of Delta cotton wearing a $7,500 Visconti laced gown with Swarovski crystal pearls. Make no mistake, Po' Monkey's seventy-plus-year-old proprietor Willie Seaberry seemingly revels in the attention, with a photograph featuring him dancing inside the landmark with a model. Undoubtedly, Seaberry benefits from the magazine's wide readership. Yet, for many who see Po' Monkey's as hallowed ground, a lens by which to see how the complicated racial turmoil of the past could create a vibrant musical culture that would later take over the world, the scene is culturally insensitive at the least, and willfully commodifying and whitewashing heritage at worst. It's a similar debate that encircles the Shack Up Inn, another site for one of the fashion shots, where tourists come and stay the night in a collection of reclaimed sharecropper cabins. Yet, the debate is still more complicated than Smirnoff's remarks imply. *Garden and Gun* editor-in-chief David DiBenedetto had this to say in response to Smirnoff:

> It would most likely come as a surprise to the many Southern artisans, craftsmen, farmers, shop owners, musicians, artists, authors, designers, dog trainers, sportsmen, chefs, barkeeps, filmmakers, pit masters, and others whom we've featured to learn that they don't represent the real South. It would also surprise the long list of great writers who have contributed to *G&G* (some of whom, as Mr. Smirnoff notes, also contribute to the *Oxford American*) to hear that their work is devoid of substance. In any case, we do agree that the South is a big, dynamic, and diverse place, and there is more than enough room for a variety of viewpoints and magazines.[38]

DiBenedetto's point is well taken. The magazine certainly represents a broad spectrum of interests, arguably appealing as much to folk-crafters, foodies, and musicians as to the abundantly affluent with their refurbished manors, perfectly manicured gardens, and collections of heirloom guns. All these people in equal measure can claim a part of Southern identity as their own, and having them share the same cultural space is an interesting commentary on the contemporary South. *Garden and Gun* offers a wide audience for little-known artists of all sorts. Critics' irks are not unfounded either. Especially in a magazine with a decidedly affluent audience, there must be a conscious effort to not gloss over the myriad issues of race, class, and gender that are infused in all conversations regarding cultural symbols, places, and art in the American South. Similarly, the *Oxford American*'s educated audience and credentialed contributors can unintentionally misrepresent the complexities of places with their own biases or treat the subject matter with the detached philosophical gaze of critical theory. It's a similar debate to Benjamin Filene's folk-fad fears in response to the influence of Burnett. Such cultural participation must hope to avoid an "idle demonstration of hip open-mindedness."[39] Within these tension points rests the crux of the difficult negotiations when the complexities of the South's past contexts are recreated in popular artistic mediums. Like Burnett's soundtracks and the host of artists he includes in his community, simple judgements regarding the propriety of such endeavors rarely do justice to the narrative's complexities. Wendell Berry's remarks on the "knowledge" and "faithfulness" of a place as the antidote to its taking on a "superficial and decorative" role are once again appropriate.[40]

With this in mind, the motivations of those with the power to provide cultural space and the creators of art themselves must hold themselves and their community accountable for addressing the complexities of Southern cultures, past and present. Interestingly, both the *Oxford American* and *Garden and Gun* share several collaborators, with names like John T. Edge and Roy Blount Jr. appearing in both. Furthermore, the inclusion of authors like Edge and Blount alongside Rick Bragg, John Currence, and Clyde Edgerton implicitly indicates an endorsement by several important figures in contemporary Southern culture, solidifying DiBenedetto's retort and further complicating any easily drawn judgments.

The Bitter Southerner seemingly occupies the middle ground between the *Oxford American*'s erudition and *Garden and Gun*'s sheen. Founded in 2013 by Chuck Reece, the spark for the Atlanta-based website came from Reece's appalled reaction to Southern establishments being left off *Drinks International*'s 2012 list of the world's top fifty bars. Sensing "a bigger story to be told," he set out to create an online space to honor his vision of the Southern cultures he felt weren't given their due. Reece did not mince words in setting his audience's parameters.

> If you are a person who buys the states' rights argument . . . or you fly the rebel flag in your front yard . . . or you still think women look really nice in hoop skirts,

we politely suggest you find other amusements on the web. The Bitter Southerner is not for you.

The Bitter Southerner is for the rest of us. It is about the South that the rest of us know: the one we live in today and the one we hope to create in the future.[41]

A trip through *The Bitter Southerner*'s archives paints the picture of what Reece's purpose statement so forcefully declares. There are photographic essays examining "Southern hip-hop's rise to domination," a look at the past, present, and future of the historically black Morris Brown College, photographic explorations of Durham, Athens, Mississippi Delta gas stations, and the back roads, railroad tracks, and hollows depicted by a self-described "conflicted" Southern photographer, among others. There are folklore stories recounting places and people, featuring fly-swatting "Mamaws," Southern speech patterns and dialects, food, politics, and all aspects of the Southern condition, as told by contributors. There are short video documentaries, featuring musicians like soul and R&B artist Leon Bridges, country musician Caleb Caudle, a trip to the barbershop with Atlanta-based hip-hop politico Killer Mike, and the Panorama Jazz Band. There are also poignant explorations of race, class, and gender in short films like *As I Am* and *The Bessemer Cutoff*, which address the hardships faced by black inner-city youths in Memphis, Tennessee, and Bessemer, Alabama.

The site's feature articles follow a similar trajectory, granting cultural space for the untold and underrepresented, yet spectacular and worthy dynamics of people, places, and events making up the contemporary Southern condition. It's multiracial and diverse, filled with the contradictory emotions of hope, heartache, anger, and joy. The site explores the full range of sensory experiences the South has to afford, attempting to leave no stone unturned to address the myriad issues facing the contemporary South. As such, *The Bitter Southerner* seeks through essays, short stories, poems, short films, and folklore to "wrestle with" Southerners and Southern places that "honor genuinely honorable traditions," covering the "musicians, cooks, designers, farmers, scientists, innovators, writers, thinkers and craftsmen" who "make the South a far better place than most folks think it is."[42]

Like Dust-to-Digital and the other narrative outlets mentioned, the Southern Foodways Alliance combines popular and scholarly mediums to look at contemporary Southern culture through the lens of food. Currently, the SFA produces a magazine and an award-winning podcast entitled *Gravy*, hosts three annual symposiums, and houses an online archive of nearly one thousand oral histories. On top of that, they partner with events like the Charleston Wine and Food Festival or Bluffton, South Carolina's Music to Your Mouth to showcase SFA content. Lastly, the organization has ventured into filmmaking. Having made their first film in 2003, the SFA has since surpassed the hundred-film mark and hired an in-house filmmaker. SFA assistant director Melissa Hall, eastern Kentucky-raised and holding a law degree from Northern Kentucky University, believes the group is on pace to make ten to twelve films a year. In an interview, she described the organization's goals in creating these films.

> [With] film and documentary work, the subject is the same: unsung heroes of Southern food. We're looking for the men and women who make, grow, and serve great Southern food, people who by and large aren't going to be on Food Network. Through their labor, through their skill, and through their compassion for their communities [they] are sustaining not only themselves but also whole communities of people.[43]

The SFA is located in the Barnard Observatory on the University of Mississippi's campus in Oxford. The building also houses the Center for the Study of Southern Culture program, which Hall states does a great job at offering "lenses through which a person can view the region, and then understand the region," ranging from the more traditional—literature and art—to the less traditional, such as music and the increasingly popular race, class, and sexuality. The SFA, for its part, focuses on food as a mode by which to discuss any of the aforementioned subjects.

> What our argument has been since the beginning is that food is as valid a lens as any of these other more expected lenses, and because food is something that everybody interacts with on some level, it's in many ways an easier entry point into the difficult discussions that divide us as Southerners. . . . If I brought fifteen people into a room and said, "We are going to talk today about race, class, gender, sexuality, and politics," everybody in the room would begin taking a position. . . . I can bring the same group in the room and say, "We're going to talk about collard greens," and I can get to all five of those things really fast, and with people who not only have their guard down, but with people who are open to the possibilities. That's why food works.

Sure, you can be the least mindful eater in the world, and just go have your meat-and-three and not think about anything on that plate, other than these are the three things I like best. [But food affords the opportunity for analysis:] Why are collards on this menu always? Why do they have corn bread at lunch, but yeast bread at supper? As you begin asking those questions, you start to understand things about Southerners. . . . That oral history archive of one thousand voices, that shouldn't just live in the library, or in a room kept in a book waiting for a researcher. These people are interesting. Their lives are interesting, the food-ways that they know and understand are interesting, and our position has always been, people probably want to know about this.

Hall doesn't discount the role traditional scholarship plays in the exploration of Southern culture, and the SFA hires trained oral historians to perform the roughly fifty to seventy-five interviews they collect per year. Yet, like the other examples throughout this book, the SFA seeks to move beyond traditional scholarship, desiring to reach an audience across media platforms, a point Hall explores:

If you look at it, I certainly think there is always going to be a vital role for folklorists, and for folks who set themselves up to go out and record the culture. No question. Particularly when you consider things like the source material that we used when we began the oral history program, when we began writing the food-ways volume of *The Encyclopedia of Southern Culture*. That source material is in no small part from the [1930s] America Eats project. Those stories were widely collected and then put away. The same thing is true in music. . . . It's terrific that somebody recorded those stories and recorded those recipes. They lived somewhere until somebody noticed. What the SFA is doing is essentially providing a snapshot of now.

Presenting such histories and conversations for public consumption, however, particularly amidst the symbolism of the Ole Miss campus, creates a tension regarding which "South" is being represented. Hall states that the center gets calls from people who say, "I want to talk to you about the Civil War." She was adamant: "That's not really the South we focus on." Instead, the SFA is interested in how the past relates to the present. "What does Southern Foodways look like now? The gauzy past is not something that holds a lot of appeal for us. Somebody's story about how they know what they know about whole hog barbecue, or how to make a biscuit, and all of those things. That's relevant only to the extent that they're actually doing it now."

Like the broader community's ethos, the SFA reads against the "moonlight and magnolia" stereotypes of the South. Hall argues that "you cannot talk about Southern food without acknowledging what we typically call 'the debt of pleasure' that all Southerners owe to the enslaved people, who created many of these food traditions we now all embrace." Relating a quote she recently heard at an event, Hall believes that "tradition is not doing things the way they've always been done. Tradition, is in fact, the choices that we make about which things we're actually carrying forward." Food, like other aspects of Southern culture, can provide a unique lens by which to test out the tension points within discussions of tradition, heritage, and contemporary contexts.

> We buy that tradition is what you choose to bring forward. Particularly with food, then, what you have here [is that] almost every ingredient, almost every preparation, almost every recipe of this region, particularly the traditional ones, come with a huge amount of strife, and struggle, and historical baggage. We are very serious about never talking about the deliciousness of, say, the rice, without talking about the history of the rice.

The discussion over "whose South" represents the complicated relationships between history, nostalgia, tradition, and heritage. Such questions that arise are particularly salient on the Ole Miss campus, whose very name—a term slaves used for plantation owners' wives—connotes problematic considerations. In 2010, the university officially changed its mascot from Colonel Reb to the Black Bear, a decision that still sparks heated debate today. The SFA's Barnard Observatory home is physically separated from the campus's Civil War monument, the James Meredith Civil Rights Monument, and the Lyceum by "the Grove." Each of these markers stands as symbolically contested heritage. The approximately twenty-foot Civil War monument bears the Lost Cause–inspired inscription, "To the heroes of Lafayette County whose valor and devotion made glorious many a battlefield." So as to hammer the point home, another side of the monument features lines from the Romantic poet Byron:

> They fell devoted, but undying;
> The very gale their names seem'd sighing:
> The waters murmur'd of their name;

The woods were peopled with their fame;
The silent pillar, lone and gray,
Claim'd kindred with their sacred clay;
Their spirits wrapp'd the dusky mountain,
Their memory sparkl'd o'er the fountain;
The meanest rill, the mightiest river
Roll'd mingling with their fame forever.[44]

Separating the ostentatious display of Confederate grandeur from the Civil Rights Monument is the Lyceum building, site of the clash between Mississippi residents and the National Guard in the fall of 1962, when James Meredith became the first African American student to enroll in the university. Bullet holes are said to still pockmark the stately old Lyceum. The monument features a bronze statue of a young Meredith walking toward a small classical pavilion. Within this structure, a 2002 quote from murdered activist Medgar Evers's widow, Myrlie, speaks to the contested historical terrain the three structures afford: "Yes, Mississippi was. But Mississippi is, and we are proud of what we have become." Myrlie's optimism is mirrored by the SFA's Hall, and perhaps with good reason. The Mississippi state flag, which features the Confederate stars and bars, will not be flown on campus anymore, after being voted on by the University of Mississippi student senate. Furthermore, Hall spoke glowingly of an explanatory plaque placed next to the Confederate soldier monument: "I wish I could tell you that wasn't a huge step forward, but oh my Lord, is that a huge step forward," she exclaimed.[45] The plaque reads:

As Confederate veterans were dying in increasing numbers, memorial associations across the South built monuments in their memory. These monuments were often used to promote an ideology known as the "Lost Cause," which claimed that the Confederacy had been established to defend states' rights and that slavery was not the principal cause of the Civil War. Residents of Oxford and Lafayette County dedicated this statue, approved by the university, in 1906. Although the monument was created to honor the sacrifice of local Confederate soldiers, it must also remind us that the defeat of the Confederacy actually meant freedom for millions of people. On the evening of September 30, 1962, this statue was a rallying point for opponents of integration.

This historic statue is a reminder of the university's divisive past. Today, the University of Mississippi draws from that past a continuing commitment to open its hallowed halls to all who seek truth, knowledge, and wisdom.[46]

The relationship between the campus's lore and the intentions of the SFA is not lost on Hall:

> Ground [it] in an academic context, rip it out of that hazy, gauzy South. I think it matters that we're here, because what I will say about Mississippi—and I think I can as not a native, but as somebody who's been fooling with this place for a long time now—I think that what's emboldening and inspiring about the place is that there are people who, I'm not even going to try to fancy this up, who know better, and who want to do better.
>
> I think that makes this uniquely a place where change can come from, because when you're dealing with us, and Southern Foodways, and we're saying we're not going to romanticize this, we're not going to sugarcoat that. I think you have to listen in a different way than you would if we were the Foodways program at the University of Indiana. At least I hope.[47]

With this forward-thinking mentality, Hall argues that the SFA is part of a growing community of change agents: "Our intent is really to be honest about, not only the region's past, but what the region is now. Then we bring a little bit about what it can become." For Hall, this potential begins with discussions over the narratives within Southern cultures. When asked what she hopes the SFA will accomplish, she hit on a foundational theme throughout this book, something seen in the soundtracks of Burnett, the songs of the Secret Sisters and Bonnie Montgomery, the production of Jason Weinheimer and Joe Henry, and the work of the other storytellers and cultural tastemakers analyzed.

> I'll tell you a personal story, and it's one that I have heard from other folks. . . . [The] 2003 theme for that year's symposium was the Appalachian South. That's my South, that's the part I grew up in, the mountains in eastern Kentucky. I think, even though I had gone to college, I had gone to law school, I had lived all over the country, I was the mother to two young children, I would say that it was not until that symposium that I understood that I had a culture, and more importantly that I had a culture that people thought something about, and thought was worth celebrating. What we hear over and over from people who become washed in the blood of the SFA is a similar story. A story of really the [work of the] SFA being the moment where they realized that their own culture, their own upbringing, was a thing of value.

One of the SFA's filmmaking partnerships represents a continuation of the spirit of Southern narratives carrying throughout these pages. The creative content studio 1504, started by college friends Nick Michael, Mark Slagle, and Tyler Jones, also embodies the philosophy of interconnected collaboration seen in Burnett's circle. The studio's documentary catalogue has traveled the lanes of food, music, and education. Along with a jazz series for NPR, the company has shot music videos for Muscle Shoals–based rock band the Civil Wars, Birmingham, Alabama, band St. Paul and the Broken Bones, Birmingham alt-rock artist Duquette Johnston, folk-pop sister duo Lily and Madeleine, and the Secret Sisters. They also recently documented the making of Donnie Fritts's solo album, chronicling how the Florence, Alabama, songwriter, studio session musician, and Kris Kristofferson's keyboardist was pushed by T Bone, who appears in the documentary, to connect with former Civil Wars front man John Paul White and his Single Lock Records. Teaming up with the Southern Foodways Alliance, the content studio also features stories highlighting the variety of Southern cultures through food. The short film *Thursdays in Hell's Half Acre* profiles Hell's Half Acre, South Carolina, resident Ricky Scott of "Ricky's BBQ," who over his cinder-block-and-metal pit barbecues meat over hickory wood every Thursday the way his family has since they were share-croppers. Similarly, *Muddy Pond* looks at sorghum farmer Mark Guenther's Mennonite-inspired agricultural philosophy in the Muddy Pond community located between Nashville and Knoxville.

Along with other SFA projects, the studio has worked with the Jones Valley Teaching Farm, a Birmingham not-for-profit that partners with local public schools to foster hands-on, experiential nutrition education, and with organizations like End Child Hunger in Alabama. Their first venture into particularly Southern stories came at the 2014 Southern Makers event in Montgomery sponsored by the Alabama Council for the Arts and the tourism department. The Southern Makers website describes the event as "bringing together highly curated, handpicked top talent that 'make' . . . music, designs, buildings, farms, art, food, beer, clothing, soap, coffee, and tea . . . ranging from experts in architecture to art, fashion, food, repurposing and everything in between." Interestingly, beyond showcasing Alabama tastemakers, the event seeks to bring people together to "network, learn, inspire and cultivate the southern soul that keeps Alabama and southern makers unique and special."[48] One of the production company's three principals, Tyler Jones, recalls the SFA, fashion designers Billy Reid and Natalie Chanin and folk-artist Butch Anthony as participants. He was inspired by the various makers' resourcefulness, noting how many artists made use of what was around them, including a basket maker weaving intricate patterns with kudzu vines, along with a strong spirit of adaptability, ingenuity, and creative support of others in the community.[49] According to Jones, the characteristic that best defines the community is an "openness for collaboration across mediums," which he saw modeled in the Florence–Muscle Shoals area with what Jones calls the "core group": Billy Reid, Natalie Chanin, photographer Robert Rausch, designer Audwin McGee, and civil rights photographer Charles Moore. They would go have dinner together out in the middle of a field, drawing on each other for inspiration and collaboration. Jones sees that in SFA and their events and other Southern cultural leaders, saying there is "a lot of cross-pollination that happens. I can see things in Natalie Chanin's work that ends up in Butch Anthony's work which then inspires the Secret Sisters to write a song."

Feeding off the spirit of creation and connectivity, and seeing the potential for a form of activism, Jones maintains that as a content studio, 1504 wanted to do more than just profile regional *distinctions*, instead looking for opportunities within the jobs they're hired for to pursue "issue-oriented work." Using their unique skills and partnerships with organizations like Jones Valley and SFA, they sought to be intentional about inclusivity and "giving the microphone" to other people, allowing for "people and perspectives that don't get shared often." On assignment for Jones Valley, Jones recalls profiling a fifth-grade student living in a Birmingham housing project whose family emigrated from West Africa. After dinner one night, the family observed the Muslim call to prayer spiritual discipline. Taken aback by his own shock, he admitted, "It was the farthest away I have ever felt from home in my own city. It was a broader picture of diversity than I was aware of, which is kind of sad." Living most of his life in the South, it was "a reminder that we so rarely get out of our network, out of groups of people who are like us, talk like us, and worship like us." Jones and 1504 are committed to "exploring similar stories and trends in the Southeast," unpacking an "evolving region" that defies "fried chicken" stereotypes, determined to complicate the notion of what it means to be "Southern."

Like Nathan Howdeshell, Bonnie Montgomery, Jason Weinheimer, Joe Henry, and many others, growing up, Jones didn't see the value in his hometown, describing himself as having the "classic prodigal son" return to the South. A Florence, Alabama, native, he moved to Los Angeles at age eighteen, "determined to go to film school and never come back to the South." Perceiving his Southern context to be "closed-minded," he soon realized that though L.A. afforded unlimited outlets for stories, he felt it lacked Alabama's "raw story resources." Influenced by men like Billy Reid and Charles Moore, who were "intentional about being in the South and fighting the good fight for it," Jones argues that such "inspirations made me totally fall in love with it and want to be an ambassador for it." After moving from L.A. to Arkansas to attend college at a small liberal arts school, Jones earned a master's degree at the University of Alabama, working as a graduate assistant for famed author Rick Bragg and later as lead research assistant on Bragg's Jerry Lee Lewis biography. Jones recalls Bragg often talking about "his people," and he took the opportunity to debate with his mentor: "How do you celebrate the South without exploiting it? . . . How do you call yourself an ambassador for a place without being an activist, with all the injustice that continues to go on?" Wanting to do work that "explores those tensions," his journalistic sensibility of wanting to listen more than speak has inspired Jones and his 1504 collaborators to strive to "let locals speak for themselves about their experiences."

A documentary produced by 1504, *America's Boulevard: A Mural on* MLK, speaks to Jones's intent. The film follows renowned artist Meg Saligman, whose group was commissioned to paint one of the largest murals in the country on the forty-three-thousand-square-foot AT&T building on Martin Luther King Jr. Boulevard in Chattanooga, Tennessee. Saligman's nine-person team's challenge was to reflect the complexities of the neighborhood's racial history and its contemporary redevelopment. Eager for local voices to be heard as they attempted to capture the neighborhood's past, present, and potential future, the team held community meetings for citizen input, piecing together what had happened over the years while providing the community a chance to speak up on the hard issues: racial and socioeconomic injustice, inner-city development, and the toll gentrification can have on those who live there.

Other than taking viewers inside Saligman's art production and philosophy, the film's producers focus on voices from the community. The former East Ninth Street, renamed in 1981, was the center of the local black community. However, in 1957 the city converted traffic from two-way to one-way, "aiding the suburban movement out of downtown," according to Councilman Moses Freeman. Freeman grew up in the area, delivering papers on his bicycle as a youth. Later, after hearing King speak in Nashville, he was inspired to join marches and sit-ins, twice being arrested. In the film, the elder statesman talks about the area's transition. The traffic, combined with the tearing down of the Liberty Theatre, a gathering spot for cultural life, and the construction of AT&T's giant blank concrete structure had the effect of creating "a solid Berlin Wall," isolating the MLK Boulevard neighborhood. These problems were compounded by buildings left abandoned and a rise in crime. Despite the neighborhood's troubled past, Saligman found within the residents great pride in the community's history and hope for the future. She recalled one woman stating, "We were proud of our businesses, we had a good life, and we want people to know that." In that spirit, the artists and filmmakers were charged with reflecting a community back to itself, honoring its experiences and showcasing its voices without whitewashing the past or the complex negotiations between the need for change and the "cultural vacuum" effect of gentrification. Saligman's team highlighted the theme of "reclaiming the past," addressing through art the community's "shared history" while remaining "careful not to project on the community." She spoke of the importance of "being true to what you find" and how it would have been "irresponsible to use the building without addressing what has happened on that street."

Part of the activist spirit of the art project included using models for the mural from the community and inviting locals in for paint-by-number painting sessions, wherein residents would paint on canvases that Saligman's team would later install. One of the models the filmmakers spotlighted was twenty-five-year-old Trell Davenport, who spoke of trying to "make the right choices" and of avoiding prison and going back to college: "I know I can finish. I don't want to be stuck in the same place forever," he admits.

In some community members' responses, the potential for art to begin neglected conversations, reflect a community back to itself and to others, and address the complexities of cultures and their past, present, and future is represented. Moses Freeman, commenting on the cultural potential of the mural's narrative, believes that "the legacy will be a symbol of hope, but it will also be a connectivity of this community to the total community . . . [and] more than that, the reconciliation is person-to-person. People will begin to say, 'they look different, they are human . . . that's not what I thought of black people, they don't look frightening up there.'" Telaine Nicholson, owner of the Wafflez Factory," a breakfast café adjacent to the mural, remembers her dad forbidding her to go down to the boulevard as a youth for fear of trouble. Yet, with her business in the community as a hopeful symbol, she can see the mural from her restaurant, with its interracial and intergenerational message. Nicholson proudly relates her adolescent daughter's take on the mural: "That's community coming together."

Saligman's art intentionally strives for "interventions." She wonders whether art "can make someone stop in their grind, in their daily routine, and wonder, question perhaps." For her, the tangible heritage begs questions for the present: "What do we want to preserve in our collective memories? How can we come down MLK Boulevard and feel the heritage of that street [and] at the same time the vibrancy of the future?" Forty thousand square feet of dialogue with models from the community past and present—a young Moses Freeman delivering papers on his bicycle and Trell reading a book—alongside images like somersaulters symbolizing a community turning over, and of past and present people dancing, leads viewers to ask "how does it change, evolve, reinvent or reclaim itself?" Saligman, and the voices the 1504 filmmakers choose to represent the community, clearly see the art as tangible heritage activism. The artist admits that the line "we will not be satisfied until. . ." from one of King's speeches, referencing Chattanooga's Lookout Mountain, inspired the work: "Things are not fully resolved, there is still work to be done on this block, in this neighborhood, in this city, in this country."⁵⁰

As the filmmakers, Jones and company are charged with crafting a narrative that is representative of the people involved while capturing the nuances and complexities of the issues at play. "Early on in our research phase, we were trying to figure out how to frame what was at stake in this story," Jones admits. "We started by reading the mural as a form of memory work. If forgetting the past is our natural mode, then what's at stake when a community actively remembers? That's where it gets complex and difficult to treat in a short film. One can look at the gentrification of public memory. Also, whose memories do we elevate? Who has the right to elevate them? To what extent are memories based on historic reality, anyway?"⁵¹

Regardless of the artistic medium—music, material culture, journalism, documentary, or any artistic outlet such as the MLK Boulevard mural—when certain memories, certain ways of engaging history with the present and future, become a norm, they have the power to fuel identity construction both at the individual and communal levels, where social activism and public policy begin to act and react accordingly. The South historically is the perfect example, where whitewashed history regarding the Civil War and Reconstruction cemented into cultural norms that justified public policy. That history carries forward into the Jim Crow South and the subsequent rise of political and social forces that helped create the current cultural environment, not unlike what is happening with Chattanooga's MLK Boulevard. Artistic mediums have the potential to tell stories that touch upon the political and cultural dynamics that truly create such circumstances, addressing, for example, the complexities of systemic racism in housing markets, lending practices, and modern-day segregated schooling systems, the effects of which are joblessness, poverty, and drugs. Art that addresses the South's past with the purpose of using those narratives to change the present carries the great potential to help us better understand all those political and cultural forces that collided throughout the South to create the all-too-common scenario on display in the film. Furthermore, cultural symbols carry enough potential to serve as catalysts for retelling history in more nuanced ways—thereby forming new cultural identities that can spark citizens' inquiries into what it means to be a Southerner and what the heritage of a place connotes—to create an interest in activism. Hopefully, politicians listen and public policy begins to reflect the change the community wishes to see. In this way, popular culture mediums, academic outlets, and artistic presentation all carry the power to influence and build on memory, identity, activism, and policy.

Jones has personal experience with the tug and pull of contemporary identity, particularly connected to place. While growing up in Florence, he always looked down on his current hometown of Birmingham: "It was the place we stopped in to use the bathroom on the way to the beach." When he moved there, he noted how many longtime residents carried a "fatalistic" mentality toward the city due to the "national shame" from the civil rights movement association. As somewhat of an outsider to the city, Jones felt attracted to the resistant narrative—notwithstanding the narrative of atrocities, with its symbols and historical figures like Bull Connor—wherein local activists "strategically and creatively" changed the world. He felt a pride about that narrative, yet he maintains that it's difficult for a middle-class white kid from Florence to say he's proud of Birmingham's civil rights heritage and to argue that we should celebrate its legacy more. In what Drive-By Truckers front man Patterson Hood calls "the duality of the Southern thing," the tension between pride, disgust, and respect when it comes to remembering and crafting narratives permeates public spaces. "It's complicated to sort through all that," Jones confesses. There is "a heritage there," he maintains, "a balance. How do you represent the past and learn from it and not forget it?"⁵² Jones cites Montgomery-based lawyer Bryan Stevenson as an example of the kind of progressive heritage work in which 1504 aims to participate. Stevenson started the Equal Justice Initiative to "litigate on behalf of condemned prisoners, juvenile offenders, people wrongly convicted or charged with violent crimes, poor people denied effective representation, and others whose trials are marked by racial bias or prosecutorial misconduct. EJI works with communities that have been marginalized by poverty and discouraged by unequal treatment."⁵³ In addition to its legal, policy, and advocacy work, the initiative has begun a project to recognize lynching sites in the South with memorials and markers. Jones partnered with EJI, documenting volunteers who are going out and gathering soil from the over three hundred lynching sites in Alabama between 1870 and 1945. Each canister is labeled with a victim's name on it, to be housed at the National Memorial for Peace and Justice in Montgomery, Alabama, a museum honoring the victims of the terrorism that was slavery and lynchings. Jones was flabbergasted by the cockeyed nature of the state's historical narratives: "There were over two hundred monuments to the Confederacy in Montgomery but none about slavery. That's mind-blowing. You can't go anywhere in Europe without seeing a marker to World War II and what happened to Jewish families."⁵⁴ What Jones terms "public memory work" complements the conversation previous chapters have addressed, arguing that popular-culture films like *O Brother, Where Art Thou?* and *Cold Mountain*, albums like *Divided and United: The Songs of the Civil War*, or film performances like Chris Thomas King's singing "Hard Times Killing Floor Blues" and productions like Dust-to-Digital's *Parchman Farm: Photographs and Field Recordings: 1947–1952*, can all, in their own small ways, contribute to complicating the unbalanced historical narratives and misguided identities often associated with heritage, history, and the South.

Furthermore, Jones and 1504 are interested in complicating the oversimplified and commodified notion of a "New South." He uses his own experience in Birmingham and with Bragg as an example.

Birmingham was not an antebellum city. It was an industrial town. And after the Civil War, all these men came together to create this new city, eager to rebrand it and the South. They called Birmingham "the New South." There are these great old posters advertising "the New South." [Jones is quick to note that this impulse has never really gone out of fashion, with many groups now recycling this idea.] The reality is, the ideas of old South and new South are fluid. There's a need to push back against the arrival of the new way it's going to be, because it's just going to change again. . . . The church building where my wife and I go to church is a hundred-year-old building built as a white Methodist church. . . . All the white people move away in the 1950s, and it becomes a Black Baptist church. There probably wasn't a white member there for fifty years. That church died off, basically consolidated, the building was left vacant, and now it's basically a millennial community church, probably 90 percent white. Over a hundred-year span, the building represents three different cultures, three different Souths, and who knows what will be next.

Jones further recalls asking his mentor Rick Bragg whether "the South is enough of a distinct thing to be a useful concept? . . . Does the South mean anything anymore?" Implied in the conversation are the negotiations argued throughout this book regarding the complexities of how labels, abstract language, artificial boundaries, trite public symbols, and stereotypes can be reacted against and complicated using artistic tools. Talking about the notion of "the South" over bad Chinese food, Bragg quoted the artist George Rodrigue from New Iberia, Louisiana, famous for his Blue Dog paintings, who Jones called "the Southern Andy Warhol." Responding to Cajun culture becoming "a thing," Rodrigue said, "By the time a culture is discovered, it's already dead." Rodrigue's point is valid, yet I take issue with the artist's finality. I would argue that the culture is not dead but has rather evolved, that it may not be the same as it was, but it has not necessarily lost its properties, its unique characteristics. The difference may seem like a matter of semantics, but the subtle declarative shift is important. Living cultures are never standing still, and Southern cultures and identities are no different. Rodrigue's comment implies the false dichotomies I have argued against throughout. Implicit in the fatalism is that a Southern culture can only be preserved and vibrant in isolation. While an understandable impulse, such logic offers little hope for cultural reinterpretation, collaboration, and creation for a contemporary South that is more interconnected than at any time in history. As such, I read Rodrigue's comment as a warning of the unintended consequences of simplemindedly commodifying vibrant Southern cultures for mass-market consumption.

In a similar vein, Nigerian writer Chimamanda Adichie says, "culture does not make people; people make culture."[55] As with Rodrigue, I agree with

Adichie's premise, that at its root people make willful decisions that contribute to culture-making. But it's also not that simple, particularly when traditions and time have codified cultural norms into systemic, faceless, so-called truths. That's why artistic mediums are increasingly important for raising awareness. If traditions can potentially create a thoughtless, deterministic identity construction, popular culture mediums can simultaneously attempt to complicate notions of "tradition" and "heritage" while seeking to purposefully confound the questions Jones, along with the Secret Sisters, Bonnie Montgomery, Jason Weinheimer, Lance Ledbetter, and others probe in their various artistic outlets. All such art can, therefore, become in some sense a form of activism. Purposeful art is not value-neutral. As such, Burnett's soundtracks, artistic productions, and broad community can represent as much what we look *at* as what we look or listen *through*, the lenses that frame how individuals, communities, and groups perceive their identities and historical realities, fueling the impulse to preserve as much as create, question as much as understand. The work is as much intangible as it is tangible, expressing a set of values or assumptions fueled by coded symbols inherently known, yet not necessarily categorized or spoken.

It is not surprising that both Jones and Melissa Hall speak about the abstract nature of "heritage" and "tradition," and particularly the need to complicate those words regarding the South. It's a message pulsating throughout the music referred to within these pages. Regarding "heritage," a search on Google reinforces the narrative cultural conundrum. The first result presents the Heritage Foundation—a controversial neoconservative Washington, DC, think tank. The search phrase "heritage, not hate" returns 27.3 million hits. Whether as fuel for political ideology or an argument for the interpretation of the Confederate flag in contemporary culture, these two results demonstrate that heritage is a loaded word, wholly dependent on context and easily co-opted for a particular argument. *Merriam Webster* defines "heritage" as "the traditions, achievements, beliefs, etc., that are part of the history of a group or nation." While this sets the parameters well, heritage and tradition vary depending on the group interpreting the beliefs, meaning that it remains possible for several different narratives to exist for the same tradition, all claiming to represent that tradition's heritage.

Furthermore, as history carries intonations of emotion, identity, and political efficacy, the nuanced complexities of heritage are often abandoned for trite sound-bites and exaggerated platitudes. Thus, multiple and conflicting narratives embedded within heritage become secondary to preserving ideals, often wrongfully excluding competing realities. Consequently, the notions of heritage and tradition can be used for ill—to pervert history, isolate social classes and races, and promote wrongheaded stereotypes. As such, any cultural representation of the contemporary American South must be grounded in its contested historical past. In the South, heritage and tradition were used to ostracize African Americans, promote white supremacy, and purposefully rewrite history. In contrast, studying the complex nuances of a culture's traditions can produce unfiltered narratives, even in film soundtracks and cover albums, for the progress of a society as it attempts to understand where it has been and where it is going. As Jones's look at his Birmingham hometown shows, a city's Civil War exhibits and civil rights monuments—a seemingly awkward juxtaposition—can speak to a progressive story of both a hurtful past and a hopeful future. Similarly, a pickup truck proudly displaying Confederate flags from homemade poles attached to the truck's bed becomes a tangible modern manifestation of a century-old dispute. As the world becomes more globalized and many parts of America grow increasingly homogenized, artistic explorations of tradition become a necessary vehicle by which to explore how the South is similar to and different from the rest of the country and to further investigate the region's cultural heritage.

At their core, the artistically interdisciplinary productions I have looked at, including film, music, art, and journalism, are concerned with answering universal philosophical worldview questions, grounded in Southern terms: Where did we come from, and what have we accomplished? Who are we? What is our relationship to each other and to the community? What does the future hold? These questions lend weight to the present and future. Grafted into these investigations are the traditions and values worth preserving, along with slippery notions of communal and individual identity. At their best, popular artistic explorations can unpack a living history, interpreting the past for the present and offering advice for the future. The interdependence of the past, present, and future displays a kaleidoscopic image of historical reality and relevance. Historian Charles Reagan Wilson argues that popular culture's broad audience appeal "contrast[s] with folklife and folk culture, which tends to be rooted in communities and built around social groups." He maintains that "in the South, pop culture is negotiated between tradition and modernity. It often draws from folklore, from folk symbols and rituals. But it is not so much concerned with authenticity as it is with reproducing these symbols for broad audiences."[56]

I would extend this one step. Yes, pop culture "reproduces traditional symbols" and is on the surface the opposite of so-called folk culture, but it has the potential to be a means of educating and encouraging participation. With its access to large numbers of people it can provoke a regeneration of traditional culture and instigate conversations regarding customs and folk-life that move beyond apologia or nostalgia to embrace the complexities of cultural experiences. In an increasingly homogenized culture, popular artistic mediums can spark an interest in cultural contexts, thereby creating social groups with similar interests on a broader scale. Herein rests the potential benefit of the Burnett-inspired community. Burnett's community pushes to make cultural heritage accessible and utilitarian, not a collection of cultural artifacts to be hidden away for a limited number of experts to handle. Making art that is inspired by historic contexts and is serviceable for a broad audience can help consumers explore both historic and contemporary cultural issues, giving the art a purpose and vitality greater than preservation alone can afford.

In this spirit, the artists on whom I have focused, with Burnett as exemplar, are translators of a Southern culture filled with symbols, traditions, values, and ways of life often taken for granted, misunderstood, or manipulated. The artistic translation and transference among the Southern-inspired cultural taste-makers aim to show why food, colloquial language, music, or rituals matter. Thus, the artistic community helps translate the nuanced complexities of history for those who may not readily see them, and strives to wrestle them away from those who seek to misrepresent. It is a mode of storytelling.

The complexities of contemporary Southern culture will continue to play out for good and ill in film, television, literature, tourism, magazines, and a host of other mediums. The debates regarding whether Southern music still inspires as it once did, and whether there is such a thing as regionalism in a world that has instant access to all regions with the swipe of a finger and the click of a mouse, will persist. As Southern demographics continue to shift and the historic racial and class divides splinter amidst migration patterns and rising economic centers, reading heritage and tradition through the lens of popular culture can provide pertinent answers to these questions.

Furthermore, the access to information and the ability of people of all walks of life to broadly participate in such conversations through a host of electronic mediums creates a democratic potential for reaching a wider audience and inviting advice and participation. Of course, such populism opens the opportunity for unintended consequences, as well, as the very democratic nature of the Internet that allows for a variety of voices to be heard and people to be connected also presents opportunities for misinformation and wrongheaded propaganda to disseminate with ease.

The two characteristics that unite all the artists portrayed here are a desire to engage the Southern contexts of the past, without trivializing them, along with the impulse to create art that is useful for the present. They are interested in complicating notions of tradition, heritage, and what it means to be a Southerner. There is a resistant desire to complicate Southern heritage as the plurality it has always been. It's no surprise that most of the artists here have experienced "prodigal son" moments, leaving the South of their youth only to return fully invested later, on reclamation missions. These artists use the tools of popular culture and all kinds of artistic venues and formats to communicate their ethic and exchange with other like-minded Southerners' principles and values across a spectrum of cultures. This study never set out to make a definitive claim regarding the South or Southerners. Instead, it offers a look at a particular community and one specific cultural tastemaker within the broad field of Southern cultures and the multiple incarnations of Southern identities. Furthermore, this was never intended to be an exhaustive look at Burnett's total cultural imprint. Such a study would take a much closer look at his navigation of the music business, commercialism, archival technology, and technical recording philosophies, among other topics. It is also not meant to idolize Burnett's role in this broad conversation. He can certainly come across at times as an alarmist, dystopian Luddite or pretentious audiophile. For example, he argues that our ability to "control the machines" will become a greater test than terrorism or climate change: "The machines tell us what music we're going to like. What girl we're going to go out with. If they can tell us that, they can tell us what God to worship and when to lay down and die."[57]

Burnett's consistent philosophy is both earnest and long-lasting and his influence is without question. Remarking on Burnett's inspiration for himself personally and 1504 collectively, Jones says,

> T Bone was always this Wizard of Oz figure for us. All roads seemed to lead to him, and we were fascinated to know what was really behind the curtain (or the sunglasses). Our friends and family were also becoming part of his circle: The

Civil Wars, The Secret Sisters, and even my stepmom who collaborated with him on the *Nashville* show. So he was definitely influencing us indirectly as this mythical figure we tried to analyze.

Once we finally were able to sit down with him and film an interview (for the Donnie Fritts film), the persona was replaced by a real person with real ideas. It's always strange to meet so-called "living legends," and I usually end up in a mental loop over debunking/validating the experience. Perhaps I'm still there with T Bone.

If I had to extract one aspect of T Bone's influence that 1504 still relies on, it would probably be the attempt to pursue creative method over medium. His vision, which drives his interdisciplinary approach and collaborations, is remarkable to me personally, and I definitely study that.[58]

Early on in the production company's infancy, Jones recalls a brainstorming session regarding what they hoped 1504 could accomplish. He admits looking to Burnett for inspiration, finding it striking how T Bone "gets to hide, reappear at will, collaborate, connect, weave, be macro, be micro. . . . He puts the craft first and thus never has to be solely dependent on marketing himself as a brand." He remembers turning the producer's name into a verb: to "T Bone" is "to dream out loud in a thrusting, forceful manner, often in stream of consciousness."[59]

All the narratives addressed throughout this study rest within or evoke Southern cultures particularly, participating in a longstanding tradition of Southern cultural analysis. William Faulkner is often recognized as the greatest Southern world-builder and most emblematic of the Southern Renascence. Through his modernist stream-of-consciousness writing Faulkner created the fictional Yoknapatawpha County from scratch—tracing its narratives from Native Americans and swamp lands through the Antebellum, Civil War, Reconstruction, and Jim Crow eras, from agrarianism to modernism, giving readers familial symbols representing the best and worst of the South's heritage: McCaslin, Compson, Sartoris, Sutpen, and Snopes. Faulkner's world-building sought to address the complex relationship between the South's past, present, and future, the degeneration of the modern world's obsession with consumption, and the emptiness and perversions of the Lost Cause ideals. Yet, the author felt all too well the complex tension between pride and shame. Though Faulkner is without peer, the Burnett-inspired present movement attempts to address similar aspects of the contemporary Southern condition. When someone asks, "What's your favorite Faulkner story?"—the joke goes—you say,

"There's only one." Most of Faulkner's novels and short stories exist separately but as part of his one story: the evolution of his creation. For Burnett, the sentiment holds true in broad comparison. Burnett's body of work, his solo career, soundtracks, and artistic productions should be read as a whole, as a cumulative treatise on how the South's past musical contexts can inform its present and how such productions can indicate a philosophy for complicating what it means to be Southern, wrestling oversimplified declarations from other popular culture mediums with a long history of relying on trite symbols and clichés.

The MLK Boulevard mural is a symbol of the Southern renaissance community's values: artistic creation buoyed by representing diverse perspectives. Whether through a mural, film, album, or novel, whether of folk, popular, or scholarly intent, the community values the creation of cultural spaces that help people better understand the virtue in complicating tired stereotypes while leading the conversations regarding where we have been, where we are, and where we're going. These case studies aim to explore a more diverse, complicated, and unedited South, with a dignity and soul all its own, a South that doesn't easily rest in preconceived categories or reality-television plot lines. The subjects are skeptical of anyone defining what the South is, of conclusions drawn: there is a sense that if you can put it into words, it's not really the South; it's a distortion of the truth, like shadows in Plato's cave. It will be unsurprising to readers that many established manifestations of Southern identity have graced these pages, yet alongside them are a host of contemporary cultural creators advocating for this fluid region. Johnny Cash, Jimmie Rodgers, and Robert Johnson have shared the bill with Ralph Stanley, Lil Wayne, and Chris Stapleton, making an argument that Burnett's soundtracks lay out clearly: that the South's songs are sung by children of roots music, a family tree connecting Robert Johnson and Mahalia Jackson to Elvis Presley, and Tina Turner to André 3000. The intermingling of genres throughout argues that black and white culture have interweaved and overlapped for generations, the latter owing a great debt to the former, so that on any trip to the South now one could just as easily encounter the trance-inducing throbs of hip-hop bass, the whines of steel guitars, and the jangles of mountain music as one could hear cicadas on a summer night. We have further explored what it means to be producers and artists within this scene, for the most part allowing them to speak for themselves regarding their desire for contemporary Southerners to resist the labels so often associated with the region and their firm commitment to carving out their Southern identities while addressing the complexities of the past with the intricacies of an ever-expanding region in the present.

In these pages a multiracial cultural stew of artists have mingled, offering their art and insight from varying perspectives: gay and straight, male and female, old and young, drunks and teetotalers, Republicans and yellow-dog Democrats—a gene-spliced collage of embraced contradictions. The study has covered a vast region—from Fort Worth, Texas, to the Appalachian Mountains, across mountain ranges, bayou swamps, and muddy rivers snaking through Delta farmland and Alabama hills. And it's extended beyond the region, as the Southern diaspora spreads around the world, from Portland, Oregon, to Paris, France, and everywhere in between. As with 1504's desire to make films that "let everybody have a seat at the table," Burnett's body of work seeks to blend and recreate genres and cultures for a new contemporary audience.[60] As Rodrigue's quote reminds us, being able to put a finger on a cultural moment means it's already started becoming something else, anyway.

Linking one Renascence to a renaissance decades apart should not imply that the negotiations over Southern cultures and identities haven't produced an ongoing and vibrant debate for decades. Great minds like C. Vann Woodward, Louis Rubin, John Egerton, John Shelton Reed, William Ferris, and Charles Reagan Wilson, authors like Eudora Welty, Walker Percy, Flannery O'Connor, Maya Angelou, Bobbie Ann Mason, Alice Walker, and Dorothy Allison, photographers like Gordon Parks, William Christenberry, and William Eggleston, artists like Carroll Cloar and Bo Bartlett, and a host of musicians, artists, filmmakers, scholars, universities, and publications have never quit exploring the tensions inherent within this region. Furthermore, there are demographics that are not explored here in depth that are clearly worth consideration: as one instance, second-generation immigrants and their experiences, fusing familial cultural heritage with Southern mores, striving to create an eclectic identity inspired by both. This study presents Burnett's work as part of a long conversation—taking place in a broad range of topical areas and mediums like food, tourism, sports, politics, journalism, film, and following a host of other avenues—that is providing a jolt of energy in the twenty-first century by using the popular-culture tools available to argue for artistry, history, storytelling, and progress, evoking the cultural past and present afforded by Southern symbols, places, and people. The community's contrarianism is fueled by an understanding that Southern culture is not dormant. Burnett's work testifies that, despite its flaws, past and present, the region boasts a cultural excitement, with a vibrant, diverse, and critical artistic spirit across many mediums. As such, Burnett is the popular culture superego of the American South, forming the moral standards and conscience by which to filter our collective criticisms, prohibitions, and inhibitions. His ideals represent the collective's aspirations as it questions what in Southern traditions and cultures is worth retaining, what is worth rejecting, and what is worth transforming.

NOTES

THE TASTEMAKER
T BONE BURNETT AND SOUTHERN CULTURES

1. Richard H. King, *A Southern Renaissance: The Cultural Awakening of the American South, 1930–1955* (New York: Oxford University Press, 1980), 7.

2. Esteemed critic, writer, and professor Louis Rubin preferred the spelling "renascence" as a statement against a lack of prior cultural output. A renaissance was a rebirth of something. Rubin felt the South lacked such a momentous cultural moment to be recovered.

3. Houston Baker Jr., "Critical Memory and the Black Public Sphere," in *Cultural Memory and the Construction of Identity*, ed. Dan Ben-Amos and Liliane Weissberg (Detroit, MI: Wayne State University Press, 1999), 264.

4. Ronald D. Cohen, *Folk Music: The Basics* (New York: Routledge, 2006), 182.

5. Barry Mazor, *Ralph Peer and the Making of Popular Roots Music* (Chicago: Chicago Review Press, 2015), 1.

6. Quoted ibid.

7. Ryan Reed, "Jack White, T Bone Burnett to Produce 'American Epic' Music Documentary," *Rolling Stone*, April 8, 2015, accessed June 15, 2015, http://www.rolling stone.com/music/news/jack-white-t-bone-burnett-to-produce-american-epic -music-documentary-20150408.

8. Brian Hiatt, "Mumford and Sons: Rattle and Strum: How Four Brits Turned Old-Timey Roots Music into the Future of Rock," *Rolling Stone*, March 28, 2013, https://www.rollingstone.com/music/music-news/mumford-sons-rattle-and -strum-78883/. Several articles have been helpful in examining *O Brother*'s cultural imprint and how the music functions within the film's narrative: Hugh Ruppersburg, "'Oh, So Many Startlements. . .': History, Race, and Myth in *O Brother, Where Art Thou?*," *Southern Cultures* 9, no. 4 (Winter 2003): 5–26; Sean Chadwell, "Inventing That 'Old-Timey' Style: Southern Authenticity in *O Brother, Where Art Thou?*," *Journal of Popular Film and Television* 32, no. 1 (2004): 3–9; Richard Middleton, "O Brother, Let's Go Down Home: Loss, Nostalgia and the Blues," *Popular Music* 26, no. 1 (January 2007): 47–64; Andrew B. Leiter, ed., *Southerners on Film: Essays on Hollywood Portrayals since the 1970s* (Jefferson, NC: McFarland, 2011); and Margaret

M. Toscano, "Homer Meets the Coen Brothers: Memory as Artistic Pastiche in *O Brother, Where Art Thou?*" *Film and History* 39, no. 2 (Fall 2009): 49–62.

9. Richie Unterberger, *Turn! Turn! Turn! The '60s Folk-Rock Revolution* (San Francisco: Backbeat Books, 2002).

10. Examples of scholarship from the so-called folk "purists" and the debate regarding the film and soundtrack will be discussed more specifically in Chapters 1 and 2.

CHAPTER 1
HISTORY, IRONY, AND CULTURAL CONDUIT

1. Joel Coen and Ethan Coen, dirs., *O Brother, Where Art Thou?*, screenplay by Ethan Coen and Joel Coen (2000; Burbank, CA: Touchstone *Home Entertainment*, 2001), 7:58–8:13.

2. Ibid., 17:37.

3. Adam Gold, "Q&A: T Bone Burnett on 'Nashville,' Elton John's Comeback and Retiring as a Producer," *Rolling Stone*, December 18, 2012, accessed October 14, 2015, http://www.rollingstone.com/music/news/q-a-t-bone-burnett-on-nashville-elton -johns-comeback-and-retiring-as-a-producer-20121218.

4. Hugh Ruppersburg, "'Oh, So Many Startlements. . .': History, Race, and Myth in *O Brother, Where Art Thou?*" *Southern Cultures* 9, no. 4 (Winter 2003): 12.

5. J. Hoberman, "100 Years of Solitude," *Village Voice*, December 19, 2000, accessed April 25, 2014, http://www.villagevoice.com/2000-12-19/film/100-years-of-solitude/2/.

6. Charles Taylor, "*O Brother, Where Art Thou?*," *Salon.com*, December 22, 2000, quoted in Andrew B. Leiter, "'That Old-Timey Music': Nostalgia and the Southern Tradition in *O Brother, Where Art Thou?*," in *Southerners on Film*, ed. Andrew B. Leiter (Jefferson, North Carolina: McFarland & Company Inc., Publishers, 2011), 66.

7. Owen Gleiberman, "*O Brother, Where Art Thou?*," *Entertainment Weekly*, January, 12, 2001, accessed April 25, 2014, http://www.ew.com/ew/article/0,,279348,00 .html.

8. Rene Rodriguez, "*O Brother, Where Art Thou? Reviews*," *Rotten Tomatoes*, accessed April 25, 2014, http://www.rottentomatoes.com/m/o_brother_where_art _thou/reviews/#type=top_critics.

9. Jonathan Rosenbaum, "*O Brother, Where Art Thou?*" *Chicago Reader*, accessed April 25, 2014, http://www.chicagoreader.com/chicago/o-brother-where-art-thou /Film?oid=1050960.

10. *Hollywood Reporter*, "*O Brother, Where Art Thou? Reviews*," *Rotten Tomatoes*, accessed April 25, 2014, http://www.rottentomatoes.com/m/o_brother_where_art _thou/reviews/#type=top_critics.

11. Stephen Hunter, "'O Brother': Ulysses On a Wacky Romp through the South,"

Washingtonpost.com, December 29, 2000, accessed April 25, 2014, http://www
.washingtonpost.com/wp-srv/entertainment/movies/reviews
/obrotherwhereartthouhunter.htm.

12. Michael Wilmington, "*O Brother, Where Art Thou?* Reviews," *Rotten Tomatoes*,
accessed April 25, 2014, http://www.rottentomatoes.com/m/o_brother_where_art
_thou/reviews/#type=top_critics.

13. A. O. Scott, "Hail, Ulysses, Escaped Convict," *NYTimes.com*, December 22,
2000, accessed April 25, 2014, http://www.nytimes.com/2000/12/22/movies/film
-review-hail-ulysses-escaped-convict.html.

14. Jay Carr, "*O Brother, Where Art Thou?* Reviews," *Rotten Tomatoes*, accessed
April 25, 2014, http://www.rottentomatoes.com/m/o_brother_where_art_thou
/reviews/#type=top_critics.

15. Roger Ebert, "*O Brother, Where Art Thou?*," *RogerEbert.com*, December 29,
2000, accessed April 25, 2014, http://www.rogerebert.com/reviews/o-brother-where
-art-thou-2000.

16. "T-Bone Burnett on 10 Years of '*O Brother, Where Art Thou?*,'" NPR, August 23,
2011, accessed May 1, 2014, http://www.npr.org/2011/08/23/139880668
/t-bone-burnett-on-10-years-of-o-brother-where-art-thou.

17. Benjamin Filene, *Romancing the Folk: Public Memory and American Roots
Music* (Chapel Hill: University of North Carolina Press, 2000), 34.

18. Ronald D. Cohen, *Folk Music: The Basics* (New York: Routledge, 2006), 31.

19. "T-Bone Burnett on 10 Years of '*O Brother*,'" NPR, 19:53–20:17.

20. Filene, *Romancing the Folk*, 46, 57.

21. Ronald D. Cohen, *Folk Music*, 52.

22. Coen and Coen, *O Brother, Where Art Thou?*, 38:52–39:39.

23. Andrew B. Leiter, "'That Old-Timey Music': Nostalgia and the Southern
Tradition in *O Brother, Where Art Thou?*," in Leiter, ed., *Southerners on Film*, 68–69.

24. Ibid., 63.

25. Christopher J. Smith, "Papa Legba and the Liminal Spaces of the Blues: Roots
Music in Deep South Film," in *American Cinema and the Southern Imaginary*, ed.
Deborah E. Barker and Kathryn McKee (Athens: University of Georgia Press, 2011),
329–30.

26. Sean Chadwell, "Inventing That 'Old-Timey' Style: Southern Authenticity in
O Brother, Where Art Thou?," *Journal of Popular Film and Television* 32, no. 1 (2004):
3–4.

27. Ibid., 5, quoting Julie Koehler, "O Brother, Why Did They Make This Movie?,"
Bluegrass Unlimited 35, no. 11 (May 2001): 14–16.

28. "T-Bone Burnett on 10 Years of '*O Brother*,'" NPR.

29. Margaret M. Toscano, "Homer Meets the Coen Brothers: Memory as Artistic

Pastiche in *O Brother, Where Art Thou?*," *Film and History* 39, no. 2 (Fall 2009): 50–51.

30. Ruppersburg, "'Oh, So Many Startlements,'" 24.

31. Toscano, "Homer Meets the Coen Brothers," 54.

32. Fredric Jameson, "Reification and Utopia in Mass Culture," *Social Text* 1 (Winter 1979), 130–48.

33. Coen and Coen, *O Brother, Where Art Thou?*, 27:48.

34. Ibid., 1:15:00.

35. James C. Cobb, *The Most Southern Place on Earth: The Mississippi Delta and the Roots of Regional Identity* (New York: Oxford University Press, 1992).

36. Bill C. Malone, *Southern Music, American Music* (Lexington: University Press of Kentucky, 1979), 3.

37. Charles Roland, quoted ibid., x.

38. Alan Lomax, *The Land Where the Blues Began* (New York: Pantheon, 1993), 258.

39. Maya Angelou, *I Know Why the Caged Bird Sings* (New York: Random House, 2009), 17–18.

40. Luke 16:19–31 (ESV).

41. Tracy Thompson, *The New Mind of the South* (New York: Simon & Schuster, 2013), 174–75. Thompson's data about the feelings particular races have toward the South is gleaned from John Shelton Reed's famous sociological polls.

42. Ralph Ellison, *Shadow and Act* (New York: Vintage International, 1995), 78.

43. For a thoughtful essay on the role of Lil Wayne's music and his increasingly legendary status in inner-city New Orleans, see David Ramsey, "I Will Forever Remain Faithful," *Oxford American* 62 (Fall 2008), accessed October 24, 2015, http://www.oxfordamerican.org/magazine/item/171-i-will-forever-remain-faithful.

44. Greil Marcus, *Mystery Train: Images of America in Rock 'n' Roll Music*, rev. and exp. ed. (New York: E. P. Dutton, 1982), 38.

45. Bill C. Malone, *Don't Get above Your Raisin': Country Music and the Southern Working Class* (Urbana: University of Illinois Press, 2002), ix.

46. "T-Bone Burnett on 10 Years of '*O Brother*,'" NPR, 20:00–21:35.

47. Malone, *Don't Get above Your Raisin'*, 126.

48. Gold, "Q&A: T Bone," *Rolling Stone*.

49. W. J. Cash, *The Mind of the South* (New York: Alfred A. Knopf, 1941), 31.

50. Ibid., 45.

51. Ibid., 51.

52. Ibid., 50.

53. Tom Moon, "The *O Brother* Revival," *Rolling Stone*, August 30, 2001, 32, quoted in Bradley Hanson, "T Bone Burnett, Roots Music, and the *O Brother* Phenomenon," master's thesis, University of Missouri–Kansas City, 2005, 111.

54. W. J. Cash, *Mind of the South*, 56.

55. Hanson, "T Bone Burnett," 11. Hanson further notes that many of the tour's participants became Christians during this time and that much speculation centered around Burnett's Christian influence on Bob Dylan (11–14). See also Lloyd Sachs's book *T Bone Burnett: A Life in Pursuit* (Austin: University of Texas Press, 2016) for a more thorough biographical exploration.

56. Bob Spitz, *Dylan: A Biography* (New York: McGraw-Hill, 1989), 527, quoted in Hanson, "T Bone Burnett," 12.

57. Sharon Gallagher, "The Alpha Band Interview," *Radix* 7, no. 6 (November–December 1978), 5, quoted in Hanson, "T Bone Burnett," 17.

58. Bill Bentley, "T-Bone Burnett: Born Again But Still Looking," *LA Weekly*, August 8–14, 1980, 37, quoted in Hanson, "T Bone Burnett," 24.

59. Mikal Gilmore, "T-Bone Burnett's Moral Messages," *Rolling Stone*, November 11, 1982, 46, quoted in Hanson, "T Bone Burnett," 24.

60. Thompson, *New Mind of the South*, 121.

61. Ibid., 125.

62. Sharon Gallagher, "Faith and Hope and Rock and Roll: An Interview with T Bone Burnett," *Radix* 21, no. 3 (Summer 1992), 15, quoted in Hanson, "T Bone Burnett," 39–40.

63. Thompson, *New Mind of the South*, 139.

64. Hanson, "T Bone Burnett," 2.

65. Andrew Dansby, "O Brother Shoots to Top," *Rolling Stone*, March 13, 2002, accessed November 9, 2015, http://www.rollingstone.com/music/news/o-brother -shoots-to-top-20020313.

CHAPTER 2

THE MUMFORD MOMENT

1. "*O Brother, Where Art Thou?* User Reviews," *IMDb*, username wilma1913, June 27, 2003, accessed April 25, 2014, http://www.imdb.com/title/tt0190590 /reviews?ref_=tt_urv.

2. Ibid., username leta36, August 25, 2006, accessed April 25, 2014, http:// www.imdb.com/title/tt0190590/reviews?start=20.

3. Ibid., username pinturricchio_juve, May 11, 2013, accessed April 25, 2014, http:// www.imdb.com/title/tt0190590/reviews?start=190.

4. Kenneth Turan, "*O Brother, Where Art Thou?* Reviews," *Rotten Tomatoes*, accessed April 25, 2014, http://www.rottentomatoes .com/m/o_brother_where_art_thou/reviews/#type=top_critics.

5. Alan Lomax, *Selected Writings, 1934–1997*, ed. Ronald D. Cohen (New York: Routledge, 2003), 86.

6. Joel Coen and Ethan Coen, dirs., *O Brother, Where Art Thou?*, screenplay by Ethan Coen and Joel Coen (2000; Burbank, CA: Touchstone Home Entertainment, 2001), 1:38:00.

7. Richard Middleton, "O Brother, Let's Go Down Home: Loss, Nostalgia and the Blues," *Popular Music* 26, no. 1 (January 2007), 48.

8. Mike Price, "T-Bone's Home, Rare and Well Done," *Fort Worth Business Press, June 11, 2004*, quoted in Bradley Hanson, "T Bone Burnett, Roots Music, and the *O Brother* Phenomenon," master's thesis, University of Missouri–Kansas City, 2005, 4–5.

9. "T-Bone Burnett on 10 Years of '*O Brother, Where Art Thou?*,'" NPR, August 23, 2011, accessed May 1, 2014, http://www.npr.org/2011/08/23/139880668/t-bone -burnett-on-10-years-of-o-brother-where-art-thou.

10. Segment beginning at 4:35 in "T-Bone Burnett on World Cafe," NPR, August 23, 2011, accessed October 26, 2015, http://www.npr.org/player/v2/mediaPlayer.html.

11. "T-Bone Burnett on 10 Years of '*O Brother*,'" NPR, 2:00–3:00.

12. Benjamin Filene, "*O Brother*, What Next? Making Sense of the Folk Fad," *Southern Cultures* 10, no. 2 (Summer 2004): 50. Other articles that are in the vein of Filene include Deborah Evans Price, "Bluegrass Music's Civil War: Why New and Heritage Acts Don't See String to String," *Rolling Stone*, October 2, 2014, accessed March 21, 2016, http://www.rollingstone.com/music/features/bluegrass-music-ricky -skaggs-jerry-douglas-old-crow-medicine-show-20141002; and Larry J. Griffin, "Give Me That Old-Time Music . . . Or Not," *Southern Cultures* 12, no. 4 (Winter 2006): 98–107.

13. Filene, "*O Brother*, What Next?," 53–54.

14. Ibid., 57–61.

15. Brian Hiatt, "Mumford and Sons: Rattle and Strum: How Four Brits Turned Old-Timey Roots Music into the Future of Rock," *Rolling Stone*, March 28, 2013, https://www.rollingstone.com/music/music-news/mumford-sons-rattle-and -strum-78883/.

16. Keith Caulfield, "Mumford & Sons' 'Babel' Scores Biggest Debut of Year, Bows at No. 1 on *Billboard* 200 Chart," *Billboard*, October 2, 2012, accessed October 31, 2015, http://www.billboard.com/articles/news/474818 /mumford-sons-babel-scores-biggest-debut-of-year-bows-at-no-1-on-billboard-200.

17. This and following quotes from Hiatt, "Mumford and Sons: Rattle and Strum."

18. Filene, "*O Brother*, What Next?," 64–65.

19. Antoinette Bueno, "Update: Mumford and Sons Banjo Player Joking about Band Break-up," *Entertainment Tonight*, March 27, 2014, accessed October 28, 2015, http://www.etonline.com/music/144844_Mumford_and_Sons_Break_Up_for_Good/.

20. Adam Gold, "Q&A: T Bone Burnett on 'Nashville,' Elton John's Comeback and Retiring as a Producer," *Rolling Stone*, December 18, 2012, accessed December 15, 2015,

http://www.rollingstone.com/music/news/q-a-t-bone-burnett-on-nashville-elton
-johns-comeback-and-retiring-as-a-producer-20121218.

21. Filene, "*O Brother*, What Next?," 52.

22. Bill C. Malone, *Don't Get above Your Raisin': Country Music and the Southern Working Class* (Urbana: University of Illinois Press, 2002), 255.

23. Greil Marcus, *Mystery Train: Images of America in Rock 'n' Roll Music*, rev. and exp. ed. (New York: E. P. Dutton, 1982), 144.

24. Lothar Hönnighausen, "The Southern Heritage and the Semiotics of Consumer Culture," in *The Southern State of Mind*, ed. Jan Nordby Gretlund (Columbia: University of South Carolina Press, 1999), 89.

25. Nicholas Lemann, "The Price of Union: The Undefeatable South," *New Yorker*, November 2, 2015, accessed November 4, 2015, http://www.newyorker.com/magazine /2015/11/02/the-price-of-union.

26. Paul Elie, "How T Bone Burnett Plays Hollywood," *Atlantic*, November 2013, accessed December 2, 2014, http://www.theatlantic.com/magazine/archive/2013/11 /how-t-bone-burnett-plays-hollywood/309521/.

27. Greil Marcus, *The History of Rock 'n' Roll in Ten Songs* (New Haven: Yale University Press, 2014), 225.

28. Filene, "*O Brother*, What Next?," 54–55.

CHAPTER 3

SOUTHERN SPIRIT IN THE T BONE SOUNDTRACK RECIPE

1. Walter Benjamin, "One-Way Street," in *Reflections: Essays, Aphorisms, Autobiographical Writings* (New York: Harcourt Brace Jovanovich, 1978), 65.

2. Andrew B. Leiter, "Introduction," in *Southerners on Film: Essays on Hollywood Portrayals since the 1970s*, ed. Andrew B. Leiter (Jefferson, NC: McFarland, 2011), 9.

3. Jack Temple Kirby, *Media-Made Dixie: The South in the American Imagination* (Athens: University of Georgia Press, 1986), xvi.

4. In his *The Ethnic Southerners* (1976), quoted in James C. Cobb, *Away Down South: A History of Southern Identity* (New York: Oxford University Press, 2005), 338.

5. Leiter, "Introduction," 2–3, 9.

6. Ibid., 2–3. On hillbilly movies released in 1914, Leiter cites J. W. Williamson, *Hillbillyland: What the Movies Did to the Mountains and What the Mountains Did to the Movies* (Chapel Hill: University of North Carolina Press, 1995), 179.

7. Kirby, *Media-Made Dixie*, xviii.

8. James C. Cobb, "'We Ain't White Trash No More': Southern Whites and the Reconstruction of Southern Identity," in *The Southern State of Mind*, ed. Jan Nordby Gretlund (Columbia: University of South Carolina Press, 1999), 135–46.

9. Quoted in Kirby, *Media-Made Dixie*, x.

10. Karen Cox, *Dreaming of Dixie: How the South Was Created in American Popular Culture* (Chapel Hill: University of North Carolina Press, 2011), 73.

11. Benjamin Filene, *Romancing the Folk: Public Memory and American Roots Music* (Chapel Hill: University of North Carolina Press, 2000), 63.

12. The quotes here and immediately below are from John Boorman, dir., *Deliverance*, screenplay by James Dickey and John Boorman (1972; Burbank, CA: Warner Home Video, 2004), DVD, 2:15, 5:15.

13. C. Scott Combs, "The Screen Kallikak: White Trash for White Guilt in Post-Vietnam American Film," in Leiter, ed., *Southerners on Film*, 106–7.

14. Roger Ebert, "Cold Mountain," *RogerEbert.com*, December 24, 2003, accessed November 15, 2013, http://www.rogerebert.com/reviews/cold-mountain-2003. Philip French, "Southern Discomfort," *Guardian*, December 21, 2003, accessed November 15, 2013, https://www.theguardian.com/film/2003/dec/21/philipfrench.

15. David W. Blight, *Race and Reunion: The Civil War in American Memory* (Cambridge, MA: Belknap, 2001), 2.

16. Ruth Landes, "A Northerner Views the South," Ruth Schlossberg Landes Papers, National Anthropological Archives, Smithsonian Institution, Museum Support Center, Suitland, MD. Quoted in Cox, *Dreaming of Dixie*, 1.

17. Cox, *Dreaming of Dixie*, 1.

18. Ibid., 5.

19. Ibid., 83.

20. Ibid., 96.

21. Victor Fleming, *Gone with the Wind*, screenplay by Sidney Howard (1939; Burbank, CA: Turner Entertainment, 2013), 6:14–6:50.

22. Tara McPherson, *Reconstructing Dixie: Race, Gender, and Nostalgia in the Imagined South* (Durham, NC: Duke University Press, 2003), 1.

23. Ibid., 3.

24. Ibid., 11.

25. Ibid., 9, quoting Nell Irvin Painter, "Of *Lily*, Linda Brent, and Freud: A Non-Exceptionalist Approach to Race, Class, and Gender in the Slave South," *Georgia Historical Quarterly* 76, no. 2 (Summer 1992): 106. The bracketed text is McPherson's.

26. Eric Bradner, "Confederate Flag Debate: A State-by-State Roundup," *CNN*, updated June 30, 2015, accessed December 9, 2015, http://www.cnn.com/2015/06/29/politics/confederate-flag-state-roundup/.

27. Kevin M. Levin, "Confederate Monuments Will Come Down in New Orleans," *Atlantic*, December 17, 2015, accessed December 18, 2015, http://www.theatlantic.com/politics/archive/2015/12/new-orleans-remove-confederate-monuments/421059/.

28. Tony Horwitz's book *Confederates in the Attic: Dispatches from the Unfinished Civil War* (New York: Vintage, 1999) is an excellent read on Civil War reenactments across the South in relationship to history and contemporary identity.

29. Kaya Herron's article "The Shame of Robert E. Lee/MLK Day in Arkansas" (*Arkansas Times*, February 11, 2015, accessed December 1, 2015, http://www.arktimes .com/ArkansasBlog/archives/2015/02/11/the-shame-of-robert-e-lee-mlk-day-in -arkansas) looks at the proceedings from an African American woman's perspective. This decision was overturned in 2017 in a bill championed by Republican governor Asa Hutchinson.

30. Blight, *Race and Reunion*, 291.

31. McPherson, *Reconstructing Dixie*, 10.

32. Quoted in Cobb, *Away Down South*, 303.

33. This is not to say, however, that poor whites were not still beneficiaries of the white supremacist culture that defined the South, particularly as Jim Crow laws became the law of the land. Rather, this particular film deals with an aspect of the Civil War and the people living in rural North Carolina mountains.

34. The line is at 1:59 in Anthony Minghella, dir., *Cold Mountain*, written and directed by Anthony Minghella (2003; Burbank, CA: Miramax Films, 2004), DVD.

35. John Cohen, "Introduction," 8, in liner notes to *Back Roads to Cold Mountain*, various artists, Smithsonian Folkways Recordings SFW40149, 2004, http://media .smithsonianfolkways.org/liner_notes/smithsonian_folkways/SFW40149.pdf.

36. Ibid., 7. See also David Roediger's *The Wages of Whiteness: Race and the Making of the American Working Class*, 3rd ed. (New York: Verso, 2007); Eric Lott's *Love and Theft: Blackface Minstrelsy and the American Working Class* (New York: Oxford University Press, 1993); and Lawrence W. Levine's *Highbrow/Lowbrow: The Emergence of Cultural Hierarchy in America* (Cambridge, MA: Harvard University Press, 1990) for a number of ways in which nineteenth-century music is contextualized in particularly racial terms.

37. Bill C. Malone, "Neither Anglo-Saxon nor Celtic: The Music of the Southern Plain Folk," in *Plain Folk of the South Revisited*, ed. Samuel C. Hyde Jr. (Baton Rouge: Louisiana State University Press), 32, 33.

38. Minghella, *Cold Mountain*, 29:59.

39. Great scholarship exists on how the instruments themselves are sources of the wide variety of musical and cultural influences in the South at this time. See Ronald D. Cohen, *Folk Music: The Basics* (New York: Routledge, 2006); and Filene, *Romancing the Folk*.

40. Alan Lomax, *Folk Songs of North America* (New York: Doubleday, 1960), quoted in Malone, "Neither Anglo-Saxon nor Celtic," 32.

41. Ibid.

42. Quoted in David Heddendorf, "Closing the Distance to Cold Mountain," *Southern Review* 36, no. 1 (Winter 2000): 188.

43. Ibid.

44. Steven Knepper, "Do you Know What the *'Hail' You're Talkin' About?*

Deliverance, Stereotypes, and the Lost Voice of the Rural Poor," *James Dickey Newsletter* 25, no. 1 (2008): 27.

45. In William Ferris, *The Storied South: Voices of Writers and Artists* (Chapel Hill: University of North Carolina Press, 2013), 35.

46. A. O. Scott, "A Country Crooner Whose Flight is Now Free Fall," *New York Times*, December 15, 2009, accessed December 1, 2015, http://www.nytimes .com/2009/12/16/movies/16crazy.html?_r=0.

47. At 28:45 in "T Bone Burnett: Zen and the Art of Music," NPR, January 13, 2010, accessed December 1, 2015, https://www.npr.org/templates/story/story .php?storyId=122526723.

48. Ibid., 6:08.

49. Ibid., 22:50.

50. Ibid., 6:21–6:25.

51. Ibid., 22:57–24:48.

52. Scott Cooper, dir., *Crazy Heart*, screenplay by Scott Cooper, based on the novel by Thomas Cobb (2009; Beverly Hills, CA: Fox Searchlight Pictures, 2010), DVD, 24:32.

53. Ibid., 9:58.

54. Ibid., 1:43:00.

55. Paul Elie, "How T Bone Burnett Plays Hollywood," *Atlantic*, November 2013, accessed December 2, 2014, http://www.theatlantic.com/magazine/archive/2013/11 /how-t-bone-burnett-plays-hollywood/309521/.

56. Adam Gold, "Q&A: T Bone Burnett on 'Nashville,' Elton John's Comeback and Retiring as a Producer," *Rolling Stone*, December 18, 2012, accessed October 14, 2015, http://www.rollingstone.com/music/news/q-a-t-bone-burnett-on-nashville-elton -johns-comeback-and-retiring-as-a-producer-20121218.

57. *True Detective: The Complete First Season*, "Bonus Features: A Conversation with Nic Pizzolatto and T Bone Burnett." Burbank, CA: HBO Home Video, 2014. DVD.

58. Ibid.

59. Julia Kristeva, "Word, Dialogue and Novel," in *The Kristeva Reader*, ed. Toril Moi (New York: Columbia University Press, 1986), 37.

60. Cooper, *Crazy Heart*, 9:58.

61. "T Bone Burnett: Zen and the Art of Music," NPR, 34:15.

CHAPTER 4
T BONE'S INNER CIRCLE AND THE SECRET SISTERS' SOUTHERN CHARACTER

1. "The South is the only place": Quoted in Greil Marcus, *Mystery Train: Images of America in Rock 'n' Roll Music*, rev. and exp. ed. (New York: E. P. Dutton, 1982), 153. Marcus also quotes Robertson as saying, "It's the only place in the country I've ever been where you can actually drive down the highway at night, and if you listen, you

can hear music. . . . I don't know if it's coming from the people or if it's coming from the air. It lives, and it's rooted there." "When they sing": "T Bone Burnett Presents . . . The Secret Sisters," *YouTube*, September 9, 2010, accessed March 29, 2016, https://www.youtube.com/watch?v=iv83BELkZxg.

2. Originally Laura auditioned alone. After a callback, she asked the panelists to wait for her sister, who was coming from Alabama. After they heard Lydia sing, the judges asked if the two could sing anything together.

3. Laura Rogers, interview with Heath Carpenter, January 8, 2016. I sat down with both sisters on their tour bus before their performance at the 2014 Fayetteville Roots Music Festival in Fayetteville, Arkansas. I also had a follow-up phone interview, quoted here, with Laura from her homestead in Happy Valley, Alabama.

4. Randy Lewis, "First Look: The Secret Sisters' PBS Special from Hollywood," *Pop & Hiss: The L.A. Times Music Blog*, September 2, 2010, accessed January 2, 2016, http://latimesblogs.latimes.com/music_blog/2010/09/secret-sisters-pbs-special-hollywood.html.

5. Steve Leggett, "AllMusic Review," *AllMusic*, accessed January 3, 2016, http://www.allmusic.com/album/put-your-needle-down-mw0002636870.

6. "The Secret Sisters," *Nash Country Weekly*, accessed January 3, 2016, http://www.countryweekly.com/reviews/secret-sisters.

7. Green Hill is seventeen miles outside its more well-known neighbor Florence, which is part of the Shoals, comprising the quad cities Muscle Shoals, Florence, Tuscumbia, and Sheffield. As the Secret Sisters, the two often refer to growing up in Florence or the Shoals as shorthand for outsiders unfamiliar with the area, and perhaps as a connection to the region's rich musical past.

8. Laura Rogers, interview, January 8, 2016.

9. Rachel Martin, "Throw-Back Harmonies Blend the Secret Sisters," NPR, April 14, 2014, accessed January 3, 2016, http://www.npr.org/2014/04/13/302532228/throw-back-harmonies-blend-the-secret-sisters.

10. When their grandfather died and grandmother moved out, former Drive-By Trucker bassist Shonna Tucker and her then-husband Jason Isbell bought and lived in the home briefly before selling it to Laura.

11. At 15:37–15:53 in "The Secret Sisters on World Cafe," NPR, January 3, 2011, accessed January 3, 2016, https://www.npr.org/2011/01/03/130510812/secret-sisters-on-world-cafe.

12. Churches of Christ are not governed by a national infrastructure in the way most denominations are. Instead, each congregation's elders are in charge of making decisions for that particular church alone.

13. "Secret Sisters on World Cafe," NPR, January 3, 2011.

14. Laura Rogers and Lydia Rogers Slagle, interview with Heath Carpenter, August 29, 2014.

15. "The Secret Sisters," *Grand Ole Opry*, accessed January 3, 2016, http://www
.opry.com/artist/secret-sisters.

16. This and following quotes from Laura Rogers and Lydia Rogers Slagle, interview, August 29, 2014.

17. Wendell Berry, "The Regional Motive," in *The Literature of the American
South: A Norton Anthology*, ed. William L. Andrews (New York: W. W. Norton, 1998),
936–37.

18. At 1:29 in Jamie Sisley, dir., "Divided and United: The Songs of the Civil War:
Short Film I," *YouTube*, October 23, 2013, accessed March 22, 2016, https://www.you
tube.com/watch?v=ZTetCEjMb00.

19. At 0:27 in Jamie Sisley, dir., "Divided and United: The Songs of the Civil War:
Short Film III," *YouTube*, October 27, 2013, accessed March 22, 2016, https://www
.youtube.com/watch?v=krNo9_onEew.

20. Ibid., 1:09.

21. Ibid., 2:03.

22. This and following quotes from Laura Rogers and Lydia Rogers Slagle, interview, August 29, 2014.

23. Meredith Ochs, "Harmony-Loving Sisters Keep It Retro," NPR, April 17, 2014,
accessed January 3, 2016, http://www.npr.org/2014/04/17/304160063/dylan
-approved-harmony-loving-sisters-keep-it-retro.

24. Alexis Petridis, "The Secret Sisters: The Secret Sisters—Review," *Guardian*,
February 17, 2011, accessed January 13, 2016, http://www.theguardian.com/music/2011
/feb/17/secret-sisters-album-review#comments.

25. Ibid.

26. This and following quotes from Laura Rogers and Lydia Rogers Slagle, interview, August 29, 2014.

27. Bruce Jackson, *Wake Up Dead Man: Hard Labor and Southern Blues* (Athens:
University of Georgia Press, 1999) xxi, xxv–xxvi. Emphasis in original.

28. This and following quotes from Laura Rogers and Lydia Rogers Slagle, interview, August 29, 2014.

29. "The 26 Albums of 2014 You Probably Didn't But Really Should Hear: The
Secret Sisters, 'Put Your Needle Down,'" *Rolling Stone*, accessed January 13, 2016,
http://www.rollingstone.com/music/lists/the-26-albums-of-2014-you-probably
-didnt-but-really-should-hear-20140807the-secret-sisters-put-your-needle-down
-20140807.

30. Leggett, "AllMusic Review."

31. Ochs, "Harmony-Loving Sisters."

32. Scott Recker, "The Secret Sisters: Put Your Needle Down," *PopMatters*, June 1,
2014, accessed January 13, 2016, http://www.popmatters.com/review/181801-the-secret
-sisters-put-your-needle-down/.

33. Laura Rogers and Lydia Rogers Slagle, interview, August 29, 2014.

34. Laura Rogers, interview, January 8, 2016.

35. Laura Rogers and Lydia Rogers Slagle, interview, August 29, 2014.

36. Ibid.

37. Laura Rogers, Instagram post, summer 2015, accessed January 16, 2016, https://www.instagram.com/p/4QZIlIrRqt/?taken-by=laurarogers.

38. Laura Rogers, interview, January 8, 2016.

39. Segment beginning at 14:54 in "T Bone Burnett on World Cafe," NPR, August 23, 2011, accessed January 3, 2016, http://www.npr.org/2011/08/23/139876977/t-bone -burnett-on-world-café.

40. Laura Rogers and Lydia Rogers Slagle, interview, August 29, 2014.

41. Travis D. Stimeling's "scenes perspective" offers a particularly perceptive manner in which to engage the complexities of music consumption and identity. Acknowledging the "competing values, practices, and goals of scene participants" in his exploration of Austin's country music scene, Stimeling explores the "role that rhetoric, fashion, song lyrics, interpersonal relationships, and local musical industries play in the formation of individual and collective identities within music scenes." These "nonmusical signifiers of identity" uncover how music consumers "actively engage with popular music and use it as a potent tool to express their political, social, economic, and aesthetic views within their communities" and "reveal . . . core values of scene participants." Stimeling notes how a scenes-studies approach helps examine the role organizations can play in "institutionalizing the scene's values." Stimeling, *Cosmic Cowboys and New Hicks: The Countercultural Sounds of Austin's Progressive Country Music Scene* (New York: Oxford University Press, 2011), viii–ix. Further influenced by Benedict Anderson's "imagined communities" and Edward Said's "imagined geographies," Stimeling's scenes perspective could be particularly useful in helping to extend the scene approach beyond a particular locale, locating it instead within communities connected by technology, shared interests, aesthetics, sounds, and perceptions.

42. This and following quotes from Laura Rogers and Lydia Rogers Slagle, interview, August 29, 2014.

43. Simon Frith, *Performing Rites: On the Value of Popular Music* (Cambridge, Mass.: Harvard University Press, 1996), 270. With this cultural influence in mind, Frith also presents an exploration of several questions swirling around the idea of performance that are useful in ethnographic study of musicians, such as "What makes something a 'performance' in the first place? What are its conditions of existence? How does performance-as-acting relate to performance-as-role-playing?" (204).

44. Laura Rogers and Lydia Rogers Slagle, interview, August 29, 2014.

45. Greil Marcus, interview by Henry Rollins, *The History of Rock 'n' Roll in Ten Songs*, audiobook (Newark, NJ: Audible Studios, 2015), 25:07–26:27.

46. Laura Rogers, interview, January 8, 2016.

47. Laura Rogers, Instagram post, January 22, 2016, accessed January 22, 2016, https://www.instagram.com/p/BA2Z_dtLRoA/?taken-by=laurarogers.

48. Brandi Carlile, Facebook post, March 9, 2016, accessed March 15, 2016, https://www.facebook.com/brandicarlile/posts/10153302338168414. Ellipses in original.

49. 1504, *The Damage: The Story Behind You Don't Own Me Anymore*, *The Bitter Southerner*, June 2018, accessed June 20, 2018, http://bittersoutherner.com/video/the-secret-sisters-the-damage/.

CHAPTER 5

THE T BONE INFLUENCE AND A MUSIC COMMUNITY'S ETHIC

1. Bonnie Montgomery, interview with Heath Carpenter, March 20, 2014, and February 23, 2016. I sat down with Montgomery at a studio loft in downtown Little Rock and over the phone from Austin, Texas.

2. For more, see Kyle Ryan, "Any Kind of Music But Country: A Decade of Indie Country, Punk Rock, and the Struggle for Country's Soul," *Punk Planet* 66 (March–April 2005): 78–82, reprinted in *The Country Music Reader*, ed. Travis D. Stimeling (New York: Oxford University Press, 2014), 304–14.

3. Bill C. Malone, *Don't Get above Your Raisin': Country Music and the Southern Working Class* (Urbana: University of Illinois Press, 2002), viii.

4. Richie Unterberger, *Turn! Turn! Turn! The '60s Folk-Rock Revolution* (San Francisco: Backbeat Books, 2002), xiii.

5. Joe Henry, interview with Heath Carpenter, August 12, 2015. Mr. Henry spoke by phone from his home in the Los Angeles area.

6. Malone, *Don't Get above Your Raisin'*, 13–14.

7. Bonnie Montgomery, interview, March 20, 2014. Richard Peterson, dealing particularly with the evolving nature of authenticity as a social construct and tracing the concept of authenticity in country music from 1923 to 1953, believes that authenticity "is continuously negotiated in an ongoing interplay between performers, diverse commercial interests, fans, and the evolving image." Through the "production perspective," Peterson examines the process of "institutionalization," focusing on how the "content of culture is influenced by the several milieus in which it is created, distributed, evaluated, and consumed." His final chapter dealing with contemporary "signifiers of artistic authenticity" is particularly useful, as many artists regularly allude to icons of music's past. In this regard, Peterson claims that new "roots" performers construct authenticity through "recasting memory." Richard A. Peterson, *Creating Country Music, Fabricating Authenticity* (Chicago: University of Chicago Press, 1997), 6, 10, 225–33.

8. Malone, *Don't Get above Your Raisin'*, ix.

9. Ibid., viii.

10. Ibid., 57.

11. Diane Pecknold, *The Selling Sound: The Rise of the Country Music Industry* (Durham, N.C.: Duke University Press, 2007), 7.

12. Ibid., 12.

13. Ibid., 243.

14. Ibid., 237.

15. Ibid., 3, citing Neil Strauss, "The Country Music Country Radio Ignores," *New York Times*, March 24, 2002. Pecknold also notes the success of the *O Brother, Where Art Thou?* soundtrack here, particularly in light of how the album was virtually ignored by contemporary country radio.

16. Quoted ibid., 237. See Aaron A. Fox, "White Trash Alchemies of the Abject Sublime: Country as 'Bad' Music," in *Bad Music: The Music We Love to Hate*, ed. Christopher J. Washburne and Maiken Derno (New York: Routledge, 2004), 52.

17. Bonnie Montgomery, interview, March 20, 2014.

18. Ibid.

19. Henry Glassie, "Tradition," *Journal of American Folklore* 108, no. 430 (Autumn 1995): 395.

20. Dell Hymes, "Folklore's Nature and the Sun's Myth," *Journal of American Folklore* 88, no. 350 (October–December 1975): 354–55.

21. Benjamin Filene, *Romancing the Folk: Public Memory and American Roots Music* (Chapel Hill: University of North Carolina Press, 2000), 71.

22. Malone, *Don't Get above Your Raisin'*, 254.

23. Johnny Cash with Patrick Carr, *Cash: The Autobiography* (New York: HarperCollins, 1997), 13.

24. Malone makes a similar point in *Don't Get above Your Raisin'* (255), noting how Top 40 songs may be more "realistic" in that "they more completely meet the needs of a majority of today's fans. The music that I and other 'traditionalists' yearn for may have more truly reflected the values, hopes, and dreams of those who lived in the past, or how we *think* they lived." Emphasis in original.

25. In dealing with music consumers at large, Thomas Turino's notions of "cultural cohorts" and "cultural formations" are informative in regards to group identity and authenticity. Turino defines cultural cohorts as "social groupings that form along the lines of specific constellations of shared habit based in similarities of *parts* of the self." Extending this to include interests and ethics, Turino argues that multiple groups can claim a version of the authentic. For example, in addressing the differences between old-time music born out of community formations and middle-class music seemingly appropriating the styles and sounds of the former, he notes that as long as they are viewed as distinct from one another, each can be "equally authentic." I do not accept

this conclusion full stop, however. His assessment, at least on the surface, appears to be too relativistic. Though distinguishing between groups clarifies—such as urban African Americans versus middle-class suburban white kids producing hip-hop—some groups could be seen as more authentic based on criteria such as proximity to the original intent, cultural demographic, or creativity. Turino nonetheless accurately explains the complications inherent within any judgments regarding the "authentic." Thomas Turino, *Music as Social Life: The Politics of Participation* (Chicago: University of Chicago Press, 2008) 111, 161–62. Turino's approach is based on Charles Sanders Peirce's theory of signs, semiotics. In the introduction to his book, Turino thoroughly outlines Peirce's aspects of signs—the sign vehicle, the object, and the effect—along with the theoretician's most famous concepts: icon, index, and symbol.

26. Glassie, "Tradition," 400–401.

27. Joe Henry, interview, August 12, 2015.

28. Ibid.

29. Nate Rau, "Chris Stapleton Sales Shake Up Music Row," *Tennessean*, updated November 12, 2015, accessed February 15, 2016, http://www.tennessean.com/story/money/industries/music/2015/11/11/chris-stapleton-traveller-album-sales-shake-up-music-row/75576568/.

30. Jon Caramanica, "Chris Stapleton Rides His Own Country Music Wave," *New York Times*, November 17, 2015, accessed February 16, 2016, http://www.nytimes.com/2015/11/18/arts/music/chris-stapleton-rides-his-own-country-music-wave.html.

31. Rau, "Chris Stapleton Sales."

32. Will Welch, "Meet Three Country Badasses Who Are Shaking Up the Nashville Establishment," *GQ*, January 7, 2016, accessed January 7, 2016, http://www.gq.com/story/meet-the-country-badasses-from-nashville.

33. Jack Dickey, "Taylor Strikes a Chord: How Pop's Savviest Romantic Conquered the Music Business," *Time*, November 24, 2014.

34. Filene, *Romancing the Folk*, 5.

35. Ibid.

36. Ibid., 65.

37. Lindsey Millar, "Hot Gossip: How White County, Ark., Thanks to Way-Larger-than-Kate Moss Singer Beth Ditto, Has Punked the World," *Arkansas Times*, October 29, 2009, accessed February 16, 2016, http://www.arktimes.com/arkansas/hot-gossip/Content?oid=964697.

38. Bonnie Montgomery, interview, February 23, 2016.

39. Beth Arnold, "The De-evolution of Arkansas," *Huffpost Politics*, May 30, 2015, accessed February 23, 2016, http://www.huffingtonpost.com/beth-arnold/the-de-evolution-of-arkan_b_6969298.html. Several recent books and articles explore the relationship of issues of class, gender, sexuality, and politics to country music:

Travis D. Stimeling, *Cosmic Cowboys and New Hicks: The Countercultural Sounds of Austin's Progressive Country Music Scene* (New York: Oxford University Press, 2011); Aaron A. Fox, *Real Country: Music and Language in Working-Class Culture* (Durham, NC: Duke University Press, 2004); Nadine Hubbs, *Rednecks, Queers, and Country Music* (Berkeley: University of California Press, 2014); Chet Flippo, "Why The Term 'Country Music' May Disappear: Marketers of the Future May Dissolve Music Genre Labels," in *The Country Music Reader*, ed. Travis D. Stimeling (New York: Oxford University Press, 2014), 353–56; and Chris Willman, *Rednecks and Bluenecks: The Politics of Country Music* (New York: New Press, 2007).

40. Bonnie Montgomery, interview, February 23, 2016.

41. Millar, "Hot Gossip."

42. Ibid.

43. "Bonnie Montgomery & Beth Ditto (Gossip) 'It Wasn't God. . .' The Fonda Oct 12, 2012," *YouTube*, October 13, 2012, accessed February 18, 2016, https://www.youtube.com/watch?v=a_weqEy4K3U.

44. "Gossip Interview @ BBC Breakfast 2012/08/17," *YouTube*, August 18, 2012, accessed February 18, 2016, https://www.youtube.com/watch?v=CNHNBSlLv3o.

45. Joe Henry, interview, August 12, 2015.

46. Ibid.

47. Quotes and information below from Jason Weinheimer, interviews with Heath Carpenter, April 4, 2014, and February 22, 2016. I interviewed Jason in his Fellowship Hall Sound studio in Little Rock, Arkansas.

48. Segment at 14:29–19:24 in "T-Bone Burnett on 10 Years of '*O Brother, Where Art Thou?*,'" NPR, August 23, 2011, accessed May 1, 2014, http://www.npr.org/2011/08/23/139880668/t-bone-burnett-on-10-years-of-o-brother-where-art-thou.

49. Segment at 14:17–15:15 in "T-Bone Burnett on World Cafe," NPR, October 31, 2011, accessed February 24, 2016, http://www.npr.org/2012/05/21/141863684/t-bone-burnett-on-world-cafe. Burnett also claims that the collapse of the Soviet Union was, at least in part, due to rock and roll.

50. Chris Willman, "T Bone Burnett vs. Silicon Valley: 'We Should Go Up There with Pitchforks and Torches' (Q&A)," *Hollywood Reporter*, October 31, 2013, accessed January 3, 2016, http://www.hollywoodreporter.com/earshot/t-bone-burnett-silicon-valley-652114. In the interview Burnett expounds beyond the subject of recording techniques into critiques of archival practices that are relevant for this conversation, discussing the pros of analog storage over the "impermanence" of digital and imploring that "with every new technological development that comes along, we have to ask ourselves, does it make us more human, or does it dehumanize us?" The producer is adamant that "digital sound has dehumanized us. . . Computers are pathetic. I feel sorry for them. They have no feelings. They have no soul. That's why they have

emoticons.”

51. Joe Henry, interview, August 12, 2015.

52. Ibid.

53. Ibid.

54. Jason Weinheimer, interview, February 22, 2016.

55. Ibid.

56. Filene, *Romancing the Folk*, 8.

57. This and following material from Bonnie Montgomery, interview, February 23, 2016.

58. Caramanica, “Chris Stapleton Rides.”

59. Welch, “Meet Three Country Badasses.”

60. Leigh H. Edwards, *Johnny Cash and the Paradox of American Identity* (Bloomington: Indiana University Press, 2009), 2.

61. Ibid., 1–2.

62. Joe Henry, interview, August 12, 2015.

63. Ibid.

64. Ibid.

65. Willman, “T Bone Burnett vs. Silicon Valley.”

66. Bonnie Montgomery, interview, March 20, 2014.

67. Bill Flanagan, “T-Bone Burnett’s Three Year Plan,” *Musician*, October 1985, quoted in Bradley Hanson, “T Bone Burnett, Roots Music, and the *O Brother* Phenomenon,” master’s thesis, University of Missouri–Kansas City, 2005, 25.

68. Hanson, “T Bone Burnett,” 27–28.

69. Ibid., 34, 29.

70. Ibid., 31.

71. “T-Bone Burnett on World Cafe,” NPR, 5:50–6:53.

72. Walter Benjamin, “The Work of Art in the Age of Mechanical Reproduction,” in *Illuminations: Essays and Reflections*, ed. Hannah Arendt (New York: Shocken, 1969), 217–51.

73. Simon Frith, *Performing Rites: On the Value of Popular Music* (Cambridge, MA: Harvard University Press, 1996), 237.

74. Peterson, *Creating Country Music*, 7.

75. The Ameripolitan Music Awards site states the awards’ purpose. “The Ameripolitan Music Awards were created to benefit and acknowledge artists whose work does not readily conform to the tastes of today’s ‘country’ or other music genres and organizations. It also provides fans with a means of finding these artists and their music. Ameripolitan—This thought provoking word is intended to be an invitation to discuss the future of the music that is important to so many of us. By leaving the hopelessly compromised word ‘country’ behind and exclusively using the

term 'Ameripolitan,' our intention is to reestablish this music's own unique identity, elevate its significance and help reinvigorate it creatively. Also, because of our place in history, we have the privilege and responsibility to pass a great musical tradition on to future generations who will otherwise have no direct connection to this music." "About Ameripolitan," *Ameripolitan Music Awards*, accessed February 25, 2016, http:// www.ameripolitan.com/copy-of-home.

CHAPTER 6
T BONE AND THE NARRATIVES OF THE SOUTHERN RENAISSANCE

1. See Greil Marcus's chapter on Sly Stone and the "Myth of Staggerlee" in his seminal book *Mystery Train: Images of America in Rock 'n' Roll Music, rev. and exp. ed. (New York: E. P. Dutton, 1982)*, 75–111.

2. "A Fake Newsman's Fake Newsman: Stephen Colbert," NPR, January 24, 2005, accessed March 24, 2016, http://www.npr.org/templates/story/story.php?storyId =4464017.

3. Richard H. King, *A Southern Renaissance: The Cultural Awakening of the American South, 1930–1955 (New York: Oxford University Press, 1980)*, 5.

4. Burkhard Bilger, "The Last Verse," *New Yorker*, April 28, 2008, accessed March 2, 2016, http://www.newyorker.com/magazine/2008/04/28/the-last-verse.

5. Quoted ibid.

6. Ibid.

7. Lance Ledbetter, interview with Heath Carpenter, July 30, 2015.

8. Ibid.

9. Bilger, "Last Verse."

10. Lance Ledbetter, interview, July 30, 2015.

11. Ibid.

12. Ibid.

13. Robert Cantwell, *When We Were Good: The Folk Revival* (Cambridge, Mass.: Harvard University Press, 1996), 190–92.

14. Lance Ledbetter, interview, July 30, 2015.

15. Ibid.

16. Chuck Reece, "Assembling the Sacred Texts: After 11 Years of Exploring Folk Music around the Globe, Atlanta's Dust-to-Digital Turns Its Sights Homeward," *The Bitter Southerner*, accessed March 2, 2016, http://bittersoutherner.com/dust-to -digital/#.Vtcw4-ZGQVA.

17. Lance Ledbetter, interview, July 30, 2015.

18. Ibid.

19. Ibid.

20. Bilger, "Last Verse."

21. Reece, "Assembling the Sacred Texts."

22. Quoted in "About," *Dust-to-Digital*, accessed March 3, 2016, http://www
.dust-digital.com/about/.

23. Quoted ibid.

24. Bilger, "Last Verse."

25. Ibid.

26. "Unforgotten Songs," *Economist*, March 9, 2013, accessed March 2, 2016, http://
www.economist.com/news/technology-quarterly/21572926-historical-audio
-specialist-record-label-digs-up-old-recordings-and-re-releases.

27. William Reece, quoted in Chuck Reece, "Assembling the Sacred Texts."

28. Lance Ledbetter, interview, July 30, 2015.

29. Reece, "Assembling the Sacred Texts." Emphasis in original.

30. William Ferris, venerable Southern folklorist, is a former chairman of the
National Endowment for the Humanities, cofounder of the Center for Southern
Folklore, founding director of the Center for the Study of Southern Culture at the
University of Mississippi, coeditor of *The Encyclopedia of Southern Culture*, and
retired associate director of the Center for the Study of the American South at the
University of North Carolina at Chapel Hill.

31. Quoted ibid.

32. "Marc Smirnoff to Samir Husni," *Mr. Magazine* (blog), March 1, 2012, accessed
March 15, 2016, https://mrmagazine.wordpress.com/2012/03/01/marc-smirnoff-to
-samir-husni.

33. Wendell Berry, "The Regional Motive," in *The Literature of the American South:
A Norton Anthology*, ed. William L. Andrews (New York: W. W. Norton, 1998), 934.

34. Eliza Borné, "Familiar as Family," *Oxford American* 92 (Spring 2016), February
25, 2016, accessed March 15, 2016, http://www.oxfordamerican.org/magazine
/item/785-familiar-as-family.

35. Ibid.

36. "Our Mission and Story," *Oxford American*, accessed March 15, 2016, http://
www.oxfordamerican.org/about/history.

37. "About Us," *Garden and Gun*, accessed March 15, 2016, http://gardenandgun
.com/about.

38. "*Garden and Gun*'s Editor-in-Chief David DiBenedetto to Samir Husni," *Mr.
Magazine* (blog), March 1, 2012, accessed March 15, 2016, https://mrmagazine
.wordpress.com/2012/03/01/garden-guns-editor-in-chief-david-dibenedetto-to
-samir-husni.

39. Benjamin Filene, "*O Brother*, What Next? Making Sense of the Folk Fad,"
Southern Cultures 10, no. 2 (Summer 2004): 54.

40. Wendell Berry, "The Regional Motive," in *The Literature of the American South: A Norton Anthology*, ed. William L. Andrews (New York: W. W. Norton, 1998), 937.

41. "A Letter from the Editor or Why We Created the Bitter Southerner in the First Place," *The Bitter Southerner*, accessed March 15, 2016, http://bittersoutherner.com/we -are-bitter. Ellipses in original.

42. Ibid.

43. This and following quotes from Melissa Hall, interview with Heath Carpenter, March 11, 2016.

44. George Gordon Byron, "The Siege of Corinth" (1816). Transcriptions and photographs of the monument can be found at the *Historical Marker Database*, https://www.hmdb.org/marker.asp?marker=102996.

45. Melissa Hall, interview, March 11, 2016.

46. "UM Takes Key Steps to Address History and Context," *Ole Miss: University of Mississippi News*, June 10, 2016, https://news.olemiss.edu/um-takes-key-steps-address -history-context/.

47. This and following quotes from Melissa Hall, interview, March 11, 2016.

48. "Southern Makers," *Southern Makers*, accessed March 8, 2016, http://southernmakers.com.

49. Following quotes from Tyler Jones, interview with Heath Carpenter, March 2, 2016.

50. 1504, *America's Boulevard*, accessed May 19, 2018, https://1504.co/work /americas-blvd.

51. Tyler Jones, email message to the author, February 4, 2016. In regards to the historical tradition of whitewashing cultural symbols, especially as it applies to urban planning and landmarks, the work of Derek Alderman, who served as an advisor to this film, is an essential resource. Alderman has written widely on what happens when streets get renamed after Dr. King. See *A Street Fit for a King*, website by Derek Alderman, accessed March 25, 2016, http://mlkstreet.com/.

52. Tyler Jones, interview, March 2, 2016.

53. "About EJI," *Equal Justice Initiative*, accessed March 14, 2016, http://www.eji.org/about.

54. This and following quotes from Tyler Jones, interview, March 2, 2016.

55. At 28:02 in Chimamanda Ngozi Adichie, "The Danger of a Single Story," *YouTube*, April 12, 2013, accessed March 18, 2016, https://www.youtube.com /watch?v=D9Ihs241zeg.

56. Charles Reagan Wilson, "Southern Food and Popular Culture," interview with Sara Camp Arnold, *Southern Foodways Alliance*, May 1, 2015, accessed March 15, 2016, https://www.southernfoodways.org/southern-food-and-pop-culture/.

57. Segment at 29:55–30:16 in "T Bone Burnett and Greg Kot @ Summit 10," *YouTube*, November 29, 2010, accessed March 18, 2016, https://www.youtube.com /watch?v=1s8zpB3ABh4. In this wide-ranging interview, Burnett tackles many topics, such as mass age "niches," digitization processes, the accessibility of music, audio quality, marketing and social networking, and the consequences of technology for the music industry and artistry. In typical Burnett fashion, he weaves in quotations from philosophers, artists, and cultural critics like Marshall McLuhan, Barnett Newman, and Pierre Teilhard de Chardin. Also of interest is a debate waged on the website *Twang Nation: The Best in Americana Music and Culture*. In the comments section to an article titled "T Bone Burnett Is Wrong," dealing with artistry and self-promotion, Burnett and writer Baron Lane debate the role artists play in promoting their art in a digital age. Baron Lane, "T Bone Burnett Is Wrong," *Twang Nation*, November 17, 2013, accessed March 18, 2016, http://www.twangnation.com/2013/11/17/t-bone -burnett-is-wrong/.

58. Tyler Jones, email to the author, March 14, 2016.

59. Ibid.

60. Tyler Jones, interview, March 2, 2016.

BIBLIOGRAPHY

1504. *America's Boulevard: A Mural on* MLK. Accessed May 19, 2018. https://1504.co /work/americas-blvd.

———. *The Damage: The Story behind You Don't Own Me Anymore. The Bitter Southerner.* June 2018. Accessed June 20, 2018. http://bittersoutherner.com/video /the-secret-sisters-the-damage/.

"About." *Dust-to-Digital.* Accessed March 3, 2016. http://www.dust-digital .com/about/.

"About Ameripolitan." *Ameripolitan Music Awards.* Accessed February 25, 2016. http://www.ameripolitan.com/about.html.

"About EJI." *Equal Justice Initiative.* Accessed March 14, 2016. http://www.eji .org/about.

"About Us." *Garden and Gun.* Accessed March 15, 2016. http://gardenandgun .com/about.

Adichie, Chimamanda Ngozi. "The Danger of a Single Story." *YouTube.* April 12, 2013. Video, 30:15. Accessed March 18, 2016. https://www.youtube .com/watch?v=D9Ihs241zeg.

Angelou, Maya. *I Know Why the Caged Bird Sings.* New York: Random House, 2009.

Arnold, Beth. "The De-evolution of Arkansas." *Huffpost Politics.* May 30, 2015. Accessed February 23, 2016. http://www.huffingtonpost.com/beth -arnold/the-de-evolution-of-arkan_b_6969298.html.

Baker, Houston, Jr. "Critical Memory and the Black Public Sphere." In *Cultural Memory and the Construction of Identity,* edited by Dan Ben-Amos and Liliane Weissberg, 264–96. Detroit, MI: Wayne State University Press, 1999.

Barker, Deborah E., and Kathryn McKee, eds. *American Cinema and the Southern Imaginary.* Athens: University of Georgia Press, 2011.

Barlow, William. *Looking Up at Down: The Emergence of Blues Culture.* Philadelphia, Pa.: Temple University Press, 1989.

Benjamin, Walter. "One-Way Street." In *Reflections: Essays, Aphorisms, Autobiographical Writings,* 61–94. Edited by Peter Demetz. New York: Harcourt Brace Jovanovich, 1978.

———. "The Work of Art in the Age of Mechanical Reproduction." In *Illumi-*

nations: Essays and Reflections, 217–51. Edited by Hannah Arendt. New York: Shocken, 1969.

Bennett, Andy, Barry Shank, and Jason Toynbee, eds. *The Popular Music Studies Reader*. Routledge: New York, 2006.

Bentley, Bill. "T-Bone Burnett: Born Again But Still Looking." *LA Weekly*, August 8–14, 1980. Quoted in Bradley Hanson, "T Bone Burnett, Roots Music, and the *O Brother* Phenomenon," master's thesis, University of Missouri–Kansas City, 2005.

Berry, Wendell. "The Regional Motive." In *The Literature of the American South: A Norton Anthology*, edited by William L. Andrews, 934–37. New York: W. W. Norton, 1998.

Bilger, Burkhard. "The Last Verse." *New Yorker*. April 28, 2008. Accessed March 2, 2016. http://www.newyorker.com/magazine/2008/04/28/the-last-verse.

Blight, David W. *Race and Reunion: The Civil War in American Memory*. Cambridge, Mass.: Belknap, 2001.

———. "Southerners Don't Lie; They Just Remember Big." In *When These Memories Grow: History, Memory, and Southern Identity*, edited by W. Fitzhugh Brundage, 347–54. Chapel Hill: University of North Carolina Press, 2000.

"Bonnie Montgomery & Beth Ditto (Gossip) 'It Wasn't God. . .' The Fonda Oct 12, 2012." *YouTube*. October 13, 2012. Accessed February 18, 2016. https://www.youtube.com/watch?v=a_weqEy4K3U.

Boorman, John, dir. *Deliverance*. Screenplay by James Dickey and John Boorman. 1972; Burbank, CA: Warner Home Video, 2004. DVD.

Borné, Eliza. "Familiar as Family." *Oxford American* 92 (Spring 2016). February 25, 2016. Accessed March 15, 2016. http://www.oxfordamerican.org/magazine/item/785-familiar-as-family.

Bradner, Eric. "Confederate Flag Debate: A State-by-State Roundup." CNN. Updated June 30, 2015. Accessed December 9, 2015. http://www.cnn.com/2015/06/29/politics/confederate-flag-state-roundup/.

Browne, Ray B. "Popular Culture as the New Humanities." In *Popular Culture Theory and Methodology: A Basic Introduction*, edited by Harold E. Hinds Jr., Marilyn F. Motz, and Angela M. S. Nelson, 75–84. Madison: University of Wisconsin Press, 2006.

Brundage, Fitzhugh W. "Introduction: No Deed But Memory." In *When These Memories Grow: History, Memory, and Southern Identity*, edited by W. Fitzhugh Brundage, 1–28. Chapel Hill: University of North Carolina Press, 2000.

Bueno, Antoinette. "Update: Mumford and Sons Banjo Player Joking about Band Break-up." *Entertainment Tonight*. March 27, 2014.Accessed October 28, 2015. http://www.etonline.com/music/144844_Mumford_and_Sons_Break_Up_for_Good/.

Cantwell, Robert. *When We Were Good: The Folk Revival.* Cambridge, MA: Harvard University Press, 1996.

Caramanica, Jon. "Chris Stapleton Rides His Own Country Music Wave." *New York Times,* November 17, 2015. Accessed February 16, 2016. http://www.nytimes .com/2015/11/18/arts/music/chris-stapleton-rides-his-own-country-music-wave .html.

Carlile, Brandi. Facebook post, March 9, 2016. Accessed March 15, 2016. https:// www.facebook.com/brandicarlile/posts/10153302338168414.

Carr, Jay. "*O Brother, Where Art Thou?* Reviews." *Rotten Tomatoes.* Accessed April 25, 2014. http://www.rottentomatoes.com/m/o_brother_where_art_thou /reviews/#type=top_critics.

Cash, Johnny, with Patrick Carr. *Cash: The Autobiography.* New York: HarperCollins, 1997.

Cash, W. J. *The Mind of the South.* New York: Alfred A. Knopf, 1941.

Caulfield, Keith. "Mumford & Sons' 'Babel' Scores Biggest Debut of Year, Bows at No. 1 on *Billboard* 200 Chart." *Billboard.* October 2, 2012. Accessed October 31, 2015. http://www.billboard.com/articles/news/474818/mumford-sons-babel -scores-biggest-debut-of-year-bows-at-no-1-on-billboard-200.

Chadwell, Sean. "Inventing That 'Old-Timey' Style: Southern Authenticity in *O Brother, Where Art Thou?*" *Journal of Popular Film and Television* 32, no. 1 (2004): 3–9.

Cobb, James, C. *Away Down South: A History of Southern Identity.* New York: Oxford University Press, 2005.

———. *The Most Southern Place on Earth: The Mississippi Delta and the Roots of Regional Identity.* New York: Oxford University Press, 1992.

———. "'We Ain't White Trash No More': Southern Whites and the Reconstruction of Southern Identity." In *The Southern State of Mind,* edited by Jan Nordby Gretlund, 135–46. Columbia: University of South Carolina Press, 1999.

Coen, Joel, and Ethan Coen, dirs. *O Brother, Where Art Thou?* Screenplay by Ethan Coen and Joel Coen. 2000; Burbank, CA: Touchstone Home Entertainment, 2001. DVD.

Cohen, John. "Introduction." Liner notes to *Back Roads to Cold Mountain,* various artists, 4–18. Smithsonian Folkways Recordings SFW40149, 2004. http://media .smithsonianfolkways.org/liner_notes/smithsonian_folkways/SFW40149.pdf.

Cohen, Ronald D. *Folk Music: The Basics.* New York: Routledge, 2006.

Combs, C. Scott. "The Screen Kallikak: White Trash for White Guilt in Post -Vietnam American Film." In *Southerners on Film: Essays on Hollywood Portrayals since the 1970s,* edited by Andrew B. Leiter, 106–22. Jefferson, NC: McFarland, 2011.

Cooper, Scott, dir. *Crazy Heart*. Screenplay by Scott Cooper, based on the novel by Thomas Cobb. 2009; Beverly Hills, CA: Fox Searchlight Pictures, 2010. DVD.

Cox, Karen L. *Dreaming of Dixie: How the South Was Created in American Popular Culture*. Chapel Hill: University of North Carolina Press, 2011.

Dansby, Andrew. "O Brother Shoots to Top." *Rolling Stone*, March 13, 2002. Accessed November 9, 2015. http://www.rollingstone.com/music/news/o -brother-shoots-to-top-20020313.

Dickey, Jack. "Taylor Strikes a Chord: How Pop's Savviest Romantic Conquered the Music Business." *Time*, November 24, 2014.

Dolan, Emily I. "'. . . This Little Ukulele Tells the Truth': Indie Pop and Kitsch Authenticity." *Popular Music* 29, no. 3 (2010): 457–69.

Ebert, Roger. "*O Brother, Where Art Thou?*" *RogerEbert.com*. December 29, 2000. Accessed April 25, 2014. http://www.rogerebert.com/reviews/o-brother-where -art-thou-2000.

———. "Cold Mountain." Accessed November 15, 2013. http://www.rogerebert.com /reviews/cold-mountain-2003.

Edwards, Leigh H. *Johnny Cash and the Paradox of American Identity*. Blooming-ton: Indiana University Press, 2009.

Elie, Paul. "How T Bone Burnett Plays Hollywood." *Atlantic*. November 2013. Accessed December 2, 2014. http://www.theatlantic.com/magazine/archive /2013/11/how-t-bone-burnett-plays-hollywood/309521/.

Ellison, Ralph. *Shadow and Act*. New York: Vintage International, 1995.

"A Fake Newsman's Fake Newsman: Stephen Colbert." NPR. January 24, 2005. Accessed March 24, 2016. http://www.npr.org/templates/story/story.php?storyId =4464017.

Ferris, William. *Blues from the Delta*. Rev. ed. Boston: Da Capo, 1988.

———. *Give My Poor Heart Ease: Voices of the Mississippi Blues*. Chapel Hill: University of North Carolina Press, 2009.

———. "Preamble: The Study of Region." In *Bridging Southern Cultures: An Interdisciplinary Approach*, edited by John Lowe, 29–36. Baton Rouge: Louisiana State University Press, 2005.

———. *The Storied South: Voices of Writers and Artists*. Chapel Hill: University of North Carolina Press, 2013.

Filene, Benjamin. "*O Brother*, What Next? Making Sense of the Folk Fad." *Southern Cultures* 10, no. 2 (Summer 2004): 50–69.

———. *Romancing the Folk: Public Memory and American Roots Music*. Chapel Hill: University of North Carolina Press, 2000.

Flanagan, Bill. "T-Bone Burnett's Three-Year Plan." *Musician*, October 1985, 25–30.

Quoted in Bradley Hanson, "T Bone Burnett, Roots Music, and the *O Brother* Phenomenon," master's thesis, University of Missouri–Kansas City, 2005.

Flippo, Chet. "Why the Term 'Country Music' May Disappear: Marketers of the Future May Dissolve Music Genre Labels." In *The Country Music Reader*, edited by Travis D. Stimeling, 353–56. New York: Oxford University Press, 2014.

Fox, Aaron A. *Real Country: Music and Language in Working-Class Culture.* Durham, N.C.: Duke University Press, 2004.

French, Philip. "Southern Discomfort." *Guardian.* December 21, 2003. Accessed November 15, 2013. https://www.theguardian.com/film/2003/dec/21/philipfrench.

Frith, Simon. *Performing Rites: On the Value of Popular Music.* Cambridge, Mass.: Harvard University Press, 1996.

Gallagher, Sharon. "The Alpha Band Interview." *Radix* 7, no. 6 (November–December 1978). Quoted in Bradley Hanson, "T Bone Burnett, Roots Music, and the *O Brother* Phenomenon," master's thesis, University of Missouri–Kansas City, 2005.

———. "Faith and Hope and Rock and Roll: An Interview with T Bone Burnett." *Radix* 21, no. 3 (Summer 1992). Quoted in Bradley Hanson, "T Bone Burnett, Roots Music, and the *O Brother* Phenomenon," master's thesis, University of Missouri–Kansas City, 2005.

"*Garden and Gun*'s Editor-in-Chief David DiBenedetto to Samir Husni." *Mr. Magazine* (blog), March 1, 2012. Accessed March 15, 2016. https://mrmagazine .wordpress.com/2012/03/01/garden-guns-editor-in-chief-david-dibenedetto -to-samir-husni.

Geertz, Clifford. "Thick Description: Toward an Interpretive Theory of Culture." In *The Interpretation of Cultures*, 3–30. New York: Basic Books, 1973.

Gilmore, Mikal. "T-Bone Burnett's Moral Messages." *Rolling Stone*, November 11, 1982, 46. Quoted in Bradley Hanson, "T Bone Burnett, Roots Music, and the *O Brother* Phenomenon," master's thesis, University of Missouri–Kansas City, 2005.

Glassie, Henry. "Tradition." *Journal of American Folklore* 108, no 430 (Autumn 1995): 395–412.

Gleiberman, Owen. "*O Brother, Where Art Thou?*" *Entertainment Weekly*. January, 12, 2001. Accessed April 25, 2014. http://www.ew.com/ew/article/0,,279348,00 .html.

Gold, Adam. "Q&A: T Bone Burnett on 'Nashville,' Elton John's Comeback and Retiring as a Producer." *Rolling Stone*. December 18, 2012. Accessed October 14, 2015. http://www.rollingstone.com/music/news/q-a-t-bone-burnett-on-nashville -elton-johns-comeback-and-retiring-as-a-producer-20121218.

"Gossip Interview @ BBC Breakfast 2012/08/17." *YouTube*. August 18, 2012. Accessed February 18, 2016. https://www.youtube.com/watch?v=CNHNBSlLv3o.

Gray, Richard. "Recorded and Unrecorded Histories: Recent Southern Writing and Social Change." In *The Southern State of Mind*, edited by Jan Nordby Gretlund, 67–79. Columbia: University of South Carolina Press, 1999.

Guralnick. Peter. *Lost Highway: Journeys and Arrivals of American Musicians*. New York: Back Bay Books, 1999.

Gretlund, Jan Nordby. "Introduction: Present States of Southern Mind." In *The Southern State of Mind*, edited by Jan Norby Gretlund, vii–xvii. Columbia: University of South Carolina Press, 1999.

Griffin, Larry J. "Give Me That Old-Time Music . . . Or Not." *Southern Cultures* 12, no. 4 (Winter 2006): 98–107.

Hall, Melissa. Interview with Heath Carpenter, March 11, 2016.

Hanson, Bradley. "T Bone Burnett, Roots Music, and the *O Brother* Phenomenon." Master's thesis, University of Missouri–Kansas City, 2005.

Harmon, Gary L. "On the Nature and Functions of Popular Culture." In *Popular Culture Theory and Methodology: A Basic Introduction*, edited by Harold E. Hinds Jr., Marilyn F. Motz, and Angela M. S. Nelson, 62–74. Madison: University of Wisconsin Press, 2006.

Heddendorf, David. "Closing the Distance to Cold Mountain." *Southern Review* 36, no. 1 (Winter 2000): 188–95.

Henry, Joe. Interview with Heath Carpenter, August 12, 2015.

Herron, Kaya. "The Shame of Robert E. Lee/MLK Day in Arkansas." *Arkansas Blog*, *Arkansas Times*. February 11, 2015. Accessed December 1, 2015. http://www.arktimes.com/ArkansasBlog/archives/2015/02/11/the-shame-of-robert-e-lee-mlk-day-in-arkansas.

Hiatt, Brian. "Mumford and Sons: Rattle and Strum: How Four Brits Turned Old-Timey Roots Music into the Future of Rock." *Rolling Stone*, March 28, 2013. https://www.rollingstone.com/music/music-news/mumford-sons-rattle-and-strum-78883/.

Hinds, Harold E., Jr. "A Holistic Approach to the Study of Popular Culture: Context, Text, Audience, and Recoding." In *Popular Culture Theory and Methodology: A Basic Introduction*, edited by Harold E. Hinds Jr., Marilyn F. Motz, and Angela M. S. Nelson, 163–80. Madison: University of Wisconsin Press, 2006.

Hoberman, J. "100 Years of Solitude." *Village Voice*, December 19, 2000. Accessed April 25, 2014. http://www.villagevoice.com/2000-12-19/film/100-years-of-solitude/2/.

Hollywood Reporter. "*O Brother, Where Art Thou?* Reviews." *Rotten Tomatoes*. Accessed April 25, 2014. http://www.rottentomatoes.com/m/o_brother_where_art_thou/reviews/#type=top_critics.

Hönnighausen, Lothar. "The Southern Heritage and the Semiotics of Consumer Culture." In *cc*, 80–94. Columbia: University of South Carolina Press, 1999.

Horwitz, Tony. *Confederates in the Attic: Dispatches from the Unfinished Civil War.* New York: Vintage, 1999.

Hubbs, Nadine. *Rednecks, Queers, and Country Music.* Berkeley: University of California Press, 2014.

Hunter, Stephen. "'O Brother': Ulysses On a Wacky Romp through the South." *Washingtonpost.com.* December 29, 2000. Accessed April 25, 2014. http://www .washingtonpost.com/wpsrv/entertainment/movies/reviews /obrotherwhereartthouhunter.htm.

Hymes, Dell. "Folklore's Nature and the Sun's Myth." *Journal of American Folklore* 88, no. 350 (October–December 1975): 345–69.

Jackson, Bruce. *Wake Up Dead Man: Hard Labor and Southern Blues.* Athens: University of Georgia Press, 1999.

Jameson, Fredric. "Reification and Utopia in Mass Culture." *Social Text* 1 (Winter 1979): 130–48.

Jones, Tyler. Interview with Heath Carpenter, March 2, 2016.

———. Email message to the author, February 4, 2016.

———. Email message to the author, March 14, 2016.

Kemp, Mark. *Dixie Lullaby: A Story of Music, Race, and New Beginnings in a New South.* New York: Free Press, 2004.

King, Richard H. *A Southern Renaissance: The Cultural Awakening of the American South, 1930–1955.* New York: Oxford University Press, 1980.

Kirby, Jack Temple. *Media-Made Dixie: The South in the American Imagination.* Athens: University of Georgia Press, 1986.

Knepper, Steven. "Do You Know What the 'Hail' You're Talkin' About? *Deliverance,* Stereotypes, and the Lost Voice of the Rural Poor." *James Dickey Newsletter* 25, no. 1 (2008): 17–29.

Koehler, Julie. "O Brother, Why Did They Make This Movie?" *Bluegrass Unlimited* 35, no. 11 (May 2001): 14–16. Quoted in Sean Chadwell, "Inventing that 'Old-Timey' Style: Southern Authenticity in *O Brother, Where Art Thou?*" *Journal of Popular Film and Television* 32, no. 1 (2004): 3–9.

Kristeva, Julia. "Word, Dialogue and Novel." In *The Kristeva Reader,* edited by Toril Moi, 34–61. New York: Columbia University Press, 1986.

Landes, Ruth. "A Northerner Views the South." Ruth Schlossberg Landes Papers. National Anthropological Archives, Smithsonian Institution, Museum Support Center, Suitland, MD. Quoted in Karen Cox, *Dreaming of Dixie: How the South Was Created in American Popular Culture* (Chapel Hill: University of North Carolina Press, 2011).

Lane, Baron. "T Bone Burnett Is Wrong." *Twang Nation*. November 17, 2013. Accessed March 18, 2016. http://www.twangnation.com/2013/11/17/t-bone -burnett-is-wrong/.

Ledbetter, Lance. Interview with Heath Carpenter, July 30, 2015.

Leggett, Steve. "AllMusic Review." *AllMusic*. Accessed January 3, 2016. http://www .allmusic.com/album/put-your-needle-down-mw0002636870.

Leiter, Andrew B. "Introduction." In *Southerners on Film: Essays on Hollywood Portrayals since the 1970s*, edited by Andrew B. Leiter, 1–13. Jefferson, N.C.: McFarland, 2011.

———. "'That Old-Timey Music': Nostalgia and the Southern Tradition in *O Brother, Where Art Thou?*" In *Southerners on Film: Essays on Hollywood Portrayals since the 1970s*, edited by Andrew B. Leiter, 62–75. Jefferson, NC: McFarland, 2011.

———, ed. *Southerners on Film: Essays on Hollywood Portrayals since the 1970s*. Jefferson, N.C.: McFarland, 2011.

Lemann, Nicholas. "The Price of Union: The Undefeatable South." *New Yorker*. November 2, 2015. Accessed November 4, 2015. http://www.newyorker.com /magazine/2015/11/02/the-price-of-union.

Levin, Kevin M. "Confederate Monuments Will Come Down in New Orleans." *Atlantic*. December 17, 2015. Accessed December 18, 2015. http://www.theatlantic .com/politics/archive/2015/12/new-orleans-remove-confederate-monuments /421059/.

Levine, Lawrence W. *Highbrow/Lowbrow: The Emergence of Cultural Hierarchy in America*. Cambridge, Mass.: Harvard University Press, 1990.

Lewis, Randy. "First Look: The Secret Sisters' PBS Special from Hollywood." *Pop & Hiss: The L.A. Times Music Blog*. September 2, 2010. Accessed January 2, 2016. http://latimesblogs.latimes.com/music_blog/2010/09/secret-sisters-pbs -special-hollywood.html.

Lomax, Alan. *Folk Songs of North America*. New York: Doubleday, 1960. Quoted in Bill C. Malone, "Neither Anglo-Saxon nor Celtic: The Music of the Southern Plain Folk," in *Plain Folk of the South Revisited*, edited by Samuel C. Hyde Jr., 21–45. Baton Rouge: Louisiana State University Press, 1997.

———. *The Land Where the Blues Began*. New York: Pantheon, 1993.

———. *Selected Writings, 1934–1997*. Edited by Ronald D. Cohen. New York: Routledge, 2003.

Lott, Eric. *Love and Theft: Blackface Minstrelsy and the American Working Class*. New York: Oxford University Press, 1993.

Lowe, John. "Introduction: Constructing a Cultural Theory for the South." In *Bridging Southern Cultures: An Interdisciplinary Approach*, edited by John Lowe, 1–28. Baton Rouge: Louisiana State University Press, 2005.

Malone, Bill C. *Don't Get above Your Raisin': Country Music and the Southern Working Class.* Urbana: University of Illinois Press, 2002.

———. "Neither Anglo-Saxon nor Celtic: The Music of the Southern Plain Folk." In *Plain Folk of the South Revisited,* edited by Samuel C. Hyde Jr., 21–45. Baton Rouge: Louisiana State University Press, 1997.

———. *Southern Music, American Music.* Lexington: University Press of Kentucky, 1979.

"Marc Smirnoff to Samir Husni." *Mr. Magazine* (blog), March 1, 2012. Accessed March 15, 2016. https://mrmagazine.wordpress.com/2012/03/01/marc-smirnoff-to-samir-husni.

Marcus, Greil. *The History of Rock 'n' Roll in Ten Songs.* New Haven: Yale University Press, 2014.

———. Interview by Henry Rollins. *The History of Rock 'n' Roll in Ten Songs.* Audiobook. Newark, NJ: Audible Studios, 2015.

———. *Mystery Train: Images of America in Rock 'n' Roll Music.* Rev. and exp. ed. New York: E. P. Dutton, 1982. *The History of Rock 'n' Roll in Ten Songs.* Audiobook.

Martin, Rachel. "Throw-Back Harmonies Blend the Secret Sisters." NPR. April 13, 2014. Accessed January 3, 2016. http://www.npr.org/2014/04/13/302532228/throw-back-harmonies-blend-the-secret-sisters.

Mazor, Barry. *Ralph Peer and the Making of Popular Roots Music.* Chicago: Chicago Review Press, 2015.

McPherson, Tara. *Reconstructing Dixie: Race, Gender, and Nostalgia in the Imagined South.* Durham, N.C.: Duke University Press, 2003.

Middleton, Richard. "O Brother, Let's Go Down Home: Loss, Nostalgia and the Blues." *Popular Music* 26, no. 1 (January 2007): 47–64.

Millar, Lindsey. "Hot Gossip: How White County, Ark., Thanks to Way-Larger-than-Kate Moss Singer Beth Ditto, Has Punked the World." *Arkansas Times,* October 29, 2009. Accessed February 16, 2016. http://www.arktimes.com/arkansas/hot-gossip/Content?oid=964697.

Minghella, Anthony, dir. *Cold Mountain.* Screenplay by Anthony Minghella, based on the novel by Charles Frazier. 2003; Burbank, CA: Miramax Films, 2004. DVD.

Montgomery, Bonnie. Interviews with Heath Carpenter, March 20, 2014, and February 23, 2016.

Moon, Tom. "The *O Brother* Revival." *Rolling Stone,* August 30, 2001. Quoted in Bradley Hanson, "T Bone Burnett, Roots Music, and the *O Brother* Phenomenon," master's thesis, University of Missouri–Kansas City, 2005.

Negus, Keith. *Popular Music in Theory: An Introduction.* Hanover, N.H.: University Press of New England, 1996.

"*O Brother, Where Art Thou?* User Reviews." IMDB. Username leta36. August 25, 2006. Accessed April 25, 2014. http://www.imdb.com/title/tt0190590/reviews?start=20.

———. Username pinturricchio_juve. May 11, 2013. Accessed April 25, 2014. http://www.imdb.com/title/tt0190590/reviews?start=190.

———. Username wilma1913. June 27, 2003. Accessed April 25, 2014. http://www.imdb.com/title/tt0190590/reviews?ref_=tt_urv.

Ochs, Meredith. "Harmony-Loving Sisters Keep It Retro." NPR. April 17, 2014. Accessed January 3, 2016. http://www.npr.org/2014/04/17/304160063/dylan-approved-harmony-loving-sisters-keep-it-retro.

"Our Mission and Story." *Oxford American.* Accessed March 15, 2016. http://www.oxfordamerican.org/about/history.

Painter, Nell Irvin. "Of *Lily*, Linda Brent, and Freud: A Non-Exceptionalist Approach to Race, Class, and Gender in the Slave South." *Georgia Historical Quarterly* 76, no. 2 (Summer 1992): 241–59. Quoted in Tara McPherson, *Reconstructing Dixie: Race, Gender, and Nostalgia in the Imagined South* (Durham, N.C.: Duke University Press, 2003).

Pecknold, Diane. *The Selling Sound: The Rise of the Country Music Industry.* Durham, N.C.: Duke University Press, 2007.

Peterson, Richard A. *Creating Country Music, Fabricating Authenticity.* Chicago: University of Chicago Press, 1997.

Petridis, Alexis. "The Secret Sisters: The Secret Sisters—Review." *Guardian.* February 17, 2011. Accessed January 13, 2016. http://www.theguardian.com/music/2011/feb/17/secret-sisters-album-review#comments.

Price, Mike. "T-Bone's Home, Rare and Well Done." *Fort Worth Business Press*, June 11, 2004. Quoted in Bradley Hanson, "T Bone Burnett, Roots Music, and the *O Brother* Phenomenon," master's thesis, University of Missouri–Kansas City, 2005.

Price, Deborah Evans. "Bluegrass Music's Civil War: Why New and Heritage Acts Don't See String to String." *Rolling Stone.* October 2, 2014. Accessed March 21, 2016. http://www.rollingstone.com/music/features/bluegrass-music-ricky-skaggs-jerry-douglas-old-crow-medicine-show-20141002.

Ramsey, David. "I Will Forever Remain Faithful." *Oxford American* 62 (Fall 2008). Accessed October 24, 2015. https://www.oxfordamerican.org/magazine/item/171-i-will-forever-remain-faithful.

Rau, Nate. "Chris Stapleton Sales Shake Up Music Row." *Tennessean.* Updated November 12, 2015. Accessed February 15, 2016. http://www.tennessean.com/story/money/industries/music/2015/11/11/chris-stapleton-traveller-album-sales-shake-up-music-row/75576568/.

Recker, Scott. "The Secret Sisters: Put Your Needle Down." *PopMatters*. June 1, 2014. Accessed January 13, 2016. http://www.popmatters.com/review/181801-the-secret -sisters-put-your-needle-down/.

Reece, Chuck. "Assembling the Sacred Texts: After 11 Years of Exploring Folk Music around the Globe, Atlanta's Dust-to-Digital Turns Its Sights Homeward." *The Bitter Southerner*. Accessed March 2, 2016. http://bittersoutherner.com /dust-to-digital/#.Vtcw4-ZGQVA.

———. "A Letter from the Editor or Why We Created the Bitter Southerner in the First Place." *The Bitter Southerner*. Accessed March 15, 2016. http://bittersoutherner.com/we-are-bitter/#.Vt8oYuZGQVC.

Reed, John Shelton. *Minding the South*. Columbia: University of Missouri Press, 2003.

———. "The South's Midlife Crisis." In *Bridging Southern Cultures: An Interdisciplinary Approach*, edited by John Lowe, 254–64. Baton Rouge: Louisiana State University Press, 2005.

Reed, Ryan. "Jack White, T Bone Burnett to Produce 'American Epic' Music Documentary." *Rolling Stone*, April 8, 2015. Accessed June 15, 2015. http://www.rollingstone.com/music/news/jack-white-t-bone-burnett-to -produce-american-epic-music-documentary-20150408.

Rodriguez, Rene. "*O Brother, Where Art Thou?* Reviews." *Rotten Tomatoes*. Accessed April 25, 2014. http://www.rottentomatoes.com/m/o_brother_where_art_thou /reviews/#type=top_critics.

Roediger, David. *The Wages of Whiteness: Race and the Making of the American Working Class*. 3rd ed. New York: Verso, 2007.

Rogers, Laura. Interview with Heath Carpenter, January 8, 2016.

———. Instagram post. Summer 2015. Accessed January 16, 2016. https:// www.instagram.com/p/4QZIlIrRqt/?taken-by=laurarogers.

———. Instagram post. January 22, 2016. Accessed January 22, 2016. https:// www.instagram.com/p/BA2Z_dtLRoA/?taken-by=laurarogers.

Rogers, Laura, and Lydia Rogers Slagle. Interview with Heath Carpenter, August 29, 2014.

Rosenbaum, Jonathan. "*O Brother, Where Art Thou?*" *Chicago Reader*. Accessed April 25, 2014. http://www.chicagoreader.com/chicago/o-brother-where-art -thou/Film?oid=1050960.

Ruppersburg, Hugh. "'Oh, So Many Startlements . . .': History, Race, and Myth in *O Brother, Where Art Thou?*" *Southern Cultures* 9, no. 4 (Winter 2003): 5–26.

Ryan, Kyle. "Any Kind of Music But Country: A Decade of Indie Country, Punk Rock, and the Struggle for Country's Soul." *Punk Planet* 66 (March–April 2005): 78–82. Reprinted in *The Country Music Reader*, edited by Travis D. Stimeling, 304–14. New York: Oxford University Press, 2014.

Sachs, Lloyd. *T Bone Burnett: A Life in Pursuit*. Austin: University of Texas Press, 2016.

Scott, A. O. "A Country Crooner Whose Flight is Now Free Fall." *New York Times*. December 15, 2009. Accessed December 1, 2015. http://www.nytimes.com/2009 /12/16/movies/16crazy.html?_r=0.

———. "Hail, Ulysses, Escaped Convict." *NYTimes.com*, December 22, 2000. Accessed April 25, 2014. http://www.nytimes.com/2000/12/22/movies/film -review-hail-ulysses-escaped-convict.html.

"The Secret Sisters." *Grand Ole Opry*. Accessed January 3, 2016. http://www.opry.com/artist/secret-sisters.

"The Secret Sisters." *Nash Country Weekly*. Accessed January 3, 2016. http://www.countryweekly.com/reviews/secret-sisters.

"The Secret Sisters on World Cafe." NPR. January 3, 2011. Accessed June 16, 2016. https://www.npr.org/2011/01/03/130510812/secret-sisters-on-world-cafe.

Sisley, James, dir. "Divided and United: The Songs of the Civil War: Short Film I." *YouTube*. October 23, 2013. Accessed March 22, 2016. https://www.youtube.com /watch?v=ZTetCEjMbo0.

———. "Divided and United: The Songs of the Civil War: Short Film II." *YouTube*. October 27, 2013. Accessed March 22, 2016. https://www.youtube.com /watch?v=XWMKqdtuYrQ.

———. "Divided and United: The Songs of the Civil War: Short Film III." *YouTube*. November 22, 2013. Accessed March 22, 2016. https://www.youtube.com /watch?v=krN09_onEew.

Smith, Barbara Herrnstein. *Contingencies of Value: Alternative Perspectives for Critical Theory*. Cambridge, MA: Harvard University Press, 1988.

Smith, Christopher J. "Papa Legba and the Liminal Spaces of the Blues: Roots Music in Deep South Film." In *American Cinema and the Southern Imaginary*, edited by Deborah E. Barker and Kathryn McKee, 317–35. Athens: University of Georgia Press, 2011.

"Southern Makers." *Southern Makers*. Accessed March 8, 2016. http://southernmakers.com.

Spitz, Bob. *Dylan: A Biography*. New York: McGraw-Hill, 1989. Quoted in Bradley Hanson, "T Bone Burnett, Roots Music, and the *O Brother* Phenomenon," master's thesis, University of Missouri–Kansas City, 2005.

Stimeling, Travis D. *Cosmic Cowboys and New Hicks: The Countercultural Sounds of Austin's Progressive Country Music Scene*. New York: Oxford University Press, 2011.

A Street Fit for a King. Website by Derek Alderman. Accessed March 25, 2016. http://mlkstreet.com/.

Szwed, John. *Alan Lomax: The Man Who Recorded the World*. New York: Viking, 2010.

"T Bone Burnett and Greg Kot @ Summit10." *YouTube*. November 29, 2010. Accessed March 18, 2016. https://www.youtube.com/watch?v=1s8zpB3ABh4.

"T-Bone Burnett on 10 Years of '*O Brother, Where Art Thou?*'" NPR. August 23, 2011. Accessed May 1, 2014. http://www.npr.org/2011/08/23/139880668/t-bone-burnett -on-10-years-of-o-brother-where-art-thou.

"T-Bone Burnett on World Cafe." NPR. August 23, 2011. Accessed October 26, 2015. https://www.npr.org/2011/08/23/139876977/t-bone-burnett-on-world-cafe.

"T-Bone Burnett on World Cafe." NPR. October 31, 2011. Accessed February 24, 2016. http://www.npr.org/2012/05/21/141863684/t-bone-burnett-on-world-cafe.

"T Bone Burnett Presents . . . The Secret Sisters." *YouTube*. September 9, 2010. Accessed March 29, 2016. https://www.youtube.com/watch?v=iv83BELkZxg.

"T Bone Burnett: Zen and the Art of Music." NPR. January 13, 2010. Accessed December 1, 2015. https://www.npr.org/templates/story/story .php?storyId=122526723.

Taylor, Charles. "*O Brother, Where Art Thou?*" *Salon.com*. December 22, 2000. Quoted in Andrew B. Leiter, "'That Old-Timey Music': Nostalgia and the Southern Tradition in *O Brother, Where Art Thou?*" in *Southerners on Film: Essays on Hollywood Portrayals since the 1970s*, edited by Andrew B. Leiter (Jefferson, N.C.: McFarland, 2011).

Thompson, Tracy. *The New Mind of the South*. New York: Simon & Schuster, 2013.

Toscano, Margaret M. "Homer Meets the Coen Brothers: Memory as Artistic Pastiche in *O Brother, Where Art Thou?*" *Film and History* 39, no. 2 (Fall 2009): 49–62.

True Detective: The Complete First Season. "Bonus Features: A Conversation with Nic Pizzolatto and T Bone Burnett." Burbank, CA: HBO Home Video, 2014. DVD.

Tullos, Allen. "What the Traffic Bares: Popular Music 'Back in the USA.'" In *A Companion to Post-1945 America*, edited by Jean-Christophe Agnew and Roy Rosenzweig, 96–112. Malden, Mass.: Blackwell, 2002.

Turan, Kenneth. "*O Brother, Where Art Thou?* Reviews." *Rotten Tomatoes*. Accessed April 25, 2014. http://www.rottentomatoes.com/m/o_brother_where_art_thou /reviews/#type=top_critics.

Turino, Thomas. *Music as Social Life: The Politics of Participation*. Chicago: University of Chicago Press, 2008.

"The 26 Albums of 2014 You Probably Didn't But Really Should Hear: The Secret Sisters, 'Put Your Needle Down.'" *Rolling Stone*. Accessed January 13, 2016. http://www.rollingstone.com/music/lists/the-26-albums-of-2014-you-probably

-didnt-but-really-should-hear-20140807/the-secret-sisters-put-your-needle
-down-20140807.

"Unforgotten Songs." *Economist*. March 9, 2013. Accessed March 2, 2016. http://
www.economist.com/news/technology-quarterly/21572926-historical-audio
-specialist-record-label-digs-up-old-recordings-and-re-releases.

Unterberger, Richie. *Turn! Turn! Turn! The '60s Folk-Rock Revolution*. San Francisco:
Backbeat Books, 2002.

Welch, Will. "Meet Three Country Badasses Who Are Shaking Up the Nashville
Establishment." *GQ*. January 7, 2016. Accessed January 7, 2016. http://www
.gq.com/story/meet-the-country-badasses-from-nashville.

Weinheimer, Jason. Interview with Heath Carpenter, April 4, 2014, and February
22, 2016.

Williamson, J. W. *Hillbillyland: What the Movies Did to the Mountains and What
the Mountains Did to the Movies*. Chapel Hill: University of North Carolina
Press, 1995. Cited in Andrew Leiter, "Introduction," in *Southerners on Film:
Essays on Hollywood Portrayals since the 1970s*, edited by Andrew B. Leiter
(Jefferson, N.C.: McFarland, 2011).

Willman, Chris. *Rednecks and Bluenecks: The Politics of Country Music*. New York:
New Press, 2007.

———."T Bone Burnett vs. Silicon Valley: 'We Should Go Up There with Pitchforks
and Torches' (Q&A)." *Hollywood Reporter*. October 31, 2013.
Accessed January 3, 2016. http://www.hollywoodreporter.com/earshot/t-bone
-burnett-silicon-valley-652114.

Wilmington, Michael. "*O Brother, Where Art Thou?* Reviews." *Rotten Tomatoes*.
Accessed April 25, 2014. http://www.rottentomatoes.com/m/o_brother
_where_art_thou/reviews/#type=top_critics.

Wilson, Charles Reagan. "The Burden of Southern Culture." In *Bridging Southern
Cultures: An Interdisciplinary Approach*, edited by John Lowe, 288–300. Baton
Rouge: Louisiana State University Press, 2005.

———. *Flashes of a Southern Spirit: Meanings of the Spirit in the U.S. South*. Athens:
University of Georgia Press, 2011.

———. *Judgment and Grace in Dixie: Southern Faiths from Faulkner to Elvis*.
Athens: University of Georgia Press, 1995.

———. "Southern Food and Popular Culture." Interview with Sara Camp Arnold.
Southern Foodways Alliance. May 1, 2015. Accessed March 15, 2016.
https://www.southernfoodways.org/southern-food-and-pop-culture/.

INDEX

MUSIC OF THE AMERICAN SOUTH

CPSIA information can be obtained
at www.ICGtesting.com
Printed in the USA
LVHW041744090519
617271LV00004B/312